Kingsley L Dennis, PhD, is a sociologist, researcher and writer. He previously worked in the Sociology Department at Lancaster University, UK, and was Research Associate at the Centre for Mobilities Research (CeMoRe) also at Lancaster University. He is also co-founder of WorldShift International.

Kingsley is the author of numerous articles on social futures; technology and new media communications; evolutionary studies; and conscious evolution. As well as academic training, Kingsley has also lived and worked for many years overseas, including five years in Turkey. He currently lives in Andalusia where he continues to research, write, travel, and grow his own vegetables.

He can be contacted at his personal website: www.kingsleydennis.com

NEW REVOLUTIONS FOR A SMALL PLANET

**A USER'S GUIDE TO HOW THE GLOBAL
SHIFT IN HUMANITY AND NATURE WILL
TRANSFORM OUR MINDS AND LIVES**

KINGSLEY L. DENNIS

WATKINS PUBLISHING
LONDON

This edition first published in the UK and USA 2012 by
Watkins Publishing, Sixth Floor, Castle House,
75–76 Wells Street, London W1T 3QH

Design and typography copyright © Watkins Publishing 2012
Text copyright © Kingsley L. Dennis 2012

1 3 5 7 9 10 8 6 4 2

Designed and typeset by Jerry Goldie Graphic Design

Printed and bound in China by Imago

British Library Cataloguing-in-Publication Data Available

Library of Congress Cataloging-in-Publication Data Available

ISBN: 978-1-78028-392-0

www.watkinspublishing.co.uk

Distributed in the USA and Canada by Sterling Publishing Co., Inc.
387 Park Avenue South, New York, NY 10016-8810

For information about custom editions, special sales, premium and
corporate purchases, please contact Sterling Special Sales
Department at 800-805-5489 or specialsales@sterlingpub.com

Contents

———

ACKNOWLEDGEMENTS

I would like to give my thanks to Michael Mann for enthusiastically
supporting my work over the years. It is a pleasure that we finally
got to publish together on this book! My thanks also to Shelagh
Boyd for her keen eye and editing skills, and for ironing out some
of my grammatical creases. Whilst this writing has been a solo
work, I have relied so much on the research done by others who
came before me – I owe a great debt to you all.

Transitions, Transformations and Revolutions

Humanity is in the midst of great transformation across the globe. This is now apparent to even casual observers of some of the changes happening on the planet at this time. Most of what we see in the daily news reports informs us of dramatic Earth changes due to climatic disruption: earthquakes, floods, hurricanes, volcanic eruptions, etc. We are also witnessing a surge in people protest as decades of corrupt or inefficient social systems are taking their toll. Yet within this outward surge of turmoil and disruption other shifts are occurring; such as the transition from the modern mind of the industrial-globalization model of the last two centuries into a life-sustaining, ecological-cosmological worldview. We are seeing a change towards fostering values that will be inherited by the world to come. During the current and upcoming years, humanity, on both an individual and collective level, will have an obligation to re-adapt itself to a world in revolution.

The revolution we are currently undergoing is not only of the physical kind, with struggle, strife and exertion. There are also revolutions now in our perceptions and worldviews – revolution in our collective psyche. Yet it doesn't stop there, as a revolution not only suggests a change or substitution in socio-cultural systems, a change in conditions, but also implies a complete orbit or rotation as well. I suggest in this book that life on planet Earth is undergoing all three types of revolutions: physical, psychic and cosmological.

Our human socio-cultural cycles are very much a part of our evolutionary history, with marked eras between hunter-gatherer, agrarian, city-state, industrial and planetary. Cultural historian William Irwin Thompson has marked these cultural ecologies or cycles as:

1 Hominization: 4000000–200000BC
2 Symbolization: 200000–10000BC
3 Agriculturalization: 10000–3500BC
4 Civilization: 3500BC–AD1500
5 Industrialization: AD1500–1945
6 Planetization: 1945–present[1]

Currently, our struggles are between a system marked by the inequalities of globalization (what I call the 'old mind') and that of an integral-ecology era (what I call the 'new mind'). This is a territorial, and psychic, dispute, which is manifesting through resource wars and the ongoing struggle for control and management. At the same time there are many forecasts trying to predict the outcome of the present geopolitical turmoil based upon what has gone before; we are unable to discern the uncertain, the unpredictable and the unexpected. The Western mindset has a preoccupation, or even obsession, with a linear view of history and progress. Yet the concept of a linear development of human civilizations is erroneous and misleading. Many ancient teachings, both spiritual and secular, and many indigenous cultures, have long known about and taught the concept of cyclic processes that are repeated over long periods of historical time. There can also be cycles within cycles; smaller cycles within larger cycles whereby social phases, from less cultured states to more cosmopolitan arrangements, can manifest within one overarching cycle. These expansions in social cycles also coincide, or are coexistent with, changes in perception and worldviews. In other words, major social revolutions are accompanied by great shifts in human consciousness. Such shifts are also, as this book attempts to explain, parallel to shifts in how the human species understands, and subsequently harnesses, varying forms of energy. This process follows a progression of discovering ever-finer energies in the world, and indeed the cosmos, of which we are living participants.

Our spiral of cultural history involves a complex interplay of various cycles and systems: of social systems, energy systems and communications revolutions – all co-dependent and integral. Ecological, biological, social and technological systems are now being reorganized because of new energy flows as our world transits a phase shift of almost revolutionary dimensions. The 21st century has been reached through a growing series of critical thresholds, moving towards current global, social and environmental limits; however, at such thresholds new arrangements are forced into being.

Eminent historian Lewis Mumford, in his *The Transformations of Man*, 1956, writes:

> Every [human] transformation ... has rested on a new
> metaphysical and ideological base; or rather, upon deeper
> stirrings and intuitions whose rationalized expression takes
> the form of a new picture of the cosmos and the nature of
> man ... we stand on the brink of [such] a new age: the age of
> an open world and of a self capable of playing its part in that
> larger sphere ... In carrying [human] ... self-transformation
> to this further stage, world culture may bring about a fresh
> release of spiritual energy that will unveil new potentialities,
> no more visible in the human self today than radium was in
> the physical world a century ago, though always present.[2]

It was prescient of Mumford to view the next era not only in terms of ideological renewal, but also as one that brings about 'a fresh release of spiritual energy'. In a similar manner, British historian Arnold Toynbee (in his *A Study of History*) referred to the possible 'transfiguration' of modern society into some kind of 're-spiritualized' form. Significant to this discussion are the work and teachings of Indian yogi Swami Sri Yukteswar Giri (teacher of Paramahansa Yogananda) who, in his book *The Holy Science*, talks of the cyclic attributes of the Hindu Yugas – the four ages of mankind. In terms of attributes, the Yugas generally highlight the rise and fall of great civilizations, as well as the ebb and flow in the morality, ethics and conscious quality of humankind. During the descending arc, not only do civilizations become more materially based but there is also a loss of truth, wisdom, sincerity and integrity amongst humanity.

According to Sri Yukteswar we are currently within the Dwapara Yuga (ascending Bronze Age) that began in AD1698 and will last for 2,400 years. In this Dwapara Yuga, humanity retains a comprehension of some of the finer forces and more subtle energies of the cosmos, and understands that all matter, all atomic form, is nothing other than the manifestation of energy and vibratory forces. Sri Yukteswar also tells us that each ascending age enhances humanity's mental faculties and clarity of understanding, which includes knowledge of the finer forces at work within the cosmos. Since we are now in the second decade of the 21st century, we are several centuries into the ascending arc of Dwapara Yuga; it is our time for discovering and working with the fundamental energies that underlie our material universe.

Western civilization has created a mindset that, although it can be termed 'modern', is one that is overly rational and logical, and which seeks to regulate and control. It has also, unfortunately, succeeded in taking the enchantment away from a mystifying universe. Some of the later chapters of this book explore the notion that technology might be enabling or giving birth to a new 're-wiring' of the human psyche that is better equipped to understand the global predicament – an empathic mind. This empathic mind, which is born out of increased physical and emotional connectivity, may then be the forerunner to new generations being born with heightened intuitive minds. We might refer to them as 'supramental' minds, where intuitive rationality, or heightened common sense, becomes the predominant state of mind. It is both a form of the transpersonal as well as the integral. In other words, it is recognizing *mindfulness* beyond our physical mind, and which encapsulates our growing awareness of our place within a grand, creatively dynamic cosmological order. We can say that it is a mindfulness that is simultaneously vertical (transpersonal) as well as horizontal (integral).

Our predominant worldviews, or the views which are the dominant conditioning forces, appear to prefer to support the 'dead universe' theory – that is, a view that assumes all life was organized by random processes thanks to a spewing out of chemical debris from a massive explosion several billion years ago. Life, it seems, is a random chance event on this rock of ours hurtling through a largely inanimate universe. Not much to tell our grandchildren! Yet perhaps there is a different story that we can learn to tell: a story of a living cosmos that is dynamic, creative and which is a continuous flow-through of energy. Within a living universe the whole underlying energetic order is recreated and sustained at each moment, rather than being a lifeless, random mass. Such a shift in perception of the meaning of our cosmos would have profound implications for our understanding of the significance of human life. It is my view that in the coming years, as humanity advances not only in its scientific discoveries of 'finer energies', but also as our species develops its innate capacities and organs of intuition, empathy and new patterns of thinking, the realization may finally dawn on us that there is no inconsistency in viewing our cosmos as a living, energetic environment. And in this way our species, in stepping further along its evolutionary journey, will see not only that the cosmos continuously sustains us but that we are all intimately related to everything that exists. After nearly 14 billion years of evolution upon Earth, humans may finally regard themselves as agents of participation within an active creative cosmos.

This book, then, is about developing the notion that we, as a species, are moving through another cycle of change within the grander scheme of historical time. Also, that this change will involve a shift in our perceptual paradigms, accompanied by a heightened understanding of ever-finer energies. Also, importantly, this book expresses the notion that this shift in worldview will increasingly come to accept the notion that in our universe, consciousness is primary. Of course, how we view the nature of our reality reflects directly upon how we live our lives as human beings. The human mind that has brought us to where we are today no longer considers our universe, our reality, as dominated by the primacy of consciousness. The revolutions that are occurring on our planet in these transitional years will have a lot of surprises in store for us.

In Chapter One of this book – 'The Birth of the Modern Mind' – I discuss how our modern mind was 'birthed' during the Renaissance, how it gradually came to be dominated by a form of scientific rationalism, and how this is a dangerous mindset for today's fractured world. Chapter Two – 'A Technological State of Mind' – continues by examining the modern post-industrial technological view of progress and advancement, and how this sets up humanity to be disenchanted from a creative cosmos, and in many respects insulates the modern person from relating to the deep crises (social, environmental, political and economic) that we are collectively facing. Chapter Three – 'Rites of Passage: Our Collective Near-Death Experience?' – speculates as to whether we are at the cusp of a transition from species infancy to species adolescence; and whether this transition involves a collective ritual experience, not dissimilar to the initiation rites of indigenous societies: a species rite of passage. In this chapter I discuss reports of the near-death experience, and other visionary accounts, and speculate whether they are manifestations of a larger, global near-death experience.

Part II begins with Chapter Four – 'The Dark Night of the Soul: The Death Throes of the Old' – and explains how the next 20 years cannot be the same as the last 20 years. Change is upon us rapidly, even if we are not aware of its pace. The world is now more starkly divided between regions that are resource sinks (importing energy) and resource sources (exporting energy) as our civilizations push towards overshoot. This chapter examines our dire finite energy resources. Chapter Five – 'Caught in Plato's Cave: The Final Trick on the Old Mind' – follows on to suggest that before humanity comes out from this darker patch (our meta-phorical initiatory period), the vestiges of our 'old mind' will attempt to increase its grip on power and our social lives. This chapter looks at our increasing global (in)security and surveillance, and the creeping systems of social control in modern societies. Chapter Six – 'End of an Era: A New Cycle in Gestation' – begins to turn the tide by examining the notion of cyclic change and renewal, and looks at some of the ideas around the 'Golden Age'. Specifically, it examines evidence that, based on the Hindu Yuga cycles, we are now entering a rising cycle whereby humanity and civilization begin an ascending path of cultural growth associated with the transition to a new world age.

The next part of the book, Part III, begins with Chapter Seven – 'Birthing the Empathic Mind: A Revolution Towards Critical Mass' – which discusses some of the consciousness raising aspects that have occurred since the late 19th century and argues that despite the seeming physical destruction and conflict happening in the world, humanity has actually been on a path of accelerated consciousness growth and awareness. As part of this, our global communications have helped a new 'empathic mind' to emerge. Chapter Eight – 'A Creative Cosmos:

Re-Aligning with a Living Universe' – continues this theme by addressing the notion that we exist in a 'living universe' and what this means for humanity. I examine how, gradually, our sciences are shifting to view consciousness as primary, and look at some of the latest findings in the sciences of consciousness, as well as our human capacity for elevated capacities of the mind. Chapter Nine – 'Field of Dreams: Participating in a New Mindful Reality' – continues from the previous chapter by delving further into notions of the 'field reality' of life, and the concept of 'quantum coherence'. Discussed here are issues of the intuitive, nonlocal mind and the possible mutation of human consciousness for an evolving species. Also discussed is the new generation of children that are exhibiting alternative perceptions of life.

The final part of the book, Part IV, which begins with Chapter Ten – 'Critical Thresholds: An Emerging New Worldview' – discusses an integral worldview, what this means for our future, as well as our views on the evolution of human consciousness. I suggest that as a species we will be moving towards a greater sense of self-reflection and empathic understanding; at the same time we need to adjust to a changing world that has bankrupted itself in terms of its current socio-economic system. I also argue that information is fast becoming a new global energy, and that each new energy revolution stimulates also a revolution in human communications. This, in turn, catalyses new patterns and organization within the human psyche. The final chapter in the book, Chapter Eleven – 'The Way Ahead: Reflections on the Coming Years' – is where I speculate upon possible events that may be a part of our next century. These include an increased global shift towards unity; future potential energy sources; technological developments; and the increasing merger between science and spirituality.

As the reader will by now have realized, our small yet wonderfully creative, adaptive and diverse planet is set to go through some mighty revolutions. I urge and support the reader to … well … to read on.

PART I

Our Critical Impasse

CHAPTER ONE

The Birth of the Modern Mind

Planetary democracy does not yet exist, but our global civilization is already preparing a place for it ... Only in this setting can the mutuality and commonality of the human race be newly created, with reverence and gratitude for that which transcends each of us singly, and all of us together. The authority of a world democratic order simply cannot be built on anything else but the revitalized authority of the universe.

Vaclav Havel, 1994, in a speech at Stanford University

We must close our eyes and invoke a new manner of seeing ... a wakefulness that is the birthright of us all, though few put it to use.

Plotinus

In many ways the Western Renaissance, beginning in the 14th century, was the birthing of the 'modern' mind. The Renaissance placed into being a manifesto for a birth of the new human self – it called for an unlimited creative mind and an explorative free will. Pico della Mirandola's *Oration On The Dignity Of Man* (1486) proclaimed this by saying:

> We have set thee at the world's center that thou mayest from thence more easily observe whatever is in the world. We have made thee neither of heaven nor of Earth, neither mortal nor immortal, so that with freedom of choice and with honor, as though the maker and molder of thyself, thou mayest fashion thyself in whatever shape thou shalt prefer.[1]

This hubris announced a new form of human being; one that would be 'dynamic creative, multidimensional, protean, unfinished, self-defining and self-creating, infinitely aspiring, set apart from the whole, overseeing the rest of the world with unique sovereignty, centrally poised in the last moments of the old cosmology to bring forth and enter into the new'.[2]

Within a single generation of this proclamation, Leonardo, Michelangelo and Raphael had given to the world splendours of High Renaissance work and the mark of the modern mind. Yet these achievements were only the openers ... within this birthing phase Columbus sailed westwards to reach the Americas; Vasco da Gama sailed eastwards to reach India; the Magellan expedition circumnavigated the watery globe; Luther posted his Ninety-five Theses on the All Saints' Church doors that brought about the Protestant Reformation; and Copernicus spurred the scientific revolution with his heliocentric theory. Shortly after, the Italian Dominican friar/astronomer Giordano Bruno went further than Copernicus's revelations to declare that the universe was an infinity of stars; many suns spinning through the heavens (for which he was burned at the stake for heresy in 1600).

These courageous acts of inspiration were, at the time, often credited as being divinely inspired, for they all sought to open up God's mysteries and to exalt the majesty of creation. In other words, they were seen as spiritual epiphanies and exalted moments. The science of the Renaissance mind was deeply imbued with a spiritual wonder and, it must be admitted, with an over-zealous religious hunger. The point, however, was that many of these discoveries were approached with awe, as an infant gazing out upon its new unfolding world. Yet, like a scolded infant, many of these 'inspired' revelations were cast aside by the religious, intellectual and general minds of the day. For, what the Renaissance mind sought was a new type of reasoning; one that went beyond the senses, moved out beyond the confines of rigid faith, and accepted with penetrating logic the new mechanisms of a far more vast, ornately designed universe. The implications went beyond the religious/spiritual, cultural, political – they were cosmological. As such, what the new rational Renaissance mind brought into being was a *metaphysical shift*; a shift that placed the mind of humanity into a new position vis-à-vis the cosmos. Our infant species was permitted to arrange the ornaments of its growth and to learn to crawl through self-exploration.

Similarly, in England, Shakespeare was writing what was to become recognized as some of the world's greatest literature, and Francis Bacon was formulating the new empiricism of the scientific method. All these incredible emergent acts sought to thrust the human infant mind into a radically new and exuberant relationship with the cosmos, heavens and Nature that irreversibly transformed humanity's mental universe.

The human mind has been grasping ever since in creative – and destructive – spurts, as the fruits of rational exploration have served to strengthen the notion that humankind has the responsibility to surge forwards, pushing against the boundaries of perceived thought and knowledge; forever probing the limits of the physical universe through an equally physical lens: the human mind. Yet the course of this seeking has also served to diminish, in ever incremental steps, the *meta* aspect of the journey, giving increasing rein to the *physical* portion. This developmental bias has opened up new and revolutionary wonders for our species and for our process of cultural evolution; yet it has simultaneously opened the doors to a world where dominance, control, possession, competition, profit and power have become accepted paradigms for the mighty few and their aspiring masses. This is exactly the paradox that underlies the growth of Western civilization.

Whilst a great deal of Western science, knowledge and architecture has been well documented to have originated from Arabian sources, the present world owes its incumbent paradox to the rational mind that leapt forth from the swaddling clothes of the Renaissance spurt. It can be said that the modern world was born from the seedbed of the Renaissance, which was flourishing in the latter half of the 15th century and continues to live on. From this inception we have derived our educational infrastructures and knowledge base that has, within the final stages of our species infancy, produced what began as the epoch of electronics (the Technological Age). Each cyclic epoch influences the next, and so our developed technological societies (or 'technocultures') have been birthed on the back of a rational drive to know – and thus conquer.

Our present accelerating Technological Age (*see* Chapter Two) may itself be a cyclic phase of growth that will influence the next seeded stage. Indeed, this book indicates this hypothesis to be the case: that immersed through our technologies we may be forced into a 'shock transition' – here referred to as an initiation rite – in order to develop into species adolescence and into an age of increased empathy and connectedness. However, in the meantime we find ourselves in a world of increasing sensory impacts, distracting stimulants and fragmentary impulses.

As wave after wave of influences carry our young species further along the evolutionary path, we inevitably experience throes of pain as well as bouts of joy. Many of these influences and impacts may necessarily be out of our control, yet the onus is on us to learn how to be resilient and adapt to change. This does not have to mean *forcing change* by combating ourselves against the world – an act of gigantic human hubris – but by accepting the nature of change and undergoing collective initiation (rites of passage) into an era where we are more attuned to the needs of our symbiotic existence. We are now required to learn new modalities of co-existence: to *learn how to learn* rather than believe, with our rational minds, that we already know what we need to know. Yet this imperative to *learn how to learn* – or to re-learn – will first have to deal with some issues of humanity's collective psyche. It appears that underneath our polished and self-accomplished exterior lie some fermenting contradictions. From an objective position it could be said that, as a species, we are clearly insane – or perhaps schizophrenic.

On the one hand, we congratulate ourselves on our sense of amazing progress, having bootstrapped ourselves up from the dark and primitive days of hunter-gathering to the sheen of technological wonder. We have, it seems, single-handedly developed the high capacities of human reason, ingenuity and ethical principles. It is the archetypal heroic journey, the struggle to survive all odds and to arrive at accomplishment. Through these trials, and errors, our species' modern mind has emerged. Progress has been validated, and history is our proof: the only way to go is forwards. However, within our collective psyche also exists an underlying thread of guilt. Surely, somewhere along the path, we left something behind; something incredible and without which we have endlessly suffered. It is this constant hum within us of incompleteness, disconnection and disharmony. In other words, we have *fallen down* – the classic scriptural 'Fall of Man', initiated with a rebellion against our original state and a break from harmony with Nature. We reneged on our duty as custodians of the Earth, and in doing so sacrificed our sense of the sacred and inter-connectedness with our planet. From this we ingeniously took on board Francis Bacon's empiricist admonition to wrench Nature's secrets from her; and the rational mind became paramount in the 'desacralization' of the world. As historian Richard Tarnas rightly noted:

> This development has coincided with an increasingly
> destructive human exploitation of nature, the devastation
> of traditional indigenous cultures, and an increasingly
> unhappy state of the human soul, which experiences itself
> as ever more isolated, shallow, and unfulfilled … The
> nadir of this fall is seen as the present time of planetary
> ecological disaster, moral disorientation, and spiritual
> emptiness, which is the direct consequence of human
> hubris as embodied above all in the structure and spirit of
> the modern Western mind and ego.[3]

The modern mind thus served to sever its ties with a unified and harmonic world. The human subject became the prime mover in world affairs; probing, prodding and wrestling with Nature's secrets in a bid to fuel advancement. This displacement from the world has resulted in humanity viewing the environment as a laboratory in which to experiment. Here the subject is divorced from object; matter creates consciousness; and consciousness impacts upon matter in order to deliver up 'meaning'. And with meaning projected externally the modern person is expected – or left – to forge and extract a sense of personal fulfilment.

This positioning is a far cry from the notion of a primal mind that not only infused the understanding of many of our ancestors but which also thrives today within indigenous communities. This primal mind senses significance embedded within the physical world; within the ebbs and flows of Nature; and within all interactions and relationships. This permeable relationship erodes boundaries and constructs a fellowship between the forces that are present upon the Earth, be they animal, vegetable, or mineral. This integrative mode of consciousness and life has sadly given way, in much of the modern world, to a mental construct that forces the external world to submit. Our hubris (now our collective responsibility) has constructed a worldview that sees the moral, ethical and conscious sensibility of humanity as the central pivots upon which the Earth spins. We have anthropomorphized our impulses, our religious ideals, whilst demystifying the universe into what are knowable facts. What we seek is less about integration and more about gaining control over our environment(s).

Further, these environmental playing fields are considered to be mechanistic, impersonal and unconscious. With our Cartesian and Newtonian tools we seek to know, calculate, predict and shape the world in which we find ourselves. In doing so we have constructed a rational cosmos in which we instinctively sense a loss, a displacement. Yet this inherent sense of loss has been wriggling its way through our individual and collective unconscious; and manifesting externally as so many incongruous acts of earthly mismanagement. Again citing Tarnas:

> … the West has played the central role in bringing about a subtly growing and seemingly inexorable crisis on our planet, a crisis of multidimensional complexity: ecological, political, social, economic, intellectual, psychological, spiritual. To say our global civilization is becoming dysfunctional scarcely conveys the gravity of the situation.[4]

This grave situation has shown clearly (for those with eyes to see) that our infantile species must quickly pass through a global form of initiation

– a rite of passage – into a more mature stage if we are to continue our symbiotic relationship with Earth. Our disconnection has only served to push us to find fulfilment and meaning within our material toys and distractions, further dislocating the human *being* from a nurturing relationship with the cosmos.

As such, our 'sentient' species continues to strive forwards within a vacuum. The consensus ideologies/beliefs that masquerade as our intelligence-gathering tools have placed modern humanity into a paradoxical schizoid relationship with our actions. On the one hand, our modern mind acts as if it is alone in the universe, and as if our actions could not possibly have other than terrestrial consequences. In other words, Earth is a bubble and we have no responsibility beyond this. The community of humankind, in this view, is alone, acts within a cosmic vacuum and has limited capacity. Yet on the other side of this we manifest arrogance over our collective ability to influence, direct, manage and control the natural systems of our planet. In cosmic terms we show a rare form of humility (or is it ignorance?), whilst terrestrially we display an unbelievable degree of delusion over our ability to act, enforce and direct Nature's affairs.

This paradoxical state of our modern mind has put us in a disharmonious relationship with both the micro and the macro environments of which we are an intrinsic part. The macro has become for us a mindless and soulless conglomerate of energy, mass and matter; whilst the micro is now the bio-building-blocks for experimentation and forced mutation. Whilst there is an acknowledgement that our environments are malleable and in flux, this is seen from a position of duality rather than unity. The human species suffers disenchantment by excluding itself from a creative, dynamic and sustaining integral cosmos.

A central argument in this book is that instead of attempting to direct our way out of the present crisis by trying to maintain our present model(s), we should rather be adapting to the changing environmental circumstances. As explained in the Gaia theory, the Earth is a living body, which moves both through her own cycles and also within larger cosmic cycles. As I outlined in *New Consciousness for a New World* there are grand evolutionary cycles that celestial bodies move through, solar and galactic, that inevitably affect terrestrial conditions. It is highly likely, then, that what we are presently experiencing in regard to Earth are manifestations of grand movements, influences and impacts that show up as erratic weather patterns, geological upheavals and changing cycles. In other words, throughout grand evolutionary time the Earth undergoes changes. And so must we.

Yet it is not as simple as us just riding on the back of Earth changes. As a species we have inherited, developed and/or grown into a mindset that creates its own problems, and which is contributing to the disharmonious state of affairs. Due to the deep schism between humanity and Nature, and our 'desacralization' of the world, we have raped and plundered our environmental resources upon an exponential scale. The complexity of our urbanized nations and competing empires has created global tentacles that require ever increasing amounts of finite energy. This is also a key issue: the question of energy. Everything is energy, whether it is matter, molecules, bodies or brains. And on this planet we have a totally misconstrued notion of energy resource, storage and use – not only physical energy but also mental, emotional and spiritual energies too. As such, we have tied ourselves into an energy-intensive mode of industrial expansion and cultural evolution that is incompatible with the energy sources at our disposal. The result, if we do not change our mode of existence, will be a mad-dog race to grab the last drop of oil and natural gas reserves whilst our energy-dependent societies reverse into contraction and eventually collapse.

Our working premise, so far, has been to shape the world into a pattern that suits us (the so-called dominant sentient species). As a species we have come to believe that it is our role to terra-form the Earth into a habitat that most suits us. In this way we have sought to impose our will upon the majesty of natural forces that have been billions of years in the making – the age of the Earth has been scientifically determined to be 4.54 billion years. This egoistic manner of thinking has brought us to a critical threshold; one where many overly urbanized and complex societies are teetering at the edge of disequilibrium. The development of advanced technological society (our modern technocultures) has also delivered the human being into a state, or place, of extreme isolation and alienation from the creative cosmos.

A reconnection with this integral living world requires a mode of resilience rather than resistance. By this I refer to intelligently adapting to an ongoing cyclical changing world rather than terra-forming a world to adapt to us. In this way, we require the attributes of *resilience* to a changing mode of life, over and above attempts to *reinforce* our perceived preferred patterns of life. The shift from reinforcement to resilience may just be a part of the monumental psychophysical transformation necessary to manage our global initiation from an infant species into an adolescent one.

If we undergo a transformation only upon the physical level then we will be entering our formative future years with the same mentality that has contributed to our present imbalance and cosmological alienation. The birth of the Western mind, although crucial for a spurt in cultural and scientific evolution, reached a plateau before the Industrial Revolution had fully risen. The rationality of being able to analyse the working parts of the world around us enabled us to more fully utilize our energy resources. As will be discussed in more detail in later chapters, the issue of energy is crucial to our human future(s). However, energy can be present in both physical and psychic forms, and just as energy can have varying forms of concentration (crude oil – refined oil), so too can psychic energy possess varying levels of potency. The paradigmatic forms of knowledge that each epoch stores, utilizes and transmits are a marker of its *essence* and the impetus through which cultural evolution operates. By way of offering a brief framework for the vessels that have consecutively transmitted cultural knowledge I cite the following three phases:

- Mythological
- Renaissance-Enlightenment
- Modernity

N.B. French philosopher Jean-François Lyotard refers respectively to these three stages as: Traditional; the Enlightenment and Scientific Knowledge; and Postmodernism.

* * *

Mythological

The mythological stage, the longest running of all our stages and still in use, includes myth, folklore, magic, mystery, occult, religious and ritual components as transmitters/carriers of knowledge, information and artefact. These elements are fundamental to most societies and have served to maintain a continuity of collective knowledge, including codes of order and behaviour. For a great deal of time the custodians of these forms of transmission, linked as they are to magic rituals and religious practices, have been shamans, priests, mystics, spiritual hierarchies and, in later times, religious institutions. Therefore, the general masses had only limited access to such knowledge in relation to their capacity and need.

To some degree, as is always inevitable within human cultures, aspects of power, domination and control crept into these lines of transmission. Institutionalized religious bodies, for example, have made great attempts to dispel practices of direct revelation in order to maintain a strict top-level hierarchy of information control. This can be seen in operation during the Inquisition in general, and crusades such as the Albigensian Crusade against the Cathars in particular. This form of cultural knowledge was gradually supplanted (through struggle and time) by the rise in individual scientific enquiry that was at the heart of the Renaissance.

Renaissance-Enlightenment

As alluded to earlier, the epiphany of 'divinely inspired' scientific discoveries were strongly resisted by religious authority. Yet the power of scientific thought and reasoning gradually won over as a legitimate means of opening up humanity's place within the cosmos. This Age of Enlightenment spurred, predominantly in the West, an intellectual, scientific and cultural life that took reason (scientific empiricism) as the legitimate mode of knowledge verification. The Renaissance-Enlightenment phase brought forward science as the new legitimizing source of truth. Thus, the transmission of knowledge was shifted from myth, parables and teaching stories into theories, observations and treatises. The new custodian was no longer the priest or the shaman, but the scientist, the person of rational argument and logical intent. Despite the ongoing struggle between religion and rationality – science and spirituality – the endeavours of scientific enquiry were able to afford Western civilization at least its means to utilize available energy sources (steam, coal, oil) that brought into being the Industrial Revolution and the modern era.

Modernity

Modernity is that name given to the phase of cultural growth (again originally associated with the Western world) that marked the shift from predominant agrarianism towards industrial nation-states and the rise of capitalism. Modernity saw the development of increasingly complex social institutions that have been instrumental in regulating social life through increased forms of rational control (*see* Chapter Two). This mode of knowledge transmission has relied heavily upon technological evolution, tied closely with economic/financial (market economy); political (democracy); and military (territorial/colonial) institutions. Because of this now vast, technically complex web of modern, largely elitist, institutions – where political, economic and military policies are closely intertwined – it has been referred to as the *military–industrial complex* (MIC). This term was first publicly popularized by the then President of the United States Dwight D Eisenhower's Farewell Address to the Nation on 17 January 1961:

> In the councils of government, we must guard against the acquisition of unwarranted influence, whether sought or unsought, by the military–industrial complex. The potential for the disastrous rise of misplaced power exists and will persist. We must never let the weight of this combination endanger our liberties or democratic processes.

> N.B. The full text of this speech is publically available and can easily be found online.

Some recent commentators now see global media corporations as comprising a part of modernity's megalithic institutions for the transmission of present forms of knowledge. The vast, complex, institutional relations that now permeate our current stage of modernity are often criticized as operating as power-knowledge-based disciplinary regimes and regulating bodies (*see* the work of French sociologist and philosopher Michel Foucault). It is little wonder then that modernity has come under heavy criticism for having developed into a corrupt and soulless age; one that corresponds to our cosmic estrangement and alienation from our environments. The epoch that brought humanity into the early stages of planetization (globalization) has been unable, so far, to develop the accompanying – and necessary – psychic presence required to establish a balanced countermeasure to cultural progress. This is one of the primary reasons, I argue here, that this current epoch of transitional change is so crucial to the future of how our species evolves in relation to planet Earth. It may be that a global initiatory experience will be thrust upon us as a means to push us collectively from our infancy into adolescence.

It would be an achingly lost opportunity if modernity – with its rationalized modern mind – were to refuse the great spiritual adventure that now lies ahead in our evolutionary species-planet unfolding. And it would be a tragedy if the modern mind, in its confused madness, were to deny such a possibility and potential future. As philosopher and scholar Jacob Needleman stated:

> The esoteric is the heart of civilization. And should the outward forms of a human civilization become totally unable to contain and adapt the energies of great spiritual teachings, then that civilization has ceased to serve its function in the universe.[5]

The modern mind of humanity will always be on a learning curve; the journey will never be completed. Some cultures are more aware of the subtleties, the dynamic interrelations, between humankind and the environment. The present stage of modernity with its push for corporate globalization, for international structures of power, regulation and knowledge control, is but the latest offering of a world mythology that is being pressed upon the majority of minds by the actions of the influential few. Below are other sets of mythologies that may be equally valid:

Analogy One
Imagine insects with a life span of two weeks, and then imagine further that they are trying to build up a science about the nature of time and history. Clearly, they cannot

build a model on the basis of a few days in summer. So let us
endow them with a language and a culture through which
they can pass on their knowledge to future generations.
Summer passes, then autumn; finally it is winter. The winter
insects are a whole new breed, and they perfect a new and
revolutionary science on the basis of the 'hard facts' of
their perceptions of snow. As for the myths and legends of
summer: certainly the intelligent insects are not going to
believe the superstitions of their primitive ancestors.

Analogy Two
Imagine a vehicle as large as a planet that began a voyage an
aeon ago. After generations of voyaging, the mechanics lose
all sense of who they are and where they are going. They
begin to grow unhappy with their condition and say that the
notion that they are on a journey in an enormous vehicle is a
myth put forth by the ruling class to disguise its oppression
of the mechanical class. There is a revolution and the captain
is killed. Elated by their triumph, the mechanics proclaim the
dictatorship of the proletariat and destroy the captain's log,
which contains, they claim, nothing but the lies of the old
ruling class.

Analogy Three
Imagine that you have just discovered a civilization as small
as a DNA molecule. You want to establish contact, but
since your dimensions prevent you from entering the same
space-time envelope, you must search for other means of
communication. From observing the civilization closely,
you find that there is an informational class that seems to
carry messages back and forth amongst parts of the society,
and you observe further that these messengers are actually
enzymes of a structure that is isomorphic to one of your own
patterns of information. Since you cannot talk directly to
the members of the civilization, you decide to talk through a
patterning of the bits of information the enzymes carry back

and forth. Unfortunately, the very act of trying to pattern an enzyme alters its structure so that a part of your own message is always shifted. It seems that the only time the enzymes are able to carry a high proportion of your own message is when their civilizational structure is either breaking apart or just about to come together again. Fascinated by the problem, you choose your opening and closing epochs carefully and begin to carry on an extended conversation with the civilization.[6]

The development of the collective modern mind of humanity is somewhat like this extended conversation: information is able to penetrate our world and be 'picked-up' at varying intervals by certain minds, which then catalyses a period of accelerated growth. The cells (individuals) of the global body (human civilization) are asked to work with these intervening mythologies. However, we may wish to consider carefully the type of mythologies we choose to live by.

We can possibly see a correspondence between this process and Walter Miller Jnr's acclaimed novel *A Canticle for Leibowitz*. The book begins at a time 600 years after a global nuclear war has destroyed 20th-century civilization. In the aftermath, those who survive are vehemently opposed to the 'modern culture' of knowledge and technology which they consider to have been responsible for the weaponry and war. Radiated tribal mutants, wandering survivors, communities and religious institutions (Abbeys) remain scattered over the wasteland. One day a monk retrieves, with the help of a wandering beggar, an old scrap of paper: the remains of a blueprint from a 20th-century engineer. The text is delivered to a local Abbey where it becomes idolized as sacred, copied, worshipped, blessed by the then Pope, and exalted to divine relic. The engineer (Leibowitz) is canonized, and the new mythology becomes the guiding manuscript. Finally, one of the monks manages to make a dynamo from Leibowitz's blueprint ... skip 600 years into the future and the Abbey has been completely modernized during The Age of Light, and space has been colonized. Yet soon war breaks out again, despite the religious guidance of St Leibowitz, patron saint of electricians ...

What we may gain from this insightful story is that, in any age, institutionalized knowledge might very well be perpetuated by outworn dogmas that are no longer understood nor of any developmental value. Further, if they maintain a fossilized religious/spiritual impulse, alongside an overly materialistic, technological civilization, then the consequences for humanity are both potentially disastrous and destructive.

As mentioned earlier, there is a notion that the modern mind suffers from the pull of contrary mythological impulses: these being 'progress' and the 'fallen state' (the cycle of death and rebirth). On the one hand we sense that it is our responsibility to forge forwards upon a developmental path towards betterment, achievement and what we may consider as 'success'. At the same time, however, a collective feeling of incompleteness and longing remains deep within us. It may well be this security/insecurity state that lies unconsciously behind the project of Western modernity. As Tarnas reminds us:

> What individuals and psychologists have long been doing has now become the collective responsibility of our culture: to make the unconscious conscious. And for a civilization, to a crucial extent, history is the great unconscious – history not so much as the external chronology of political and military milestones, but as the interior history of a civilization: that unfolding drama evidenced in a culture's evolving cosmology, its philosophy and science, its religious consciousness, its art, its myths.[7]

It is the interior history that maps out our potential future(s) – an internal drama that shifts amongst the myths, cosmology and religious/spiritual consciousness. The transition that human life on planet Earth now finds itself a part of is a psychophysical transmutation; that is, of physically adapting to a changing environment whilst simultaneously adopting regenerative and developmental myths that correspond to the new needs.

In the next chapter I will explore how our present myths have succeeded in placing developed nations – and the modern mind – within the rational grip of a Technological Age.

CHAPTER TWO

A Technological State of Mind

I can imagine the world being held together and kept at peace in the year 2000 by an atrociously tyrannical dictatorship which would not hesitate to kill or torture anyone who, in its eyes, was a menace to the unquestioning acceptance of its absolute authority ...

Arnold Toynbee, historian

To be absolutely modern means to be the ally of one's gravediggers.

Milan Kundera, novelist

Modernity ... to involve a degree of alienation or homelessness, a sense we have become strangers to ourselves and to others.

John Jervis, sociologist

Science explores: Technology executes: Man conforms

(motto of 1933 World's Fair in Chicago)

It is difficult to say definitively what it means to be modern, or a part of modernity. Nor do I wish to attempt a categorical definition. Rather, it is enough to recognize some of the shapes, flows and traits that characterize this formative epoch that emerged within Western civilization. What I wish to discuss in this chapter is how the modernizing process came to construct the social and technological framework that now constitutes many of our developed societies. Also, how this socio-technical structure is responsible for modulating a specific mentality. It is this mentality, I argue, that is prone to rationalism, is possessed of a disenchantment from a creative cosmos, and in many respects detaches the 'modern person' from relating to the deep crises (social, environmental, political and economic) that we are collectively facing. From the Renaissance to Modernity the human being has gone through various adaptations, influences and impacts. The question is: has the most recent adaptation towards a 'modern life' been a successful one?

The physical restructuring towards a 'modern life' came about through what is known as the Industrial Revolution. This industrializing shift instigated a move away from geographically dispersed, mixed cottage-style and agrarian lifestyles into the urbanized, mechanically driven workspaces most of us are so familiar with today. This movement occurred in a series of developmental waves, beginning in late 18th-century England. The first of these waves introduced early mechanical devices that made a dramatic impact upon cottage industries such as textiles; upon hard manual-labour industries such as mining (with the introduction of steam pumps); and upon animal-driven agrarian work. The technology of steam pumps made mining more efficient and thus expanded the extraction and use of coal. This development was instrumental in the early establishment of factories, factory towns, institutionalized urban labour, and early forms of transporting goods.

This was followed by a second wave of advancement that expanded the technological and economic base, opened up extensive transport routes (shipping, railways) and further centralized the workforce. The expansion of international travel developed in tandem with the Morse code, the telegraph – referred to as the 'Victorian Internet' – tourism and standardized time. Extensive communication routes were also opened up through the sending of mail. The establishment of the postal system was very much a precursor to today's modern telecommunication systems. As nation-states emerged they established 'national mail systems as government monopolies or near-monopolies' with the result that the postal global network was 'the first of many such large-scale information distribution systems that were to follow'.[1]

This early telecommunication network was followed by the invention of the telephone and the wireless, which further succeeded in reducing the size of the globe for the industrializing world. The patenting of the telephone in 1876 began not with the apocalyptic tone of Morse's '*What hath God wrought?*' but, on 10 March 1876, with the more playful '*Mr Watson – come here – I want to see you!*' as Alexander Graham Bell spoke to his assistant in the next room. By 1880 a concert in Zurich was broadcast over the telephone wires to the town of Basel 50 miles away; and in 1880 the London *Times* installed a direct telephone line to the House of Commons.[2] Yet it wasn't long after such physical communication networks had been established that the 19th century went wireless.

The Italian inventor Guglielmo Marconi sent and received his first radio signal in Italy in 1895 (although Nikola Tesla is now credited with having invented the modern radio as in 1943 the Supreme Court overturned Marconi's patent in favour of Tesla's). The first wireless signal was broadcast across the English Channel in 1899, and the first successful transatlantic wireless radiotelegraph message – between England and Newfoundland – was sent in 1902. This proved especially important for maritime use and soon oceanic vessels were equipped with wireless receiving and sending equipment. By 1912 the wireless had become central to international communication, traversing land and sea in the first instantaneous, worldwide network. Just how important 'always on' connectivity was to become was revealed in the early hours of 15 April 1912. It was the wireless station in Newfoundland that informed the world, at 01.20 hours, of the sinking of the *Titanic*. The distress call, first put out by the captain of *Titanic* at 12.15am, was picked up immediately by those ships within relatively close range. However, the ship closest to *Titanic*, the *Californian*, which was approximately 19 miles away and thus near enough to have saved a majority of the stricken passengers, was not in wireless contact and had gone 'off line' about 10 minutes before *Titanic*'s first wireless distress signal.[3] The rest, as we say, is history. This incident, amongst others at the time, emphasized to the rapidly modernizing world that it was important not only to be in contact but to be connected; in other words, to be networked.

Yet to be efficiently networked also gave rise to the issues of management, time, conduct and regulation. Such an emerging modern environment, with its increasingly urbanized workforce and automated machinery, required that efficiency and regulation become central to notions of progress. It was said that a person could not hope to know the world if they could not know what time was. Further, the rhythm of social life, it was noted, was becoming increasingly faster. In 1881 the psychiatrist George Beard (who introduced the concept of 'nervous exhaustion' into psychiatric parlance) published a report titled 'American Nervousness', which blamed the invention, use and increasing reliance upon clocks and watches for causing general social nervousness. According to Beard's report: 'a delay of a few moments might destroy the hopes of a lifetime'.[4]

This type of conduct went hand in hand with the new form of workforce behaviour that was being implemented as a means of developing mass production: namely, Frederick Taylor's 'Scientific Management'. In brief, scientific management introduced empirical, statistical analysis into work methods, including time ratio and division of labour, in order to calculate the most efficient means of completing a particular job function. Such methods were not popular amongst the workers and generally led to feelings of alienation and lack of satisfaction with work.

Also of importance, the second wave of the Industrial Revolution can be said to have ended with the beginning of commercial oil drilling and the subsequent explosion of the oil age. It was this newly discovered form of energy that not only brought the world closer together in terms of transport, but also accelerated technological developments towards a more energy-intensive industrialized landscape.

Finally, the third wave of the Industrial Revolution ushered in the electronic revolution of the early 20th century. This, as we know, has led to an unbelievable acceleration in our technologies, to a point where we are symbiotically bound to and dependent upon our exterior electronic nervous system. Energy was thus transformed from 'heavy' sources such as fossil fuels (coal, oil), to the 'soft' sources of electronics. Each industrializing phase of the Western modernization project has correlated with a simultaneous transition in energy. The increasing complexity of our societies has been tightly bound with a trajectory of increasing energy-intensive dependency. This, as I shall discuss in later chapters, is part of the predicament of our global future(s).

To summarize, then, the three waves of industrialization that formed the backbone to the current epoch of modernity called for a standardization of behaviour through new conduct, codes and a work mentality; increased urbanization and labour-intensive communities; and a top-down structure of bureaucratization and rationalization. We may also speculate that it contributed greatly to the disenchantment of a person's work life (leading to almost forced slavery), alienation and loss of community. In the rush to modernize our minds, our practices, our very selves, we ended up constricting our interior life in sacrifice to ever-greater forms of mechanized labour. However, somewhat paradoxically, our physical constraints of time and space were simultaneously being expanded through successive communications revolutions. Within a short span of time the industrialized nations went from domestic canals and railroads, to global shipping, telegraph, telephone and wireless; and eventually to an electronics explosion that has brought the world into a virtual communications embrace. This radical restructuring of human society has utilized what historian Lewis Mumford referred to as the human 'mega-machine' – the ordered management of human labour. Being modern entails being a part of this 'mega-machine' within the increasing complexity of everyday life.

What it Means to be Modern

The complexity of modern life has necessitated its own efficiency. Obviously, you cannot have stability, order and control over millions of people, operations, transactions, etc., if there is no effective management. The history of our known civilizations has, in general, been the history of increasing social complexity (it has also been the downfall of our civilizations!).[5] This in turn has required an increase in rationalization and bureaucracy. Rationalization, in general terms, refers to those processes that subject almost all areas of human life (personal, political, religious, economic, etc.) to calculated, logical and administrative regulation. These various socio-cultural institutions are rational because they are structured according to rules that determine the most efficient means for achieving any given goal. In order to achieve these goals a relative degree of bureaucracy is required; the two seem to go hand in hand. And bureaucracy is the means whereby a structured, administrative hierarchy puts into operation increasing specialization or division of function; structures of authority; governing/legal bodies; and formalized procedures. In this way social bureaucracy is further enhanced and strengthened by the expansion of administrative functioning.

Once fully established, bureaucracy becomes a dominant, almost indestructible, often faceless, force of social power and domination. The dominant forces of these bureaucratic structures are further empowered because they have a technical superiority over other forms of management and control. And, as you may have already surmised, these structures are then further enhanced through the increasingly technological means with which to enforce and implement them. Rationalization, then, is upheld and empowered by a technological logic to supply greater capacity to order and manage.

It is, in all its lucidity, a maddening logical relationship and one which we can all perhaps understand whilst despising. This frustrating relationship between a person and their increasingly bureaucratic environs has been well presented in such works as Kafka's *The Trial* and Gilliam's *Brazil*. Max Weber, the sociologist who researched in depth and published on rationality and bureaucracy, himself stated that 'the individual bureaucrat cannot squirm out of the apparatus into which he has been harnessed'. Weber also commented that 'the fate of our times is characterized by rationalization and intellectualization and, above all, by the "disenchantment of the world"'.

And here Weber was accurate, and acute, to realize not only that such socializing structures were resulting in dehumanizing the individual but that such dehumanization was feeding back into the system to further empower it. Like a positive feedback loop, the bureaucratic system was becoming strengthened the more it tightened its calculating, rational and regulating structures. This, Weber referred to as the 'iron cage' in which individuals were being trapped by the increasingly logical, rational structures of efficiency, management, regulation and control. We might say that in today's modern world we have shifted towards a 'technological iron cage'.[6]

This dehumanizing bureaucracy has resulted in what many people feel to be *disenchantment* with the world. Perhaps it is partly out of this disenchantment that a certain affinity with fragmentation, abstraction and incompleteness has arisen in Western socio-cultural life that has been referred to as Postmodernism. This term refers to what some commentators have seen as a disbelief in grand truths,[7] a deconstruction of language, the growth of indeterminacy, experimentation, hyperreality,[8] denial of reality and meaninglessness. This incredulity towards truth, reality and meaning was controversially explored and popularized when Jean Baudrillard published, in 1991, his book *The Gulf War Did Not Take Place*. However, despite these academic and popular debates, the hard reality was that colonial expansion continued to be exercised under the guise of globalization, and market economic forces have strengthened into the 21st century. Whatever the debates over modern social trends, movements, or tendencies, the reality of physical life is that global technologies have ushered into being a high technical level of management and regulation that is now evolving as part of our way of life.

Technology as Technique

It is hard to deny that technology has proven useful to us; nor would I wish to pretend it has not enabled great advancements within human civilization. We can see the effects around us: medical knowledge and tools; international travel; instant global telecommunications; better quality of life; scientific understanding; space travel etc. These are just some of the technological accomplishments that have come as a result of an increasingly complex and technologically evolving culture. Many worthy books have been written on the subject of our technological benefits (as well as some dubious books having speculated upon our technological futures). Yet we can't say that we didn't see this coming, since the logical end of a developing (or evolving) technology is an increase in a given society's capacity for forming and maintaining complex arrangements and thus, by default, regulating their management and control. Technology, in whatever form, is a means of effectively dealing with energy – the source behind all physical and non-physical existence.

In the case of the general evolution of human societies it has been argued that the factor that has enabled societies to access and consume ever more available energy can be identified as 'technology'.[9] In other words, technology is the means of exploiting available energies from the environment, which then transforms human societies, leading to the ever-increasing complexity of social arrangements. What this implies is that the more energy that is available for exploitation (physical use) the greater the organizational complexity that may result from this. Taking these issues in mind, it is now possible to see how technology can be viewed as a vast organizing principle that either directly or indirectly functions to manage and regulate increasing socio-cultural complexity.

As a consequence, human societies are able to develop more intricate relations amongst their diverse components and to create more intensive, flexible and regulated modes of interaction. In this manner, socio-cultural evolution has passed through many stages of growth as technologies have harnessed physical energy (and energy-storage) mechanisms. However, the latter half of the 20th century – as the third wave of the Industrial Revolution moved into the Technological Age – saw the shift away from high material energy inputs towards the more subtle energy input of information. The dramatically increasing sophistication of information communication technologies has enabled modern societies to be ordered within ever more complex patterns of relationships and interconnectedness. The central component here is how information is handled.

It is possible to see how information has become the new primary mode of energy after the earlier coarser energy of steam, electricity and raw materials that were catalysts behind the preceding waves of the Industrial Revolution. Information technologies are a transformation from earlier technologies in that they allow a further, i.e. more profound, enmeshment between technology and the environment. In other words, an embedded experience is being established that has begun to erode the parameters between 'outside/inside'. Our modern technologically developing societies have become more *information-intensive*. Media analyst Nicholas Negroponte has referred to this as the shift 'from atoms to bits'.[11] As such, the time intervals between the emergence, integration and development of technology within a socio-cultural environment are decreasing. This pattern is set to speed up even further – perhaps exponentially so – as information catalyses new and emerging technological paradigms.

With this in mind, we can think of our present technologies not only as tools but also (perhaps increasingly more so) as immersive, pervasive and digital processes. In this respect, these processes are catalysing the shift towards the convergence of more highly integrated systems. This in turn remodels social, cultural, economic and political structures into more managed, regulated and – dare we say it – rationally organized processes. This, I argue, outlines in brief some of the processes of how a Western modernity project has enabled a rapid expansion towards an increasingly interconnected world. This 'Modernity Project', however, has proven itself to be one based on establishing a global 'technical' civilization, constructed on techniques of power and control, rather than a truly human liberating paradigm.

The 'logical' and rational extreme of this mindset is towards increasing reliance on scientific methods for dealing with human nature. The temptation to use rational logic to solve social/civil issues can be too great to deny. As the old joke goes – *someone who thinks logically provides a nice contrast to the real world.* Yet ironically, the Western mind that is the conditioned product of a technological modernity is re-making the 'real world' in the image of logic; or at least attempting to. The corollary is that the same way of thinking will not be useful to us for solving our current global problems; as Einstein famously remarked – 'You cannot solve a problem from the same consciousness that created it.' The technological frame of mind, now widespread amongst the governing bodies of our 'modern' societies, is a combination of scientific analysis, experimentation and organization; rationalization and bureaucracy; and technological logic. The result is what the well-known philosopher Bertrand Russell explains as *scientific technique*:

> Scientific technique is much more than just the impact of new technology on the machinations of society. It is the use of science, in its most calculating and inhumane ways, to analyse, control and guide societies in a desired direction.[12]

As Russell suggests, modern scientific enquiry, coupled with technical capacity, provides the capability, techniques and know-how for the better analysis, management and control of modern societies. Yet this form of scientific technique, rather than being a diabolical plot for world domination (as is often depicted in film) is, instead, the inevitable outcome of increasingly mechanized and rational societies. In other words, with improved methods for the organization and management of social practices, more highly concentrated forms of power and control are made possible.

A recent 20th-century illustration of the extremes of this rational use of technological organization was demonstrated during Nazi Germany's 'Final Solution' programme, with the orchestrated use of the IBM Hollerith punched card to cross-tabulate and organize the prisoners. According to investigative journalist Edwin Black, the punched card technology was used to gather identity information about European Jewry by collating censuses, registrations and ancestral tracing programs; this led to the classification of concentration camp slave labour and associated work projects.[13] Other examples of the use of scientific technique in modern society include the various eugenic programs, the Human Genome Project, and national criminal DNA databases. (The UK National Criminal Intelligence DNA Database is currently the world's biggest DNA database with several million profiles, adding tens of thousands each month.) Films that explore the 'logical' extensions of such issues for future scenarios include *Code 46* (Michael Winterbottom) and *Gattaca* (Andrew Niccol). The modern technologies of humankind can be both frivolous and destructive: tools for pleasure or for annihilation in the hands of infants.

This same type of thinking has also been responsible in recent years for the vast machinery of agricultural farming and global food distribution; energy monopolization and distribution; the medical establishment; and global trade, etc. These almost universal institutions have served to push modern societies further towards a modernity that is increasingly faceless and untouchable, where the individual is left without any 'person' to blame or hold accountable. How many times have we rung a service for enquiry or help only to be answered by an endless rotating series of voice programs? In such a complex, computerized labyrinth everything is well until something goes wrong: convenience is then replaced by frustration and surrealism. As one 20th-century critic once said about modern society, it is 'not only a terroristic political coordination of society, but also a non-terroristic economic-technical coordination which operates through the manipulation of needs by vested interests.'[14]

For many of us, our daily lives resemble a technical embrace where technological infrastructures become an extension of ourselves. We could say, as did media guru Marshall McLuhan nearly half a century ago, that our technological extensions have become our externalized nervous systems. According to McLuhan:

> Today, after more than a century of electric technology,
> we have extended our central nervous system itself in a
> global embrace ... when our central nervous system is
> technologically extended to involve us in the whole of
> mankind and to incorporate the whole of mankind in us, we
> necessarily participate, in depth, in the consequences of our
> every action ...[15]

Yet in terms of our present stage, metaphorically we are like an infant with their rattle – in the early stages of using a new tool. This is why, as I suggest in the following chapters, humanity needs (or will be forced through) an initiation, a growing up, from childhood to adolescence. We need to reach childhood's end and, just as in Arthur C Clarke's novel of the same name, merge towards a new collective evolved mind.

* * *

What I have attempted to describe in these few pages is that the accelerated development of modern cultural life from the Renaissance, the Enlightenment period, and the Industrial Revolution, was followed by an even more rapid period of technological growth. Within the last half-century alone we have witnessed a tremendous increase in urban growth, paralleled by the spread of organized economic markets and cultural conditions (and conditioning) that are receptive to the rise of technical structures. The result of this is that our modern societies are exhibiting a 'technical consciousness' that operates through regulation, rationality and calculated efficiency – the very opposite of the natural, the organic and the spiritual. These traits mark a further shift, or decline, away from an enchanted, vibrant and dynamic universe towards a disenchanted, mechanical, rational and clockwork universe. It is these traits, this mode of thinking, that are central to the state we now find ourselves in concerning our global affairs.

As modern, complex, developed (and developing) societies move ever further towards a convergence and centralization of power and control, there is increasing need to fuel this complex expansion through more advanced networks of supply. The obvious primary necessity here is energy requirement – oil and natural gas supplies; electricity production/distribution; nuclear power; and all alternative forms. The technological mindset that is most predominant is still that of an *old technological mind* – one that requires expansion, organization, power and control. As will be discussed in later chapters, this old mindset is attempting, as the world goes through tremendous shifts, to hold onto power through centralizing control over the production, supply and distribution of such vital commodities as energy and food. This is the top-down approach to technology. Yet the next two decades – in fact the next decade – will see radical changes in the world simply because these technological structures and systems are not compatible with dwindling resources, contracting economies and overall shortages. What some of the later chapters will also explore is the notion that technology might be enabling, or giving birth to, a new form of technological mind that is better equipped to understand the global predicament – an empathic mind. This empathic mind, which is born out of better physical and emotional connectivity, may then be the forerunner to new generations being born with heightened intuitive minds.

However, as the social scientist Michael Harrington commented back in 1962: 'If there is technological advance without social advance, there is, almost automatically, an increase in human misery.' This was followed only seven years later, in 1969, by Harvard psychologist B F Skinner's remark that 'the real problem is not whether machines think but whether men do'. What we are facing now is the prospect that as our technological civilization evolves, it does so without an accompanying evolution of the human mind towards an enchanted, empathic and entangled creative cosmos.

Disenchantment of the Technological Mind

Increasingly, many of us are now living everyday lives in an environment that is ever more unreal and disembodied. By just taking a look at our worldwide, digitalized financial markets we can see how the peak of unreality and the digital operate. Now this illusory environment is becoming stretched to exhaustion: credit-debt economies; consumerism; media and entertainment; even warfare. There is a danger that the illusion will overtake the actual, pushing real human experience and values into the background. The cultural critic and philosopher Jean Baudrillard often expressed how he felt that many societies were becoming so reliant upon the simulation that they were losing contact with the physical 'real' world.[16]

The Argentinean writer Jorge Luis Borges famously wrote of a great Empire that created a map that was so detailed it was as large as the Empire itself. The actual map grew and decayed as the Empire itself conquered or lost territory. When the Empire finally crumbled, all that remained was the map. This 'imaginary map' finally became the only *remaining reality* of the great Empire: a virtual simulation of the physical reality that now encompasses everyone. In some sense we can say that the modern technological world is moving further towards existing within its own simulation.

This is further exemplified by numerous news stories about people 'losing the plot' and disappearing into virtual environments. In February 2010, a 22-year-old South Korean man was charged with murdering his mother after she nagged him for spending too much time playing online games. After murdering his mother the young killer then went to a nearby Internet café to continue playing his games. Another recent example is that of a young couple, again in South Korea, who in September 2009 returned home from an all-night 12-hour gaming binge to find their three-month-old daughter dead. The couple were later arrested and charged for starving their daughter to death, after it emerged that they were more interested in raising an online baby (called Anima) in a popular role-playing game called Prius Online. A recent UK example is a news story, published 12 September 2010 in the *Daily Mail*, that tells of a young mother who, after the untimely death of her husband, retreated into an online fantasy game to the extent that her three children were badly neglected for six months. Her children were forced to feed themselves from cans of cold beans whilst her two dogs were left in a room to starve to death. Research published by Leeds University in the UK, earlier in the year in February 2010, also showed evidence of a link between excessive Internet use and depression.

The modern global economy has brought new levels of the consumerist mass-production of objects and desirables. Whilst this has contributed to the rising economies and living standards of newly industrializing nations, it has also resulted in people's attention and focus being increasingly driven towards superficial attainments and false values. Further, the global media, through movies, television and printed material, shoulders a high responsibility for blurring the sense of meaning and values between the superficial and the real; and, of course, for the incredible amount of propaganda and mental/emotional manipulation that lies at its heart. When there is intent to flood people's consciousness with images that are often *more real than the real*, this sense of hyperreality is in danger of eroding the presence of meaning and significance.

The landscape of modernity gives us a rich tapestry of transient impressions, bright lights and advertising slogans, mixed with the temptations and pleasures of urban convenience and instant excess. Within such a highly distracting environment the lines between fulfilment/emptiness; pleasure/saturation; and magical/monotonous begin to blur into subjective unknowns, unease, disquiet and general malaise. All these contribute to increased disenchantment with the world, with people's lives, and an encroaching sense of emptiness, grief, stress, boredom and anxiety may creep in.

The danger is that as people become accustomed to being immersed in highly techno-mechanized systems, they then become mentally attuned and influenced psychologically by the traits of extreme logic. This type of environmental influence may already have succeeded, to some degree, in making the rational appear irrational, and the irrational as rational. Or, as some mystics like to assert, we live in an upside-down, topsy-turvy world. The result is that we have learned to accept the 'efficient' and the 'functional' as inevitable and agreeable aspects of the progress of civilization. This step-by-step drive towards what may be considered as a form of technological determinism also, by its intrinsic nature, contributes to disenchantment through forces that standardize and normalize rather than inspire and empower.

It is well to remember that having *more* will never compensate us for being *less*. As the thinker Idries Shah put it:

> People today are in danger of drowning in information;
> but, because they have been taught that information is useful,
> they are more willing to drown than they need be. If they
> could handle information, they would not have to drown
> at all.[17]

The flood of information that now characterizes our technological frame of mind can lead to cultural amnesia through overload. This can also be seen in the ever-widening consumer choices that flood the shelves. Yet, instead of having extended choices between products, we are facing a monopoly that actually shrinks consumer choice by making us select between competing brands of the same products. Therefore the politics of commodity provides the illusion that we have greater choice whilst, in effect, diminishing the range of options by flooding the market with more of the same. As the old teaching adage goes – *real freedom is having no choice at all.* One effect of this perceived increase in choice and availability is that it has served to disempower us; as Richard Heinberg notes:

> As civilization has provided more and more for us, it's made
> us more and more infantile, so that we are less and less
> able to think for ourselves, less and less able to provide for
> ourselves, and this makes us more like a herd – we develop
> more of a herd mentality – where we take our cues from the
> people around us, the authority figures around us.[18]

More than ever we are becoming less able to provide essential resources for ourselves. Complex societies move towards specialization, resulting in a majority of people being dependent upon those who possess the relevant skills. The ability to work with natural materials and resources (wood and soil) has been shifting away from the hands of most people. How many of us have the aptitude to repair, build, or invent with solid materials? Most likely we ring for voicemail services. Soon we will lose the ability to read maps because we are so accustomed to the sweet or husky voice of the in-built satellite navigation. Such an increased reliance on technology, without a corresponding development of human skills, may in fact be working against our natural human traits of adaptability, resourcefulness and inner authority. Our dependency upon technological infrastructures is, I argue, part of the *old technological mind* whereby we expect technology to work for us instead of alongside us. This relationship will require a fundamental re-balance if humanity wishes to evolve harmoniously into adolescence as a participating force upon planet Earth. As I argue in later chapters, this transition is in the works, albeit at a critical, vulnerable and unstable stage.

A planetary consciousness, in the sense of a shared collective mindfulness towards harmonious and balanced development, is not yet formed. It has been in gestation for the past century, as I discuss in a later chapter. Yet the *old technological mind* that still persists from the Industrial Revolution is having a continued influence upon the human psyche. The shift from a divinely inspired universe to a mechanical, rational one has reverberated until the present where it is manifest in a general state of frustration and disappointment. I argue that collective human existence, as an imperative to evolution, requires nourishment from a sense of organic unity and involvement within a larger universal scheme. Reckless resource exploitation, the inhumanity of humans against themselves, and the exploitation of power are signs of spiritual estrangement; they are the nervous impulses of a modern psyche thrashing about in a disenchanted world. As Richard Tarnas notes:

> And if this disenchanted vision were elevated to the status of
> being the *only* legitimate vision of the nature of the cosmos
> upheld by an entire civilization, what an incalculable loss,
> an impoverishment, a tragic deformation, a grief, would
> ultimately be suffered by both knower and known.[17]

This period of critical vulnerability and transition upon our planet and within our global societies is part of a transformation that, I contend, will see a shift in our shared mindset, out of its shell of separatism and towards a unifying integral consciousness and vision. Should this not happen, as the above quote reveals, a great impoverishment of our civilization and a disappointing legacy of our species would result.

Thus, there follows a period of initiation – a dark night of the soul – whereby a crisis of global proportions may signal the descent, struggle, and final emergence of a sentient species prepared for adolescent responsibility. Yet such an initiation suggests first a near-death experience of planetary proportions. Such signs have been noted for some time, as the following chapter explains.

CHAPTER THREE

Rites of Passage:

Our Collective Near-Death Experience?

[A] mood of universal destruction and renewal ... has set
its mark on our age. This mood makes itself felt everywhere,
politically, socially, and philosophically ... This peculiarity of
our time, which is certainly not of our conscious choosing,
is the expression of the unconscious human within us who is
changing. Coming generations will have to take account of
this momentous transformation if humanity is not to destroy
itself through the might of its own technology and science ...
So much is at stake and so much depends on the psychological
constitution of the modern human.

Carl Gustav Jung

Until you know this deep secret – 'Die and become' –
you will be a stranger on this dark Earth.

Goethe

Something is dying, and something is being born.
The stakes are high, for the future of humanity and the
future of the Earth.

Richard Tarnas

The rapid cultural rise towards a technological state of mind – a Western-birthed epoch of modernization and scientific technique – is simultaneously in danger of rushing humanity towards an irreversible abyss. We are an infant species that is literally 'growing up in public', and thus forced to live out – and hopefully outlive – all our errors and transgressions. As a relatively new addition to our planet, we have passed through consecutive waves of civilization and civilizing processes to emerge at the cusp of a new era: the transition from species infancy to species adolescence. This transition, I argue, will itself involve a collective ritual experience, not dissimilar to the initiation rites of indigenous societies: a species *rite of passage*. It is becoming increasingly evident that we will need to pass through such an intense 'initiatory experience' if we are to continue the evolutionary unfolding upon our terrestrial Earth. Upon this journey we have passed through various phases of socio-cultural organization, energy utilization and communication revolutions. In each epoch these traits have converged to characterize its specific phase; i.e. social organization is intrinsically related to energy use and communication technologies. These reconfigurations have defined social relationships and the temporal-spatial perceptions of the time, which, in turn, influences the way human brains perceive their reality. It has been noted that there has been a general succession from mythological consciousness (oral cultures), to theological consciousness (script cultures), to ideological consciousness (print cultures), to psychological consciousness (electricity cultures).[1] Modern technocultures are very much tied to an underlying psychological consciousness, aided in the last 100 years by the birth of psychoanalysis and a wealth of psychiatric studies and applications. Our modern forms of warfare embody a mixture of ideological consciousness (nationality, religion, etc.) and psychological consciousness (fear of loss/scarcity, need for security, etc.) that have only exacerbated a mental warfare against individuals and pushed us collectively towards a global state of psychosis. In a similar manner philosopher Jean Gebser described the five structures of consciousness as archaic, magical, mythical, mental and integral. We are thus struggling with our mental stage, an unbalanced and overly rational era, until we can be thrust into the age of integral consciousness – the next transformation.

Yet whilst the Earth is in ecological turmoil, humanity is in psychological and spiritual turmoil. As turbulent events on both sides are accelerating exponentially, time is running out in which this almost vertical curve can continue. The natural equilibrium between human and Earth seems to have been lost, and this disequilibrium is now feeding upon a kind of chaotic energy that pushes the situation further out of balance. In the past, human societies managed their time, work and social balance by integrating their activities with seasonal time and movements, whereas our mega-societies have now virtually abandoned these cycles and bodies of knowledge. With this loss of functional cosmology and planet-solar-cosmic rhythm we have glided into a period of technical progress divorced from a grander significance and belonging. The once enchanted human mind, inspired by epiphany, revelation, intuition and cosmic connection, has ventured into disenchantment and what for many is drudgery.

Despite having developed through various stages of consciousness, of states of mind, and having reached the final step in this sequence, we are now desperately in need of *leaping into a new mind*. In other words, our current psychological consciousness may seem to be a new mind, even a radical mind, yet I argue that it is a mindset that represents a successive growth of the old consciousness; as such, it is the final stage of the old sequence. Just as the octave of the musical scale needs an interval to 'jump' to the next pitch, so too does our present octave of consciousness require an interval in which to jump to a new sequence. Our present sequence (which I shall refer to as the old consciousness or old mind) has culminated in creating an artificial context for our present living. Through extravagant use of energy and a leaning towards 'mechanism' we have slipped away from the organic flow of an ever-renewing world. In the words of one 20th-century commentator:

> The civilization of our time, with its unlimited means for
> extending its influence, has wrenched man [sic] from the
> normal conditions in which he should be living. It is true
> that civilization has opened up for man new paths in the
> domain of knowledge, science and economic life, and thereby
> enlarged his world perception. But, instead of raising him
> to a higher all-round level of development, civilization has

developed only certain sides of his nature to the detriment of other faculties, some of which it has destroyed altogether … modern man's world perception and his own mode of living are not the conscious expression of his being taken as a complete whole. Quite on the contrary, they are only the unconscious manifestation of one or another part of him. From this point of view our psychic life, both as regards our world perception and our expression of it, fails to present an unique and indivisible whole.[2]

This suggests that we have adopted a lopsided, inharmonious manner of development. Our old mind has spurred the growth of particular physical aspects of life – science, technology, management, control, etc. – to the detriment of a holistic, integrated 'whole mind' that incorporates the sustainable, natural cycles of an organic Earth. A shift to alternative cultural forms, one that would serve to place humanity within the dynamics of our planet, is required. We need to adapt to an evolving, changing planet rather than attempting to force a much more resilient planet to adopt an ego-driven, ravenous late-comer species.

Nothing short of a global revelatory experience is required. An experience that would be able to awaken a collective human consciousness towards the grand evolutionary journey ahead: both for our species and for planet Earth. We have moved into our *Crisis Window* – a period for intense change whereby we are called upon to make the leap from the octave of the old mind (characterized by the pathology of power) to the beginning sequence of a new integral mind (characterized by collaboration and sustainability). For the past several thousand years the human race has defined itself through crisis and calamity, struggle and greed. We have crammed ourselves into conurbations; densely packed city spaces where, daily, we pass thousands of people, with tens of thousands more living within a few minutes of where we are, and yet we each act independently of each other, unaware of our intrinsic interdependence. Individually we act out our differentiated roles, utilizing bonds, networks when we need to, often feeling isolated at the same time. Psychologically we are separated, placed alone in our endeavours, whilst collectively being socially organized and effectively regulated and managed. Such a state of collective existential aloneness (perhaps aloofness?) reflects the old-mind energies of competition and struggle, which is an anti-social psychology and behaviour, and one that is damaging to our planet and may be forced into sudden change. In some ways this state-of-mind behaviour reflects the mythological 'Fall' which, as described in Chapter One, supposes an underlying form of subconscious collective guilt. As mythologist Richard Heinberg notes:

> As human consciousness lost contact with its internal,
> heavenly source of power, technology emerged as a power
> substitute. Its first appearance was as sympathetic magic
> and as the invocation of spiritual beings to change Nature
> for human benefit. However, as human awareness became
> increasingly restricted to the material world, purely
> mechanical technologies appeared.[3]

Our relatively modern mechanical-technological societies are in need of an overhaul – a psychophysical transformation – if we are to successfully navigate a global shift/initiation towards a future that is sustainable for the planet.

We are struggling through a corridor of dwindling energy; as we are extending our reach through ever more extensive infrastructures (communication, travel, supply chains, etc.) we are relying more and more upon structures that are energy-intensive. Further, people are racing to reach out to one another whilst corporate and national interests race to control, store, utilize and manage the fundamental resources of civilization. We need to fundamentally alter how we use and manage both our material and psychic energies. It is for this very reason that I state we are heading towards a psychophysical transformation of life on planet Earth.

It is almost certainly a race between an emerging global consciousness (a new sequence of psychic evolution) and major social and cultural disruptions. Despite our modern era of social and human rights, ethnic sensibilities and ethical sensitivities, we have already been pushed to a critical threshold whereby a dramatic, and relatively sudden, change is upon us. Indeed, we may already have reserved our ticket for a collective near-death experience: the shock initiation required for our global wake-up call and psychophysical transition.

Rites of Passage

Michael Grosso echoes the words of Russian sociologist Pitirim Sorokin when he says that:

> ... ours is a disintegrating sensate culture on the threshold
> of becoming a new ideational culture, a culture of higher
> consciousness. We are, we could say, in the midst of the
> near-death experience of our sensate civilization.[4]

Although our 'sensate culture' (read 'secular culture') is beset by the denial of death, the signs of a dying cycle – a death before renewal – are all around us. We have accelerated (exploded) towards the overstretched reaches of our energy-intensive systems. The only alternative available to us, if we do not now wish to face a sudden implosion, is to undergo a *rite of passage*: an initiatory experience of death and renewal to mark our passage from species infancy to species adolescence. According to Elizabeth Kubler-Ross, a psychiatrist in near-death studies, the terminal condition is a challenge to growth; it shakes up the basic structure of personality and allows new possibilities of perception and relationship. In a play by Luigi Pirandello – *The Man with a Flower in his Mouth* – a man emerges from the doctor's office with a fatal diagnosis; with this knowledge of impending death the man's world suddenly changes and every small thing has significance. He undergoes a conversion of consciousness: a bleak diagnosis and shock followed by a courageous renewal. Similarly, humanity may be caught up in a forced fatal diagnosis for change as our global civilizations begin to enter their near-death throes. Perhaps ours is a world with a flower in its mouth.

Another way to view the passage of Western civilization is as a preparatory stage towards an initiatory event; a movement geared towards arriving at a rite of passage, a transition period, in which we must encounter a dark period. This dark period is to be characterized by warfare and the nuclear crisis; environmental degradation and the ecological crisis; cosmic alienation and spiritual crisis; to arrive finally at a transformation for individuals, our species, and our planet. It is perhaps a historical encounter with mortality on an epic scale, signalled by spiralling unrest in the collective consciousness of humanity. Just what this encounter will entail cannot be entirely known, yet the signs of global stresses are now becoming increasingly visible: problems with natural resources (fuel, food and fresh water); climatic disruptions; biodiversity loss; deforestation; ocean acidification; loss of agricultural land; chemical pollution of the stratosphere; weakening of the Earth's magnetosphere, and more. Our initiation encounter is thus likely to place us face to face with the darker, mortal aspects of our existence; with death, disruption, chaos and a crisis of community and civilization. That we have no cultural memory of having encountered such an epochal transition before places us in frightening new territory. As Richard Tarnas states:

> Perhaps the fact that our culture does not provide rituals of initiation is not simply a massive cultural error, but rather reflects and even impels the immersion of the entire culture in its own massive collective initiation. Perhaps we, as a civilization and a species, are undergoing a rite of passage of the most epochal and profound kind, acted out on the stage of history with, as it were, the cosmos itself as the tribal matrix of the initiatory drama.[5]

Tarnas goes on to say that as a species we may now be engaged in a race between initiation and catastrophe.

At the same time, however, we do not fully understand the process of initiation – of having to face our dark side, pass through a series of struggles, and emerge the hero. Part of the initiation – the suffering and the inner/outer struggles – is an intrinsic search for meaning; the journey to the underworld and back is not only an external test of fortitude, willpower and determination, it is also a necessary journey to purge and prepare. The ordeal sets us up to emerge after the trial as a matured and, hopefully, wiser being. The collective consciousness of humanity is currently manifesting tremors that are all too often manipulated by social forces into fear and insecurity. Yet we are required to transform our species mind, our global thinking, into a more energized, focused and integral mind-at-large. We are teetering on the edge of the hero's journey – the descent into the underworld and back – the initiation, rite of passage, our dark night of the soul.[6] The 'dark night of the soul' may involve a personal and collective crisis of meaning, a disorientation (perhaps even despair) where identity of the self is dissolved and renewed. This process has often been depicted in myth as rites of passage. According to famed mythologist Joseph Campbell there are three phases in the rites of passage: separation, initiation and return. The middle phase – the initiation – is the transformative stage, the transitional impulse, the transfiguration, that sets up the way forwards for the return: a return to the world as a renewed force.

Our own global 'dark night of the soul' may very well symbolize humanity's own death–rebirth ritual that shamanistic and indigenous cultures recognize during transitions, such as that from childhood to adulthood; from dependence to independence; from innocence to maturity. By passing through a global initiation period, a mass psychical immersion, we may be provided with the energies and impulses to catalyse a growth in psychical awareness and understanding – a transition from a psychological to integral stage of consciousness. As Duane Elgin says:

> At the core of our history as a species is the story of our movement through a series of perceptual paradigms as we work to achieve our initial maturity as a self-reflective and self-organizing planetary civilization.[7]

Elgin believes that we are passing through a series of 'superheated decades' from which a 'new human alloy may emerge'. Yet such fiery decades will see the suffering of millions as destruction and disorder compel us to act against our collective complacency:

> Needless suffering is the psychological and psychic fire that can awaken our compassion and fuse individuals, communities, and nations into a cohesive and consciously organized global civilization.[8]

Physical discomfort, distress, anguish and insecurity may have to be the price we pay in order to catalyse integral consciousness and a new planetary era. As Elgin puts it:

> Eventually we will see that we have an unyielding choice between a badly injured (or even stillborn) species-civilization and the birth of a bruised, but relatively healthy, human family and biosphere.[9]

A shared psychological trauma combined with a series of profound physical crises may be the necessary requirements – the minimum price of admission – for the global initiatory immersion towards a psycho-physical transformation of life on planet Earth.

On a related matter it is interesting to note that in the early to mid 1980s two hypnotherapists in the US – Chet Snow and Helen Wambach – performed a series of hypnotic future-life progressions with groups (in both the US and Europe) consisting of varied age ranges. This experimental project initially began as a means to effect a patient's cure, then expanded as it became clear that a series of unusual data was being gathered. It began to emerge that nearly all of the patients, when progressed to a future life, witnessed living in a post-disaster scenario. All groups of patients were then progressed to a time much further into the future; again, all accounts were of civilizations that had emerged after a global cataclysm of some unknown type. Snow and Wambach were able to classify 90 per cent of these future scenarios into what they termed as four future types:

1 In-Space Habitats – off-Earth in space stations, colonies, or other planets;
2 New Age Communities on Earth – usually near mountains or the coasts, in natural surroundings;
3 Hi-Tech Urban Centres – usually in domed cities, artificially enclosed centres, or underground;
4 Rural Survivors – in more basic villages with little resources, living amongst the rubble of once-great cities.[10]

Whilst this is not a verification of future catastrophes, what it does show, at the very least, is a subconscious concern, or anxiety, about our future. It also demonstrates a potential collective unconscious psychosis that acts to warn us of potential impending worldwide crises. Chet Snow, one of the initiators of the future-life progressions, comments that:

If a species or planetary consciousness does exist,
then today's subconscious premonitions of impending
catastrophes … may mirror collective unspoken fears that

only drastic, dramatic change can solve our current world order's many thorny problems.[11]

Snow goes on to say that in order to choose and develop positive alternatives for our future it is first necessary to face our 'deeply programmed fears of disaster'; in effect, to step into the underworld journey, struggle through the initiatory event, and return/emerge as a renewed hero.

Somewhat surprisingly this mythological hero's journey of darkness and return is also mirrored in the now extensively documented cases of individual near-death experiences (NDEs). As in the case of future-life progressions, many people who experienced a close call, to the extent that they had an out-of-body experience as a result of nearly dying (or in some cases being clinically dead for a short period), reported unusual insights. Psychologist Kenneth Ring, who has studied the near-death experience for nearly 40 years, has found that people return from the experience with a changed worldview, often one that leans towards a (re)energized psyche and consciousness. Perhaps, to use the previous symbolism, they returned with a flower in their mouth. In one series of sessions Ring noted how more than 50 per cent (compared to less than 20 per cent of control group) stated that after the NDE they were flooded with more information than they could absorb, and that they also claimed to be able to process new information better than before. There was also widespread agreement across all of Ring's groups that those who had the near-death experience felt that humanity was in the midst of an evolutionary shift towards greater spiritual awareness and higher consciousness:

> … all groups tend to agree that these experiences reflect
> a purposive intelligence and that they are part of an
> accelerating evolutionary current that is propelling the
> human race toward higher consciousness and heightened
> spirituality.[12]

Ring remarks that the real significance of the 'extraordinary encounters' of NDEs may in fact lie in their 'evolutionary implications for humanity'. Similarly, another NDE researcher, Margot Grey, came to an almost identical conclusion in her book *Return from Death*:

It would seem that similar physiological mechanisms are operating in both the NDE and kundalini phenomena and that they are both aspects of the same evolutionary force. Taken together, these spectacular instances of transformation add up to a surprisingly large and increasing percentage of the population and might therefore be expected to have a growing influence on the collective awareness of the rest of the species, at both a conscious and subconscious level ... It would appear that a new breed of mankind may be about to be born, and that in order for this to happen our consciousness and biological structure is undergoing a radical transformation. What we seem to be observing is a rebirth process which ... will eventually culminate in bringing forth an enlightened human being who has knowledge of the life and order of the universe.[13]

These are indeed weighty and profound speculations – that the near-death experience is a forerunner, or part of a grander process, which provides a 'rebirth process' that will culminate in the next stage of humanity's evolution.

These 'otherworld' or out-of-body experiences (OBEs), including the hypnotic future-life progressions, all share similar patterns in that the mind-at-large (a phrase used initially by philosopher Michael Grosso), or the collective consciousness of humanity, is working with images/signals that tell of both physical and psychical grand shifts. In other words, the Earth herself may be entering a period of instability and disruption whilst simultaneously catalysing a dramatic, and perhaps unsettling, transformation in human consciousness. The global initiation – our *rites of passage* – may thus entail a collective near-death experience that will not only affect us physically and psychically but also directly involve our planet Earth.

Our Collective Near-Death Experience

There may still be a lingering unconscious guilt in humankind's collective mind over some great evolutionary *Fall*. Myths abound in many cultures that tell of a once utopian Golden Age, where peace and harmony reigned supreme. In some ways the myth of the hero reflects this need/desire to undergo trials and tribulations in order to re-emerge victorious, renewed and re-spirited. The signs and reminders are everywhere in our cultural artefacts, tales/stories/myths, histories and beliefs. Our Earth is scattered with the remains of many long-passed civilizations as if to remind us that *this too will pass*. We are fascinated with tales of the lost lands of Lemuria and Atlantis; of speculations about lost civilizations at the bottom of our oceans, or even more ancient cultures now washed away with the sands of millennial time. Rather than living in linear time many of us are beginning to realize that the passing of events – terrestrial and cosmic – occurs in cycles. What has gone before may be re-encountered, and thus the signs of past experiences may be of deep value to us.

The Tibetans have an account whereupon humanity is living at the end of a 26,000-year period of darkness, and that this dark period will be followed by a 'a period of purification'. However, we will first have to face a series of catastrophes and political/social upheavals before the next epoch emerges. This account is remarkably similar to Mayan and Hopi prophecy accounts which both tell of a dark period of upheaval and great change before the next cycle fully materializes. The time frame of 26,000 years is identical to the Mayan calendar which indicates that the 'Age of Jaguar', the 13th *baktun*, or long period of 144,000 days, will come to an end with the fifth and final Sun on 22 December 2012. This time frame indicates a cyclic Great Year; that is, the time required for one cycle of the precession of the equinoxes to be completed, which is calculated to be approximately 25,765 years. According to the Mayan system, 22 December 2012 will mark the 'switch' to a new era of planetary evolution, one that requires a radically different kind of consciousness. Similarly, there exist Teutonic Norse myths which state that 'a renewal of the world would only come after great destruction in which a period of anarchy would arise that would see humans commit many foul acts'.[14]

Another example of eras as part of what are called 'Great Ages' is the 'Yugas' of Hindu philosophy (epochs within a cycle of four ages from Satya, Treta, Dvapara and Kali). Such ages are known cycles within celestial motion, and within these macro cycles occur significant periods of planetary change. Many commentators speak of present conditions on Earth being under the influence of the Kali Yuga, which is 'always oppressed by bad rulers with burdens of taxes; the foremost of the best classes will, in those terrible times, take leave of all patience and do improper acts'.[15] It is said that the Kali Yuga will come to an end after much chaos and disruption.[16] This doesn't seem so different from present conditions today – bad rulers with burdens of taxes! However, as I discuss in Chapter Six, we may in fact already have entered an ascending Yuga cycle.

Biblical accounts, too, abound with times that denote the end of one cycle: 'For nation shall rise against nation, and kingdom against kingdom: and there shall be famines, and pestilences, and earthquakes, in divers places.' (Matthew 24:6) Again, not too dissimilar to present global conditions.

These examples are only a few of the many Earth myths that contain references to celestial cycles and cyclical epochs. According to the book *Hamlet's Mill*, a work of comparative mythology, there are over 200 myths/folk stories from over 30 ancient cultures that refer to the 'Great Year' – the precession of the equinoxes. Celestial calendars have been the central structure for many past civilizations, whose rituals and social lifestyles were arranged in resonance with celestial cycles. It appears that our ancestors were much more aware of cyclic change than we are today, and so the nature of rise and fall, dark and light ages, catastrophe and catharsis, are common themes within the long journey of evolutionary time. Mythologist Richard Heinberg sums up this rise–fall–rise cycle when he says 'Humanity's moral or spiritual decline must eventually culminate in a catharsis of cataclysmic dimensions, from which will emerge the seed of a restored age of peace and perfection.'[17]

The idea, then, of a planetary near-death experience doesn't seem so fantastical when placed in the context of cyclical change. It may well be that our current age is experiencing the beginnings of this upswing – a rising cycle, rising mind – and as it does so it must first witness the Earth shaking as the planet passes through its own cosmic spiral as part of the precession of the equinoxes. This begins to make more sense when we put together James Lovelock's Gaia hypothesis, Jung's collective unconscious, and the increasing crisis in our ecosystems, biodiversity, geophysical disruptions and climatic variations. The warning signs are all around us, for those with eyes to see, and a mind to care. This is why I use the near-death experience as a metaphor for the transition period we are passing through now, and which is likely to become more distressed in years to come.

Our old mind is one where we wish to intervene with the planet to restore 'business as usual'; i.e. restoring the planet to how we wish it to be rather than adapting to a planet that is in need of readjustment. As scientist James Lovelock, originator of the Gaia hypothesis, recently put it:

> The real Earth does not need saving. It can, will and always has saved itself and it is now starting to do so by changing to a state much less favourable for us and other animals. What people mean by the plea is 'save the planet as we know it' and that is now impossible.[18]

The old mind is one of the greatest obstacles to successfully passing our global initiation. Indeed, this is no child's play, no page of poesy metaphors: astrophysicist Martin Rees (President of the Royal Society 2005–10) has publically stated that he considers the odds of our civilization on Earth surviving to the end of the present century as being no more than 50/50. Rees believes that we are currently at risk from both 'malignant intent' and 'misadventure', citing that the 21st century could be a foreclosure upon the human journey. In his 2003 book *Our Final Century* he writes that 'A catastrophic collapse of civilization could destroy continuity, creating a gap as wide as the cultural chasm that we would now experience with a remote Amazonian tribe.'[19] Again, this reminds us of the scenario put forth in Miller's apocalyptic novel *A Canticle for Leibowitz*, in which a global catastrophe sends civilization back to the Dark Ages, before it again ascends to technological heights. Lovelock is acutely aware of this possibility, which is perhaps why he has proposed creating a 'start-up manual for civilization' including information on how to make fire, agricultural techniques and practices, genetics and technology. This manual would then be distributed far and wide, proposes Lovelock, in order to safeguard some of our treasured knowledge should … should something happen?

In a similar direction NASA once proposed creating a repository on the Moon to preserve humanity's learning, culture and technology. This plan was dubbed the Lunar Ark and intended to preserve technology, art, crops, and both animal and human DNA. Parallel to this is the recently opened (February 2008) Svalbard Global Seed Vault, which is a secure underground seed-bank on the Norwegian island of Spitsbergen, about 1,300 kilometres from the North Pole. The seed vault preserves duplicate seeds from gene banks worldwide and will provide refuge for seeds in the case of large-scale regional or global crises. It is almost as if there are moves underway to prepare for our collective near-death experience. After all, we have been building up for it – it has been estimated that 187 million people perished in the 20th century alone from human agency (war, massacres and persecution). Then in the second half of the 20th century we had the threat of all-out nuclear annihilation hanging over our heads. Now we are in the second decade of the 21st century, and it looks as if things are about to get worse.

A near-death experience may be a sudden event; a sharp shock that literally throws one out-of-the-body and into a terminal phase. In later chapters I will look at some of the factors that may be involved during the transition from the old mind of species infancy to the new mind of adolescence. Yet here I wish to take a brief foray into some of the sudden impacts that might be considered unpredictable and/or unknown, and which could provide a dramatic shock awakening and force a necessary rapid reorganization upon human civilization.

Bio-threats

In 2002 *Wired* magazine ran an article asking prominent scientists for 'long bets'; astrophysicist Martin Rees bet 1,000 dollars 'that by the year 2020 an instance of bioerror or bioterror will have killed a million people'. He countered this by adding – 'Of course, I fervently hope to lose this bet. But I honestly do not expect to.'[20] The issue of bio-threats is a Pandora's box waiting to be opened. In reality only a total police state could offer hope of protection for a world where no bioweapons were manufactured – and even this may not be possible. The reason is that 'biological super-weapons' are so easy to manufacture that they can be created in low-key labs with moderate skill; for example, the Aum Shrinrikyo sect in Japan (now known as Aleph) which released the nerve gas sarin in the Tokyo subway in 1995 killing 12 people. Similarly, we had the mysterious (and never fully explained) anthrax scare in the US after September 2001 where envelopes containing anthrax spores were sent to two US Senators and several media organizations. Five people are known to have died during this amateur, and modest, operation.

Interestingly, only a few months before, on 22–3 June 2001, a bio-terrorist attack simulation was conducted, codenamed 'Operation Dark Winter'. It was designed to carry out a mock version of a covert and widespread smallpox attack on the United States. The scenario involved a localized smallpox attack on Oklahoma City which was then designed to spiral out of control. The simulation was then expected to deal with a catastrophic situation as the disease's rapid spread meant the contagion could not be contained. The mock attack was meant to highlight the consequences of a massive loss of civilian life and the widespread panic, social breakdown and mob violence that would ensue as infrastructures were left unable to cope with the strain.

In what appeared to be another bout of strange coincidence, earlier in the year, in February 2001, a BBC film crew began work on filming a 'docu-drama' that they titled *Smallpox 2002*. The BBC website description – 'This docu-drama reports on a fictitious attack made by terrorists using the smallpox virus. Starting in New York the virus is ruthlessly carried out by one man travelling around the city.' As we know, several months later the anthrax scare in the US became a reality, which was not lost on BBC producer Simon Chinn:

> We began production on Smallpox 2002 in February 2001. 'This is not science fiction', had been our mantra, this could happen. This film is not about a distant future, it's about tomorrow. Suddenly, seven months later, bioterrorism became a reality and Smallpox 2002 acquired the kind of prescience it had never sought.

The BBC docu-drama dealt with the social consequences of a pandemic and how families have to deal with such issues as martial law and enforced quarantine. It is clear that a well-orchestrated bio-terror attack could have disastrous consequences with a knock-on effect on world markets and financial trading; upon a grand enough scale, it could bring the world to a virtual lock-down.

This scenario is not fictitious, as revealed by top Soviet bioweapons expert Colonel Kanatjan Alibekov (now known as Ken Alibek) who published his memoirs *Biohazard* in 1999. Before Alibek defected to the US he was the First Deputy Director of the Soviet Biopreparat programme where he oversaw more than 30,000 workers engaged in modifying organisms to make them extra virulent and resistant to vaccines. In other words, his role was in creating the most virulent forms of biological weapons that had no known antidotes.

Biotechnology has been at a stage for many decades where viruses can be engineered, and equipment is now commercially available to manufacture new pathological agents. In 2002 research scientists at the University of New York at Stony Brook assembled the first synthetic virus from scratch by using the genome sequence for polio. The researchers then injected the artificial virus into mice whereby they were first paralysed and then died. What is even more unsettling is that the researchers say they followed a recipe they downloaded from the Internet and used gene sequences from a mail-order supplier. With these possibilities at stake Martin Rees' 1,000-dollar bet may not seem so far-fetched after all. The situation could also become much worse if knowledge of the human genome were to be incorporated into bio-weapons in order to create targeted DNA bio-weapons. This would be nothing less than 'genetic genocide'.

The threat of a pandemic 'scare' has already been experienced by the media-encircled world through the 2009 swine flu fracas. In this incident a global outbreak of the H1N1 influenza virus (commonly referred to as 'swine flu', and which appeared to be a new strain) began in the state of Veracruz, Mexico, in March 2009. By June 2009 the World Health Organization (WHO) and the US Centers for Disease Control (CDC) declared the outbreak to be a pandemic, despite the relatively few cases of infection. The new 'outbreak', however, had the world's full attention by this time – it was a global pandemic and nations were rushing to secure millions of vaccine doses. Major pharmaceutical companies such as GlaxoSmithKline and Baxter were racing to get vaccines tested, prepared and shipped out to desperately waiting governments worldwide. On 24 October 2009, US President Obama declared swine flu a national emergency, thus releasing federal powers. However, between March 2009 and August 2010 – when WHO finally announced the end of the H1N1 pandemic – there had been officially recorded a worldwide total of 14,286 deaths. Whilst seemingly sizeable, this is well below the annual average of 'normal' flu-related seasonal deaths which is between 250,000 and 500,000 globally every year. The figures from the swine flu 2009 outbreak were well below what should have been designated as a pandemic.

In January 2010 a member of the health committee at the Council of Europe, Wolfgang Wodarg, joined other critics to claim that major pharmaceutical firms had organized a 'campaign of panic' to pressurize the WHO into declaring a 'false pandemic' in order to make profit for selling vaccines. Whatever the specifics here, it does show that virus outbreaks such as H1N1 swine flu, a variation on bird flu (H5N1), SARS (severe acute respiratory syndrome), foot and mouth disease, etc., are all in danger of becoming global pandemics due to our human chains of transmission. In a world of high mobility and interconnectedness, localized outbreaks can easily become global threats. It is perhaps only a matter of time before the next mutated virus becomes a 'near-death' catalyst for a slumbering mass mind.

Technology Shock

Being integrated makes us vulnerable, not only as human chains of transmission but also as dependent technological chains. We have never been a species in isolation; we have always existed within a complex ecosystem of animal, vegetable and mineral (as the old guessing game used to go). Now we have an added ecosystem which is a technological one. As such, we have co-evolved a world that is entwined symbiotically between the biological and the technological. Philosopher Joël de Rosnay considers that our species is now symbiotic and, as such, information and energy regularly transfers through both biological and technical networks, enmeshing all processes together.[21] In such a symbiotic world of increased integration and interdependence there is increased potential for disruptive technological shocks:

> We are entering an era when a single person can, by
> one clandestine act, cause millions of deaths or render a
> city uninhabitable for years, and when a malfunction in
> cyberspace can cause havoc worldwide to a significant
> segment of the economy: air transport, power generation,

> or the financial system. Indeed, disaster could be caused by
> someone who is merely incompetent rather than malign.[22]

The reality of the world is that we are moving from physical interventions-invasions into cyber-warfare and sabotage. This is becoming all too common over recent years with such incidents as the Titan Rain and Estonia cyber-attacks. Titan Rain was the name given to a series of well-coordinated attacks against US computer systems beginning in 2003 which were aimed against sensitive military information. A few years later on 27 April 2007 the cyber-attacks against the country of Estonia (known as the Estonian Cyberwar) crashed, hijacked and defaced the websites of the Estonian parliament, banks, ministries, media outlets and political sites. It was a highly sophisticated attack, considered to have been the second largest instance of state-sponsored cyber-warfare after Titan Rain. That accolade, however, was challenged in 2010 with the arrival of the computer worm known as Stuxnet.

The Stuxnet computer worm, which was first discovered in June 2010, was specifically created and programmed to attack critical infrastructure systems (what are referred to as Supervisory Control and Data Acquisition systems – SCADA). This worm, now dubbed the world's 'first cyber- superweapon' by experts, has infected a high number of critical energy infrastructure systems in Iran, notably its nuclear facilities, as well as a large number of Chinese facilities. One expert digital security company stated that the Stuxnet computer attacks could only have been produced with nation-state support, thus making it a specific cyber-weapon that will lead to the creation of a new arms race in the world.

Imagine a state suddenly having its energy and communication networks crash: electricity networks go offline; all Internet communication is stopped; transportation grounds to a halt as transport networks cease to function. The food would stop reaching the shops, people would be told to stay indoors and not to travel as traffic signals may not be working. Hospitals would revert to generators for power back-up whilst desperately needed medicines may not be distributed to those home-bound. It would create wide-scale panic leading to civil unrest and looting. If the infrastructures were not immediately restored then eventually everyone would turn to fending for themselves. The country would be put under martial law and some areas would revert to tribal organization and brute force. In such complex 'civilized' societies it only takes a critical disturbance to create widespread breakdown.

In late September 2010 the US Department of Homeland Security hosted a massive simulated cyber-attack exercise named Cyber Storm III, which is aimed at testing the security of both government and private-sector organizations. The US government has also recently launched a grand programme dubbed 'Perfect Citizen' that aims to detect cyber-attacks against private companies and governmental agencies responsible for infrastructures such as energy, transportation and security networks. This shows that the threat to a nation's critical infrastructures is being taken seriously. In May 2010 Cyber Command (CYBERCOM) officially became operational in the US after several years of preparation. It plans a rapid expansion to ensure that all military computer networks are free from hackers and that military activities are fully protected against cyber-spies. Procedures are also allegedly underway for CYBERCOM to offer assistance to governmental and civilian networks, effectively intertwining military and civilian defence systems.

Similarly, the UK government released its National Security Strategy in October 2010, listing cyber-attacks as one of the most important challenges faced, alongside international terrorism. Following this, the UK's Strategic Defence and Security Review explained how Britain will use the new £500-million boost to defend itself against such attacks. The head of Britain's Intelligence and Security Committee (ISC) is alleged to have warned that cyber-attacks against both government and corporate computer systems could be 'the next Pearl Harbor'.

The rise of cyber-warfare is another aspect of the growing arsenal of 'silent weapons' that are filling the technosphere. The technological arms race now includes an array of space-based weapons and electromagnetic pulse weapons that can be operated through an invisible landscape. In this regard we may not even see the near-death experience coming; it will be shrouded in a virtual ether. However, the ensuing technological shock will be all too real, and may be reminiscent of a throw-back to the pre-technological Dark Ages. Our over-reliance upon external, internal, and behind-the-scenes systems may turn out to be our greatest weakness.

Natural Hazards

We may not need to worry about near-Earth objects (NEOs) hitting us, such as asteroids from space that have left us a crater-pocked Earth, since we have our own natural hazards to worry about. Despite the 50 per cent risk of an asteroid impact in this century on the scale of the Tunguska event that occurred in June 1908, we are likely to have concerns closer to home. The Earth is currently experiencing an unpredictable set of geological changes and disruptions, including hurricanes, earthquakes and volcanic eruptions. The year 2010 especially highlighted the fragility of the human species upon a dynamic and shifting planet.

Early 2010 opened with a record seismic bang with the earthquake in Haiti on 12 January that was of a magnitude of 7 (on the moment magnitude scale). Due to the geology of the island and its living conditions it suffered a dramatic impact. It has been estimated that 3 million people were affected by the earthquake; a reported 230,000 fatalities; 300,000 injuries; 1 million homeless; and nearly 300,000 buildings damaged or destroyed. Such huge figures have made the Haiti earthquake the sixth deadliest earthquake in recorded history – and yet this was soon followed by the fifth strongest since the 19th century. On 27 February an 8.8 earthquake (moment magnitude scale) struck off the coast of Chile causing huge tremors across 80 per cent of the country, and being felt as far away as major cities in Argentina and Peru. The earthquake also triggered a tsunami which resulted in warnings being issued in 53 countries; the San Diego area of California and northeastern parts of Japan were also affected. Chile experienced a blackout for 93 per cent of its population that, for some, lasted for several days. Looting ensued and the military were called in to restore peace and control damaged areas. The year 2010 was surely off to an explosive start – all that remained was for a volcanic eruption to add to the mix.

On 14 April 2010 the Icelandic volcano Eyjafjallajökull, which had had some minor eruptions the previous month, finally bellowed volcanic ash several kilometres into the atmosphere causing havoc and affecting economic, political and cultural events throughout the world. A European air travel ban was put in place causing extensive worldwide travel disruption. The International Air Transport Association has estimated that the airline industry was losing £130 million per day. Fears grew that daily deliveries of food supplies would be affected and that some countries, such as the UK, would experience shortages. Spoilage concerns also disrupted stocks of medications; global transport companies such as FedEx and DHL had to initiate road routes to compensate for closed air space; travel firms reported daily losses in the millions; some car manufacturers and IT firms were forced to suspend production because of interruptions in the supply chain of electronics. Kenya suffered greatly because of its time-sensitive flower export industry which, reported its Flower Council, had to destroy 3,000 tonnes of flowers due to spoilage. On top of this, cultural and sporting events saw widespread cancellations and disruptions; royal and state visits were suspended; and political dignitaries were forced to cancel their travel plans.

From just a few days of cloud ash the world was brought into chaos and upheaval. Not only companies suffered but people were given a brief picture of the fragility of such on-time delivery economies and lifestyles. We expect fresh food on the shelves each day; we expect to step onto an airplane and be halfway around the world in just a few hours; we are used to everything around us being *on time, in time,* and *timely.* The Icelandic ash cloud cracked this illusion and revealed, to those who could see, that our global systems may be efficient and convenient yet they are not resilient.

The Eyjafjallajökull volcanic eruption was estimated to have emitted about 150,000 tonnes of carbon dioxide each day into the atmosphere. The US Geological Survey says that worldwide volcanoes release about 200 million tonnes of carbon dioxide into the Earth's atmosphere each year. Natural hazards are often beyond our reach and responsibility, yet they have the potential to throw the world into great tremors and shocks. Such shocks are part of living upon a shifting Earth – a molten-core rock – that is hurtling through cosmic-radiated space. The quicker we grasp this fact the better it will help us realize that security can never be taken for granted. Each day that passes brings our civilization one step closer to a near-death experience through natural hazards. And it may even be a 'natural' hazard that is human-made.

Man-made Hazards

We may not need any natural hazards to force us into an uncomfortable rite of passage; it seems we are quite capable as a species of providing the necessary shocks ourselves. Within the industrial period of our techno-logical phase we have had our fair share of disastrous accidents. In truth there are industrial accidents occurring throughout the world virtually all the time; many of these are minor and do not make (or are forced not to make) the headlines. There are, no doubt, countless 'near misses' that are left under the radar, and of which the general public know nothing. For the sake of brevity, I shall refer to only a few of the most infamous human hazards that have occurred over the last three decades.

The Bhopal gas tragedy is infamous the world over as being the worst industrial catastrophe to date. On the night of 2 December 1984 the Union Carbide India Limited pesticide plant in Bhopal, India, leaked a poisonous gas – methyl isocyanate – along with other chemicals. The immediate death toll was in the thousands; and there have since been several thousand more fatalities from gas-related diseases. A government statement in 2006 claimed that the gas leak caused 558,125 injuries in total, including many thousands of partial and permanently disabling injuries. Compensation has never been adequately forthcoming, according to those families affected by the tragedy.

Less than two years later, on 26 April 1986, what is considered to be the worst nuclear power plant accident in history occurred. The Chernobyl Nuclear Power Plant in Ukraine (then part of the Soviet Union) had a series of ruptures when a surge in power output damaged a reactor vessel. The ensuing explosions sent radioactive plumes of smoke into the atmosphere, and then began to drift over large parts of the western Soviet Union, and across much of Europe. It has been estimated that 400 times more radioactive material was released during the Chernobyl accident than the atomic bombing of Hiroshima. Although relatively few deaths were related directly to the disaster (mostly plant workers and rescue teams), it is calculated that several thousand will ultimately die from cancer-related illnesses.

The aftermath of such hazards is not only immediate but is also longer lasting and farther reaching. In the case of radioactivity it can enter the environmental ecosystems and leave residual traces for many years.

Radioactivity enters rivers, reservoirs, lakes and groundwater, leading to contamination of fish stocks and drinking water. Fauna, flora and livestock are also affected, with many forests and local animals dying as a result. Even in Europe many cattle were found to have radiation contamination with some herds having to be kept out of the human food chain. Such man-made hazards inject artificial and unnatural substances into natural ecosystems, adding to an invisible landscape of human pollution and contamination.

This was further shown only three years later, on 24 March 1989, by the Exxon Valdez oil spill in the Gulf of Alaska, which has been long considered one of the most destructive environmental disasters. This is not because of the volume of oil spilled, which was between 260,000 and 750,000 barrels, but because its remote location meant the clean-up operation was slow and difficult. The oil spill was eventually to cover 1,300 miles of coastline and 11,000 square miles of ocean. The Alaskan waters are home to a wide variety of organisms, and the massive damage to the environment included the killing of around 250,000 seabirds, 3,000 sea otters, 300 harbour seals, 250 bald eagles and 22 killer whales. The oil spill also devastated the Alaskan fishing industry, leading to bankruptcies and several suicides. The Exxon Valdez disaster remained as one of the worst oil spills in the public mind due to the huge media coverage and exposure it received. This, however, was eclipsed by the BP oil disaster of 2010.

On 20 April 2010 the Deepwater Horizon drilling rig suffered an explosion, killing 11 platform workers, and causing an oil spill that flowed for 3 months from a sea-floor oil gusher. This oil spill in the Gulf of Mexico (referred to as the BP oil spill) is now considered the greatest environmental disaster in US history, and is the largest accidental marine oil spill in the history of the petroleum industry. It may never be possible to accurately estimate the number of millions of barrels that gushed into the sea over the three-month period, not to mention the huge amounts of chemical dispersants used, most notably Corexit 9500. The Gulf seas may take decades to fully recover from the contamination, with fish stocks being severely affected. Due to the nature of the oil spill; i.e. from a sea-floor blowout rather than a sea-level spill, the longer-term consequences of the disaster may never be fully known. Also, unlike the Valdez spill, media coverage of the BP spill was severely limited and, according to many reports, actively suppressed. What is known, however, is that the spill has caused extensive damage to marine and wildlife habitat, fisheries, tourism, wetlands and shorelines, and allegedly people's health.

Bearing in mind the few incidents mentioned here it may become obvious to many of us that we have had plenty of notice – so we can't say we were not warned! Yet still we have neither awoken nor passed through our global initiation: we are still struggling with species infancy, teetering on the brink of our rite of passage; at the threshold of the underworld. Yet all these incidents have also accumulated within our environments and ecosystems. Whilst we have not yet been overwhelmingly shocked into realization of our crisis window, we will still suffer in the coming years from the damage we inflict today.

The attack on the Twin Towers on 11 September 2001 was a wake-up call for many. Perhaps an insecure future of nuclear 'guerrilla terrorism' will provide the final alarm: so-called 'dirty bombs' (conventional bombs coated with plutonium) placed in crowded urban centres. With plutonium/uranium more or less 'easily' available on black markets, it is a plausible scenario. Again, as Martin Rees, President of the Royal Society (2005–10) states:

> … in the twenty-first century, humanity is more at risk
> than ever before from misapplication of science. And the
> environmental pressures induced by collective human
> actions could trigger catastrophes more threatening than any
> natural hazards … New sciences will soon empower small
> groups, even individuals, with similar leverage over society.
> Our increasingly interconnected world is vulnerable to new
> risks; 'bio' or 'cyber', terror or error. These risks can't be
> eliminated: indeed it will be hard to stop them from growing
> without encroaching on some cherished personal freedoms.[23]

Indeed, individuals and small groups are empowered like never before with the misapplication of science, the crowning gems from our technological age. With such potential catastrophes we may find the human species being thrown suddenly into a collective psychological near-death experience. After all, we are doing it to many of the species with which we share the planet. Before the arrival of *homo sapiens* one species in one million became extinct each year; now it is closer to one in a thousand. Some are directly killed off whilst many other extinctions are due to human-induced changes to habitat or from the introduction of non-indigenous species into the ecosystem by human intervention. Global biodiversity is now being eroded like never before through interventionist practices, whether knowingly or otherwise.

Dr John Alroy, a palaeobiologist from Macquarie University, recently compiled data from nearly 100,000 fossil collections worldwide, tracking the fate of marine animals during extreme extinction events some 250 million years ago. His findings, which were published in the international journal *Science*, showed a major extinction event was currently underway that had the potential to be more severe than any others in history. Geological records show that there have been five great extinctions within Earth's known history. Of all the species that ever existed, fewer than 10 per cent remain on Earth today, so it may be that the human species is bringing about its own near extinction – its collective initiation into an uncomfortable yet very necessary rite of passage. We are, it seems, fast approaching the end of our childhood.

Childhood's End

Our human collective mind has been full of creative ideas concerning the progression to the next stage of evolutionary consciousness for a long time. It appears we are all tapping into a creative vision that exists as a non-physical shared mind. As the interconnectivity of our global species intensifies, it is as if this convergence will push us to another level. This idea has become popular through the writings of the Jesuit priest Pierre Teilhard de Chardin, who in taking Vladimir Vernadsky's notion of *noosphere*, conceptualized the emergence of a shared mind through the increasing interaction of human minds. Just as the biosphere is the global sum of all ecosystems, the *noosphere* would represent the sum of all human shared minds. This would emerge as the organization of humankind becomes ever more complex, and social networks ever more intricate and expansive. Of course, with the dramatic and sudden rise of the Internet, ideas about the *noosphere* are now rampant and popular. They also represent the concept of a global brain which, according to systems-philosopher Ervin Laszlo, is 'the quasi-neural energy – and information – processing network created by six and a half billion humans on the planet, interacting in many ways, private as well as public, and on many levels, local as well as global.'[24] Both concepts are alike in that they express the notion of an emerging planetary conscious-ness which, it is speculated, would be the natural state of our evolving species mind.

For Teilhard, the natural law of complex systems indicates that all life, including the universe, is developing/growing towards ever greater integration and unification. This, Teilhard states, will eventually culminate in a point of singularity, what he calls the 'Omega Point'. The trajectory of evolution, therefore, is towards an ultimate unification of all mind/consciousness. At an earlier stage, however, is the formation of a planetary consciousness, which is more akin to the global brain concept. The further integration of human civilization is often supported by the exponential increase in information (since information is itself a form of energy). In 2005 experts noted that information generated was doubling every 36 months; in 2007 this had accelerated to doubling every 11 months. On 4 August 2010 Google CEO Eric Schmidt stated at the Techonomy conference that every two days we are now creating as much information 'as we did from the dawn of civilization up until 2003', and most of this new information is 'user-generated content'; i.e. it's the information that the people create themselves and add to the digital world. A recent study by IBM concluded that as of 2010 the amount of information is now doubling every 11 hours. With these statistics, it does appear that our global digital civilization is moving towards some form of informational 'Omega Point' (or 'singularity'). Creative minds have, however, seen this more as a singularity of mind-consciousness rather than physical information.

Science-fiction is the realm that contains perhaps more representa-tions of the collective evolutionary mind than any other medium. Olaf Stapledon's writings have the recurring theme of a 'supermind' that is composed of many individual consciousnesses. His most famous novel – *Star Maker* – has as its central idea the formation of collective minds from many telepathically linked individuals, as well as the linking with higher collective minds of planets, galaxies, and eventually the cosmos itself. One of the most well-known science-fiction writers, Arthur C Clarke, wrote a popular book titled *Childhood's End* which depicted all the Earth's children eventually displaying psychic powers. A race of technically superior beings – the Overlords – are sent to Earth to protect and guide the Earth's younger generation as they evolve beyond their material bodies and eventually merge with the universal 'Overmind'. In a similar manner, the narrative of Doris Lessing's *The Making of the Representative for Planet 8* involves a planet undergoing an ice age that eventually covers the whole planet and destroys its civilization and peoples. However, as the final 'representatives' of the planet journey to the pole in their final endeavour, their physical bodies die but their conscious minds transcend and merge into a single collective consciousness that becomes the planetary mind and thus its final collective representative for the now frozen planet.

Psychologist and near-death expert Kenneth Ring sees such creative visions as heralding the *shamanizing of modern humanity* – that is, helping to develop 'our latent capacities for imaginal perception'.[25] The human capacity for exercising 'imaginal perception', for creative visions, may indeed help our species to experience – or endure – the 'shamanizing process' of our global rites of passage towards a more functional planetary mind. Philosopher Michael Grosso also notes how a new type of species mind arises out of critical times, amid the collective possibility of annihilation; in other words, the threat of species death catalyses the rise of a species 'mind-at-large'.[26] The transition to a planetary mind, a more evolved state of human consciousness, will be crucial for the continuation of our species upon Earth. As Vaclav Havel pointed out in 1991 in a speech to the joint session of US Congress:

> Without a global revolution in the sphere of human
> consciousness, nothing will change for the better ... and
> the catastrophe towards which this world is headed – the
> ecological, social, demographic, or general breakdown of
> civilization – will be unavoidable.

A more empathic mindset is needed for our planetary future; an empathic consciousness that recognizes the evolutionary process and acts responsibly in light of this perception.

The future is more likely to drive towards a singularity of mindset than a technological singularity, as when the finite energy sources upon our planet dwindle we will be required to increase the psychic potency of our collective thinking. It is this transition that will be discussed in the following chapters. So far, the first part of this book has dealt with the formation of our current mindset, and how our modern technological state of mind has now brought us to a critical impasse. We have now entered the crisis window, the transition phase – that heroic journey into the underworld – where we will be forced to experience a shamanic initiatory experience, perhaps a near-death experience, before we can emerge as an adolescent species with a new, more mature mind. Until we reach that stage, however, we will have to struggle with the death throes of the old mind, as old systems cling to power and global infrastructures attempt to remain in control of a world in transition.

PART II

Passing Through the Underworld

CHAPTER FOUR

The Dark Night of the Soul:

The Death Throes of the Old

You say that this society will come to an end, because societies always have done so. I wonder whether they have ended because they were not really societies at all.

Idries Shah

No sensible decision can be made without taking into account not only the world as it is, but the world as it will be.

Isaac Asimov

The crew of spacecraft Earth is in virtual mutiny to the order of the universe.

Edgar Mitchell, astronaut

The preceding chapters of this book took a peek at how human life on planet Earth might have arrived at its point of great transition; i.e. at the gates of initiation, awaiting a transformational rite of passage. I speculated that global unease exists within the collective mind and that some of these intuitions have played out within people's individual visions, dreams, or during hypnotic sessions. The 'modern' mind that has exerted itself upon the present world and which developed on a trajectory of Western industrialization, until arriving at the technological age, exhibits a great deal of short-sightedness. It is a mind-at-large that doesn't quite seem to understand past patterns of change. It seems to possess a great amount of guilt (myth of the Fall?); a large amount of blindness (the myth of progress?); and little historical remembrance (ignorance is bliss?). It is little wonder then that a majority of people today, especially in the developed nations, are surprised, bemused, and somewhat dazed to find themselves staring into a melting pot of uncertainty. Why does the world have to change? Why can't it continue on its present path? Well, growth is about experiencing great change, and cyclic renewal as infinite growth is not possible upon a finite planet.

Part II of this book will take a brief tour through the 'dark passage' that we are now venturing into. This is part of our collective *rites of passage*: it will shake us, reshuffle and reorientate a great deal of life on the planet; and it will also, hopefully, catalyse and prepare us for a psychophysical transformation. The reorientation required – both psychological and physical – may be far from linear, I contend. The next few chapters, however, will largely concentrate on the physical aspect of the situation as we wrestle with the cloak of the old world system that clings onto a *modus operandi*, refusing to let go without a fight. Despite our glorious, gleaming, polished achievements that the world displays with pride, our current systems (social, cultural, political and economic) are remarkably anachronistic, cunningly deceptive, opaque, and in dire need of renovation. Yet in order to sweep out the brushwood we may be forced to endure a metaphorical, and literal, *dark night of the soul*.

The next 20 years cannot be the same as the last 20 years. Change is upon us rapidly, even if we are not aware of its pace. As mentioned in the previous chapter, every two days the world is creating as much information as was created from the dawn of civilization up until 2003. The somewhat ethereal (i.e. non-physical) nature of information, however, is not the only thing that is speeding up – the whole growth of the world is. Nation states have expanded into regional blocs: EU (European Union); AU (African Union); UNASUR (Union of South American Nations); AL (Arab League); and ASEAN (Association of Southeast Asian Nations), to name but a few. Nations that were once considered less developed are now expanding extensively into global players – e.g. China and India – and nations/regions that are strong in resources – Russia, Iran, Brazil, etc. – are shifting their positions in the geopolitical arena of the 'Great Game'. The world is now swaying between regions that are resource sinks (importing energy) and resource sources (exporting energy) as our globalizing civilizations push towards overshoot. Overshoot is an ecological term for a population exceeding the environment's carrying capacity; i.e. the ability to supply the needs of the population. The result, as I will discuss in this chapter, is usually an implosion or slow decline and/or migration.

What makes this transitional period so precarious is that it is based around the transaction of energy: both physical and psychic. Let me qualify this – yes, everything *is* energy if we take the view that matter is a construct of 'dense energy' out of the universal energy vacuum. The new quantum paradigm is revealing much about the nature of universal energy and how matter and energy fields interrelate (as I discuss in Part III). Yet information, food, sunlight, thoughts, oil, all these things are energy too: energy is that source which allows any system to continue to grow against the forces of decay. That is, anything that goes against the classic law of entropy. Entropy, as part of the second law of thermodynamics, states that all energy moves from a more intensive state to a less intensive state; i.e. energy dissipates. We continue to grow because we can take in constant amounts of energy each day to store and use – we eat, we drink and we breathe. We have more energy than we need to maintain our body and thus we are generally able to grow; until, that is, our bodily systems deteriorate with age to the point whereby no amount of energy is sufficient to maintain them. The same also applies to our nations, our regional blocs, our civilizations and our ecosystems. Each cycle of growth and change is about the balance between energy and entropy. And this is why the next 20 years are going to see a lot of change.

Energy & Entropy

Taking a leaf out of the science of complex systems, any given system (whether biological or social) requires sufficient energy to maintain internal structure, so the system does not break apart. Now when this is amplified on a larger scale we see that as a state/nation/civilization increases its level of internal relationships, more energy is required to stabilize the system and maintain its working capacity. In other words, for any system to maintain its stability it must be regularly fed by an appropriate degree of available energy. Not only does this functioning cause a great strain on resources, but it also makes the 'efficiency' and running of the system sensitive and vulnerable to shocks. As a system expands and increases its degree of interconnections, it generally becomes less resilient and more fragile to shock impacts.

Anthropologist and historian Joseph Tainter, in his book *The Collapse of Complex Societies*, noted how these very same principles could be seen as triggers for the collapse of the Mayan and Roman civilizations.[1] The significant trigger for societal collapse was not solely environmental mismanagement but, importantly, the rate of return of energetic investments required to maintain the level of social complexity. The notion of 'net energy' is the crucial equation: if more energy is invested or put into any given system than the amount of energy gained as a result, then we well and truly have a problem. For example, if a person works 7 days a week, 12 hours each day, only to gain a slice of stale bread at the end of the week, then this is a bad energy investment and is likely to lead to an early death. And it is this predicament that has faced many cultures and civilizations in the past, resulting in the tragic nature of historical cyclic collapse.

According to anthropological studies, the ancient Sumerian civilization went into terminal decline because of the inability of its agricultural land to feed and maintain a growing population. In Sumer's case it was likely that soil salinity played an important part in its break-up, as increasing soil salinity led to massive crop failures in the Indus Valley 4,000 years ago. Similarly, archaeologists also believe that soil salinity lead to massive crop failures and the abandoning of lands in Central America, affecting such civilizations as the Maya.[2] The loss of soil fertility has been a major factor in the collapse of several major civilizations throughout history. Another case in point is Easter Island, a very insular society that, like the Mayans, succumbed to topsoil erosion due to cutting down virtually all of their trees to build boats. The exposed topsoil was thus eroded leading to loss of soil fertility and the depletion of their food source. Those that didn't migrate, eventually starved to death leaving an 'empty' island for future explorers. This is a classic example of the struggle between rising entropy in the face of weakening energy sources.

The same thing happened to one of the world's mightiest empires. The implosion of the Roman Empire can be said to be another case of overshoot – the inability to supply its expanding empire with the necessary resources; in other words, imperial over-reach. The more Rome conquered territories both at home and abroad, the more it needed to supply and maintain its expanding infrastructures. Yet as the empire increasingly failed to recoup its energy investment (e.g. through enough new taxes to pay for the military expansion), the fringes of the empire ceased to be supported. The power infrastructure weakened, allowing invading hordes to enter; less taxes were thus flowing into Rome, which meant that the Roman Empire was being supported by diminishing returns. When no longer able to maintain its empire by new conquests and plunder, Rome was forced to turn more heavily towards agriculture for sustenance. However, as the Roman Empire began to draw more heavily upon its agriculture, this led to declining soil fertility and decreases in agricultural yields. At its height the Roman Empire relied on grain being delivered by barges through the port of Ostia, which were then transported up the Tiber to Rome. It is reported that by the 1st century AD more than 30 million *modii* (1 *modius* is about 1 quarter of a bushel) of grain was being imported annually to Rome from northern Africa and Egypt. The anthropologist Joseph Tainter suggests that:

> During the later period of the Roman empire, agriculture provided more than 90 percent of the government's revenue. Food production had become the critical linchpin in the survival of Rome.[3]

The final collapse of Rome ushered in what became known as the Dark Ages, and the world was set back a few hundred years as energy use became more localized and 'low-capacity'.

Continuing with the theme of the energy-entropy cycle, the Dark Ages finally entered a new period of 'energetic' growth as new farming practices in the late Middle Ages – horse and plough – created increased harvests and new food crops. Again there followed the cyclic pattern of population expansion, growth in urban settlements, and commerce. The new energy sources were wood, wind and water. By 1086 there were more than 5,600 watermills in England alone, spread out amongst over 3,000 communities. Watermills soon were put into widespread use throughout Europe, including milling grain, tanning, sawing, crushing ore and operating bellows for furnaces. Watermills, however, as their name suggests, had to be constructed near a source of flowing water, usually beside a river. It is said that in the 1790s there were more than 500,000 watermills operating in Europe alone.[4] Windmills, on the other hand, could be constructed almost anywhere there was available land as wind is essentially free. Thus, windmills also emerged into widespread use, especially amongst the rural communities (hence, 'commoners' mills'). Yet nothing is for free – not even wind power – as with energy there is always a cost. For nearly 800 years the European expansion used trees to build watermills, windmills, farm equipment, ships; also to fire the furnaces and heat the homes. This then resulted in a depletion of energy resources; namely, a wood crisis. Yet how did Europe subsequently manage to upgrade into the first Industrial Revolution? Because a new energy source was found in time before the onslaught of collapse – coal.

Coal proved to be a hard-working industrial energy source, quite literally. It powered the heavy machinery that constructed the infrastructure for a new 'modern' world and fuelled the new imperial reach – the British Empire. This period of history marks the world's discovery of the magic of fossil fuels, and it has continued to rush ahead with accelerating growth without as much as a look back to earlier historical lessons. It has been fossil fuel energy that made it possible to have such a radical break from the old agrarian world and to leap into an increasingly urbanized industrial one. And yet this newly discovered energy source has been on Earth long before any human ever set foot on it. As John Michael Greer notes:

No human being had to put a single day's work or a single gallon of diesel fuel into growing the tree ferns of the Carboniferous period that turned into the Pennsylvanian coal beds, nor did they have to raise the Jurassic sea life that became the oil fields of Texas.[5]

What we've been doing so well for the past 150 years is living off the fruits of 'free' energy. Millions of years of stored energy came gushing out of the ground into blackened greedy hands. And now it seems that our present civilizations have all but wasted it in a century and a half of extreme extravagance. In going global we have entered – and entertained – a new myth: infinite growth within a world of finite resources.

There's No Infinity in a Finite World

Despite some of the optimistic claims from the energy industry, planet Earth is a finite resource. Let's face it – planet Earth cannot import oil. Yes, countries can – and more often than not they do – but a planet does not have this luxury. Our planet imports plentiful supplies of sunlight and solar radiation constantly (otherwise the planet would not sustain life). Now that we are more or less living upon an industrialized, urbanized planet, our local, physical energy needs are primary. And oil is a pervasive energy that is the lifeblood of modern civilization. It fuels the vast majority of the world's travel and transport means – cars, trucks, airplanes, trains, ships, farm equipment, the military, etc. Oil is also the primary source for many of our fundamental, everyday needs: fertilizers; cosmetics; plastics; packaging; lubricants; asphalt/road building; mechanical components; etc. It took the last 150 years, and huge investments of time and money, to construct the industrial, economic and social infrastructures that process the black gold from liquid slime into some of our most precious components. These infrastructures are now embedded throughout our world, providing the veins that carry our precious lifeblood.

As the human need (greed?) for this energy source exploded, each generation constructed more complex, pervasive and interdependent technologies that formed linking systems into many areas of human life – for better or for worse. Industrializing society now forms an intricate and entangled web of interconnections, dependencies and dubious alliances. Our modern global energy system is now so integrated that components, equipment, etc., are outsourced and involved in an elaborate oil-dependent chain of transport and delivery. Furthermore, oil prices play a key role in the global economy: increasing food prices; transport; delivery; travel; increased unemployment and rising living costs. And if these negative impacts occur during an economic downturn then their effects are exacerbated. This energy-intensive weak spot of our globalizing civilization was exposed, decades ago, by Roberto Vacca in his popular book *The Coming Dark Age*, warning that the interdependence of technological systems could turn out to be our Achilles heel. Yet our energy-intensive lifestyles (especially in the industrializing nations) are addicted to oil; and with a current consumption of 84 million barrels per day, how are we ever going to replace this?

Many people still don't fully understand the energy situation we are facing; and many of those who *do* know are in active denial. Either way, we should all know better. Yet reform rarely occurs during a smooth patch, and is seldom initiated without drastic reasons. In other words, reform is more generally the result of revolution than the rational implementation of foresight and vision. What I am trying to outline here is that our rapidly expanding, economically-driven, global civilization is the result of a once readily available and plentiful supply of fossil fuel energy – oil. Our reliance has been placed upon a finite physical energy to fuel our living industrial organism. Now that situation is changing. The predicament facing us now is not only a technical one; it is also a social and cultural crisis as we have allowed our dependence upon oil to embed itself into virtually every aspect of life throughout the world, whether it has been for convenience, comfort, or colonialism. Yet perhaps it has been the privileged minority in the more developed societies that have benefited most from what has become a culture of excess and extravagant waste. Our globalizing empires of human construct are Babel towers of illusory wealth and permanence. How close are they to a tipping point?

The influential 2005 Hirsch report that was prepared for the US government stated that 'peaking will happen, but the timing is uncertain'. And peaking means that there will still be large reserves remaining, only that the half-way mark has been reached. Therefore the rate of world oil production cannot increase, and thus will decrease with time. It also means that the remaining oil reserves will be harder to extract, of lower quality, needing more refining processes and greater investments; all costing more money. The last super giant oil reservoirs worldwide were found in 1967 and 1968. The Hirsch report states that:

> As peaking is approached, liquid fuel prices and price volatility will increase dramatically, and, without timely mitigation, the economic, social, and political costs will be unprecedented. Viable mitigation options exist on both the supply and demand sides, but to have substantial impact, they must be initiated more than a decade in advance of peaking.[6]

The report continues by saying that to deal with the issue of world oil production peaking will involve literally trillions of dollars and require many years of intense effort. Further, that past energy crises will provide little guidance for these times ahead as they are uncharted waters. Increasing global demand has been so far supplied through the continued use of older oil reservoirs, which are now more likely to be within a phase of declining production. With no new significant oil reserves being developed, and with global oil demand expected to grow 50 per cent by 2025, the future looks troubling. The Hirsch report closes by saying: 'In summary, the problem of the peaking of world conventional oil production is unlike any yet faced by modern industrial society.'[7] Well, we might ask – has peak oil arrived?

Below is a list of the estimated dates/time frame for peak oil alongside the status of the speaker:

2006–07 –	Bakhitari, A M S, Iranian oil executive
2007–09 –	Simmons, M R, investment banker
After 2007 –	Skrebowski, C, petroleum journal editor
Before 2009 –	Deffeyes, K S, oil company geologist, ret.
Before 2010 –	Goodstein, D, Vice Provost, Cal Tech
Around 2010 –	Campbell, C J, oil company geologist, ret.
After 2010 –	World Energy Council (NGO)
2010–20 –	Laherrere, J, oil company geologist, ret.

2016 –	EIA/DOE analysis
After 2020 –	CERA, energy consultants
2025 or later –	Shell, major oil company
No visible peak –	Lynch, M C, energy economist[8]

This is an interesting sliding scale, especially when we note the affiliation of the respective speakers. It is thus inevitable that peak oil will be, if it is not already, a physical reality. We therefore have to accept that a future of declining fossil fuel energy is upon us, with all this implies for our global futures. Intervention by governments is likely to become more overt as the economic and social implications of a dwindling energy supply become more visible; and before the chaos begins. Will this be the beginning of a long drawn-out descent as some commentators predict[9]; or will it be, as some others suggest, a terrific fall with a big bang?[10] Either way, we are assured that energy is the lifeblood of any living organism; and we have been pumping our global body with the blood of a finite, dwindling sticky source.

The initiatory passage through the underworld, as alluded to in the previous chapter, is a dark journey. There is little light, and the trial is about passing through this darkened terrain in order to arrive back to the light of the awaiting world above. Only when the hero returns is it with a new light: that of vision, experience and an altered state of consciousness. So, too, may our global society be pushed through a 'dark night of the soul' in order to find a new collective, creative vision of light. Consciousness may well be the energy of the future – *our new lifeblood* – that fuels our global society into adolescence and renewed growth. In the meantime, we are struggling with the older energies of black goo, sulphuric slime, and the dangerous blackened coal pits where humans dig like slaves.

The world we are moving into requires new myths, whereby we are not constrained by the powers of corporate greed, political tyranny and the suppression of human creative vision. Fossil fuels feed an economic control system, which benefits the few at the top of the social hierarchy. Profits line the pockets of the major global players, and pipelines cross, cut into and devastate the lands of the impoverished majority. It is an energy system that perpetuates a lower form of *psychical energy*. It is a physical network that coerces – both covertly and overtly – the lifestyles and circumstances of our present social systems. This is why I suggest that the transitional initiatory period, our *dark night of the soul*, will be replaced by a psychophysical transformation of life on planet Earth. It is my view that the human race is in line for some great changes as a more creative, empathic, collectively integrated field of consciousness begins to emerge across the planet.

Yet it would certainly help if we could break away from the culture of cultivating uselessness. As if bored with our experiences, we create a whole array of artless gadgets to amuse us and fill the infantile hours. We live in distracting times, racing towards the cliff edge like a convoy of excited, pharma-fuelled lemmings. Instead we should be putting both our physical and our psychical energies into moving through this shift and preparing for a rearrangement of life circumstances. Rather than hoping to maintain the cracking, crumbling status quo we should be thinking about creating an alternative path. The industrial cultures created Modernity, which is attempting to model itself as a global culture, and which is an artificial device that devalues our original and creative component. We may be in danger of replacing the creative capacity of the human mind with technological crutches; unless, that is, we are shocked back into our 'rightful minds'.[11]

As it stands, our collective 'dark night' may last longer than is needed because the incumbent power structures are determined to hang onto their control until the very last drop has been squeezed. They know very well, and have known for a long time, that it's all about energy.

It is all about ENERGY

We live in highly materialistic times where the main focus of human life is upon exterior gains and external systems. This is partly a symptom of our modernist myth of progress. It may also be a part of our historical 'Fall' whereby the long-ago (now mythological) 'Golden Age' of spiritual, harmonious and egalitarian tendencies has been all but forgotten and replaced by the 'dark ages' of matter. Whatever the speculative hypotheses at this point, we can say that the majority of our earthly human systems are firmly rooted within the physical. On this level, 'energy' is that which fuels our mechanistic societies; yet it does not solely include the fossil fuels. It also consists of other resource energies such as food and water. Importantly, it also involves the energies of fear and control (*see* next chapter).

The energies of control go hand in hand with the control of the flow of resource energies. In other words, by controlling the lifeblood that flows through the channels of our global societies a minority (often referred to as the global elite) is able to manage an otherwise burgeoning chaotic population. In the modernist, materialist race to construct a global empire, the architects of such control have been relying upon the pattern of increasing gains (both economically and energetically). Now that these energetic resources (oil, natural gas, food, water) are becoming ever more scarce, there is increased activity on the part of the elite minority to covet these precious sources. These are symptoms belonging to the behaviour of the old psychic energy. Such desperate grasping for control of these physical energy resources will make the transition to finer energies (*see* later chapters) much more difficult and traumatic.

For example, if we take a look at our human staples of food and water we will see that there have been some covert, strategic moves operating behind the political scenes for quite some time. The control and management of global food supplies has been a priority for decades. The 1974 UN World Food Conference in Rome outlined the necessity of maintaining sufficient world grain reserves, especially since the price of world grain had shot up dramatically because of the huge increase in oil price during the early 1970s' oil crisis (at one point world oil prices had risen by 400 per cent). The US export strategy in the 1970s was to further control food trade supplies, which led to moves to consolidate power as 95 per cent of all grain reserves in the world were under the control of 6 multinational agribusiness corporations – Cargill Grain Company; Continental Grain Company; Cook Industries, Inc; Dreyfus; Bunge Company; and Archer Daniels Midland – all of which were US-based companies. The US long-term strategy was to dominate the global market in grain and agriculture commodities, as outlined in the early 1970s by Richard Nixon. This policy coincided with taking the dollar off the gold exchange standard in August 1971 to make US grain exports competitive in the rest of the world. However, in order for the US to become the world's most competitive agribusiness producer it had to replace the traditional American family-based farm with the now widespread huge 'factory-farm' production. In other words, traditional agriculture was systematically replaced with agribusiness production through changes in domestic policy. For example, domestic farm programmes that had previously protected smaller farm incomes were phased out during Nixon's term in office. This policy was then exported to developing countries in a bid to make US agribusiness more competitive and to get a foothold into foreign markets:

> The Nixon Administration began the process of destroying the domestic food production of developing countries as the opening shot in an undeclared war to create a vast new global market in 'efficient' American food exports. Nixon also used the post-war trade regime known as the General Agreement on Tariffs and Trade (GATT) to advance this new global agribusiness export agenda.[12]

In Henry Kissinger's 1974 report 'National Security Study Memorandum 200' (NSSM 200) he directly targeted overseas food aid as an 'instrument of national power', suggesting that the US would ration its food aid to 'help people who can't or won't control their population growth'.[13] Also, the policy shifts during the 1970s were towards increased deregulation, which meant increased private regulation by the large and powerful global corporations. This led to an increase in corporate mergers and the rise of transnational corporations (which today often have larger GDPs than many nation states).[14]

As large corporate agribusinesses were creating their food production, storage and distribution monopoly, smaller domestic farms were going bankrupt and closing. (Although this trend was predominantly occurring within the US, it was also later spreading to other developed nations who were forced to 'modernize' their agricultural industry to compete with global trade.) For example, between 1979 and 1998 the number of US farmers dropped by 300,000 as by the end of the 1990s the agriculture market (in the US at least) was dominated by large commercial agribusiness interests. The US also operated a foreign policy of offering financial assistance 'to developing countries via the World Bank in return for these countries to open their markets up to cheap US food imports and hybridized seeds'.[15]

By the beginning of the 21st century world supplies of cereal were under the control of a few US-based monopolies. Only four large agro-chemical/seed companies – Monsanto, Novartis, Dow Chemical and DuPont – controlled more than 75 per cent of the US's seed corn sales and 60 per cent of soybean seed sales. By the merging of giant agrochemical and seed companies, livestock could be fed on a huge diet of drugs in order to stimulate increased growth. It has been estimated that in recent years the largest users of antibiotics and similar pharmaceutical products have been not humans but animals, which consumed 70 per cent of all pharmaceutical antibiotics. Statistics show, quite shockingly, that the use of antibiotics by US agribusiness increased from 500,000 pounds to 40 million pounds (an 80-fold increase by weight) from 1954 to 2005. As a consequence, the Centers for Disease Control in the US has reported an 'epidemic' rise in food-related diseases in humans as a result of eating meat containing large quantities of antibiotics. One Harvard University researcher, Ray Goldberg, who set up a research group to examine the revolution in agribusiness (including genetically modified organisms) reported that: 'the genetic revolution is leading to an industrial convergence of food, health, medicine, fiber and energy business'.[16]

However, as the global demand for agriculture increases so will the need for increased water supplies. To date, agricultural farming accounts for 66 per cent of the world's water supplies; and this is without including industrial and personal/household use. It has been calculated that 'the world will nearly have run out of existing water supplies by the mid twenty-first century'.[17] Just as in the case of oil/fossil fuels, water will become the focus of an 'energy war' in the very near future with various nation states arguing over how much disputed and/or shared water sources belong to a given area. In fact, there have already been instances of nations attempting to redirect water sources: for example, in 2006 Uganda decided to cut the flow out of Lake Victoria into the River Nile.

One of the major problems is that there is a significant discrepancy between available fresh water (run off) and population; for example, Asia has 36 per cent of run off but 60 per cent of the world's population. By contrast, South America has 26 per cent of run off but only 6 per cent of the population. In areas where there are large urban populations it is likely we will see increased instances of water being redirected from agricultural land/food production to supply urban cities; such as is the case in China. Desalination, too, will prove to be important, for those nations not naturally supplied by fresh water will struggle to keep the input energies flowing. Saudi Arabia alone accounts for 20 per cent of global desalination but at the expense of huge amounts of energy. Whilst Saudi Arabia has oil to use as energy for desalination projects *now*, this is liable to change in the future, at which time Saudi Arabia, as well as other Middle Eastern nations, will find themselves struggling to quench their needs.

The 'dark night' that I have alluded to, which signifies the initiation – or incubation period if you will – describes a time whereby the material gross energies will dominate the global scene. The old energetic world order has indeed been dependent upon these types of physical fuels for maintaining social and global structures. Yet as I have already suggested, this gross-matter energy focus is indicative of our planetary infancy. Just as the 'near-death' period is a time of struggle as our world has to deal with moving away from its dependency upon these gross and 'dirty' energies, on the other side lies the discovery and use of finer, cleaner energies. For now, though, we may see the last throes of a struggle to control the final flows of energy lines.

Dark Night Death Throes

The signs are there for anybody to see; energy colonialism is as old as slavery, which is itself an ancient form of energy colonialism. Uninvited incursions and occupations, such as in Iraq and Afghanistan, are purely means to control energy sources and supply routes. The 'Great Game' of oil routes is now often derogatively referred to as 'Pipelinestan' after the many pipelines that run through the Central Asian 'stan' states. A major new Western oil route in Pipelinestan is the Baku-Tbilisi-Ceyhan pipeline (BTC) which was conceived to allow Western states to gain oil independence from the Persian Gulf. This pipeline at 1,768 km long begins in the Caspian Sea, running though Azerbaijan, Georgia and Turkey, before arriving at the Mediterranean coast. This serpentine metallic energy pipeline first began to supply the West with crude oil in 2006.

More recently, however, Pipelinestan has now become home to the Central Asia–China gas pipeline (known also as Turkmenistan–China gas pipeline) which runs at 1,833 km. This natural gas pipeline begins in the gas fields of Turkmenistan and runs through Uzbekistan and Kazakhstan to connect with the west–east gas pipeline in China. The complete pipeline was inaugurated on 14 December 2009 when China's Hu Jintao visited Turkmenistan, alongside the leaders of Turkmenistan, Uzbekistan and Kazakhstan. Energy makes for interesting bed-partners indeed.

As well as the mad scramble for securing oil routes, food chains and water supplies, the world is also desperate to secure what are known as rare earth metals. These metals, as their name implies, are found in relatively small quantities; their uses, however, are wide and varied, and are included in superconductors, magnets, car components, radar, optical-fibre communications, televisions, computers, mobile phones and various sensitive military applications. Furthermore, China currently produces over 97 per cent of the world's supply of rare earth metals, and in late 2009 announced plans to extensively cut its export quota over the upcoming years in order to conserve domestic supply. There have also been signs that recent disputes, with Japan over disputed maritime boundaries for example, have led to China cutting off supplies of rare earth metals. After all, in these times, it's all about ENERGY.

As existing global systems are hit by multiple stresses and strains there will be increased vulnerabilities in the supply chains. We will witness increasing 'shocks' to the system as the 'old energy' paradigm tries to continue managing 'business as usual'. One of the major casualties here will be the global food chains. A recent example is the severe drought in Russia which destroyed 25 per cent of its wheat crop. As a result, Russia declared a ban on all wheat exports, sending up the price of food world-wide. Hikes in bread prices in various countries led to local food riots, such as the deadly ones in Mozambique. Following this, the UN's Food and Agricultural Organization held a special meeting in Rome on 24 September 2010 to discuss the issue of food security. Julian Cribb, scientist and author of *The Coming Famine*, has stated that 'The most urgent issue confronting humanity in the next 50 years is not climate change or the financial crisis, it is whether we can achieve and sustain such a harvest.[18] Already there have been notable increases worldwide in the prices of wheat, cocoa, coffee, sugar and meat. Experts believe that increasing food prices will lead to further civil unrest and rioting, especially in developing countries. And for the first time in modern history China became a net importer of corn, largely used for animal feed.

The scales are shifting, and the world equilibrium of energy (fuel, food, water) supplies is becoming dangerously unbalanced. We are slipping (or perhaps are being pushed) down through the underworld tunnel that, by necessity, we are forced to pass in order to deal with the potential re-emergence that faces us. Yet when it is dark we might be tempted to avoid seeking out the new and to look instead where we think there is light – still within the old comfort zones/systems. The following is a classic tale that illustrates this human tendency:

> Some local villagers came upon Nasrudin one night crawling around on his hands and knees under a lamppost.
>
> 'What are you looking for?' they asked him.
>
> 'I've lost the key to my house,' he replied.
>
> They all got down to help him look, but after a fruitless time of searching, someone thought to ask him where he had lost the key in the first place.
>
> 'In the house,' Nasrudin answered.
>
> 'Then why are you looking under the lamppost?' he is asked.
>
> 'Because there is more light here,' Nasrudin replied.

Humanity's period of initiation may appear to be deceiving for a time. There are likely to be various shortages and system breakdowns as the energy overshoot begins to become apparent. There may be many instances of 'looking for the key' in the wrong places just because that is where we feel more secure and safe. The desire for security may well be a catch that keeps us in the shadows and away from the real light of discovery (*see* Chapter Five).

On a physical level the more complex a living entity (animal, city, nation, civilization) becomes, the more energy is required in order to maintain its equilibrium – and even more energy to sustain its continual growth. Anthropologists often refer to the degree of a civilization by its ability to utilize energy for human advancement or needs. In other words, energy can be used to measure the level of social achievement of a culture. Yet there also needs to be a balance between physical and psychic energy; that is, the progress of any civilization needs to be balanced between our vision and inspiration and our use of available gross energy. After all, the most important constraint for every society is available energy, whether it is from the ground (fossil fuels) or from within the human mind (vision/inspiration).

Often a third mediating force can be seen in human civilizations as contributing to this energy equation – that of *communication*. Revolutions in communications can be indicative of changes in how the human mind perceives the world and interacts with it:

> The convergence of energy and communications
> revolutions not only reconfigure society and social roles
> and relationships but also human consciousness itself.
> Communications revolutions change the temporal and
> spatial orientation of human beings and, by so doing, change
> the way the human brain comprehends reality. Oral cultures
> are steeped in mythological consciousness. Script cultures
> give rise to theological consciousness. Print cultures are
> accompanied by ideologicial consciousness, while early
> electricity cultures spawn psychological consciousness.[19]

As civilizations become more complex and energy-consuming they often develop more sophisticated communications in order to better organize and manage these resources. These communication revolutions, in their turn, compress time and space differently for the human experience. It is thus possible that certain developments in human cognition and psychic awareness have come about through a simultaneous advancement in energy communications. As more complex systems in energy and communications emerge they reposition social arrangements. People are required to adapt to reinterpret the new environments and social contexts, which then also affects human perceptions. Marshall McLuhan noted how the emergence of print and the printing press revolutionized the production, storage and distribution of information and knowledge.[20] This then led to printed treatises and ever-deepening probes into the human psyche and the nature of consciousness.

It is interesting to note that the first modern definition of consciousness appeared in English in 1620; and in 1690 *self* was combined with *consciousness* to produce *self-consciousness*. The written form was therefore important to the evolution of human consciousness. Now today's modern global communications have shrunk the paradigms of space-time into an almost instantaneous 'now'. This has had remarkable effects upon the human psyche, cultivating increased empathy, connectivity and feelings of a global family. These are the significant stirrings of a collective consciousness awakening; of a species developing from infancy to adolescence. With this new collective mind rising, I postulate, we can transition into the next stage of our planetary-species evolution. As I shall endeavour to explain in later chapters, these are the early signs of a new planetary mind in gestation that is connected to the discovery and utilization of finer energies. And it just may be these finer energy discoveries that allow us to move away from our dire dependency upon the dirty finite fossil fuels.

Yet this is not likely to happen overnight. We should not expect to awaken one morning (e.g. on 22 December 2012) and expect to be in a lighter, etheric fifth dimension. Of course, it might be nice for this to happen, yet I suspect the reality may be somewhat more drawn out than this. In other words, we will have to work for it – and towards it.

The upcoming years and decades will provide much opportunity for transitioning from the older 'gross' to the new 'finer' energies in both physical and psychic domains. However, as this occurs we may also see, as is evident even today, ever-increasing totalitarian/draconian control measures being put into place by the governing elite to maintain its grip on the old world. These final desperate acts of 'old energy' control in order to preserve the illusion, and to keep the majority of humankind in the shadows, are what I refer to as the 'shadow fire', which is the subject of the next chapter.

CHAPTER FIVE

Caught in Plato's Cave:
The Final Trick on the Old Mind

None are more enslaved than those who falsely believe they are free.

Goethe

In adversity, everything that surrounds you is a kind of medicine that helps you refine your conduct, yet you are unaware of it. In pleasant situations, you are faced with weapons that will tear you apart, yet you do not realize it.

Huanchu Daoren, Taoist philosopher, circa 1600

Hope, when bold, is strength. Hope, with doubt, is cowardice. Hope, with fear, is weakness.

G I Gurdjieff

I made several references in earlier chapters to the fact that our modern societies have entered a period of intense technological development, whilst our actual state of consciousness has in general been lacking a parallel state of development. This has led to a technological 'state of mind' (Chapter Two) whereby a rising feature of those societies adopting global technologies is a technical consciousness that learns to operate through regulation, rationality and calculated efficiency. These traits, I argue, mark a further shift and decline away from the more ancient notions of an enchanted, vibrant and dynamic universe. The technological mindset that is emerging as the dominant ruling ideology is that of an *old technological mind* – one that requires expansion, organization, power and control.

I also stated in Chapter Two how information is nowadays utilized as an energy flow, and that many technological systems operate through the management and control of information flows. How information circulates within a given society – i.e. open and free, or closed and restricted – indicates the degree of conscious and spiritual energy that is (or is not) present. A society that propagates and encourages the free flow of information is more likely to also embrace individual rights and spiritual, evolutionary values. Likewise, any society that works to suppress and control information (like East Germany's Stasi) is indicative of a repressive ruling ideology. And information, whether gathered, stored and managed by technical systems or not, has always been a crucial energy force. After all, information has the power to liberate, empower and revolutionize, just as much as it has the power to incarcerate, pacify and decimate.

Therefore I am suggesting that before humanity emerges from this dark passage, the governing structures representing the 'old mind' will attempt to increase their grip of power over our social lives. Further, this agenda is already in place since most nations are now irrevocably entwined within global networks of interdependence, and tied in to mutual needs. To combat an emerging planetary consciousness, as this book outlines, more and more nations, regimes and power hierarchies will increase their infrastructures of control and human management. These are the signs that the material, grosser energies are still being relied upon whilst the more subtle and finer energies are yet to emerge in our collective and social consciousness.

This old-energy agenda entails that modern technology be put to use to further regulate and manipulate the free expression of human activity. In this sense people/citizens are very much *disciplined* into specific behaviour that is most suitable to their particular nation and form of governance. These processes, of course, also act as a form of regulation for the active expression of human consciousness.

The notion of discipline is an important and intriguing one, and its operation often goes unnoticed in our more 'democratic' societies. In past societies there were public executions and very real physical threats to one's life to instil discipline; whereas nowadays this has shifted to more covert forms of control and influence. In today's more modern social setting this has been replaced by fluid and pervasive control environments that permeate most aspects of our lives and integrate with our own behaviour patterns. As philosopher Michel Foucault noted, the mechanism for creating and sustaining power should be able to exist independent of the body exercising the power; i.e. the people under the sway of power should be caught up in the situation so that they render themselves as bearers of the power structure. Thus, the ultimate dystopian future, for example, could be described as:

> It will not be a universal concentration camp, for it will be guilty of no atrocity. It will not seem insane, for everything will be ordered, and the stains of human passion will be lost amid the chromium gleam. We shall have nothing more to lose, and nothing to win. Our deepest instincts and our most secret passions will be analyzed, published, and exploited. We shall be rewarded with everything our hearts ever desired. And the supreme luxury of the society of technical necessity will be to grant the bonus of useless revolt and of an acquiescent smile.[1]

We should be careful, therefore, to note that the illusion of liberty can be used as a powerful form of control and domination. For example, the democratic 'right' to free and fair elections is provided as an illusion of our liberty; yet the 'free election of masters does not abolish the masters or the slaves'.[2] This is all part of maintaining the illusion; of keeping society under control as cracks rise and the façade begins to break down.

Shadow Fire – Maintaining the Illusion

The allegory of Plato's Cave is now a famous one, and to which the above subtitle makes reference; it is also a highly telling metaphor of our situation in which an illusionary sense of reality is maintained. In this allegory Plato describes a group of people who have lived all their lives chained, facing the wall of a cave. All they can see is the blank wall that lies in front of them. Upon this wall, day after day, the chained people watch shadows move across – these are the images projected on the wall by things passing in front of a fire behind them. The chained people cannot turn around and see the 'real' objects that pass behind them. Thus, they view these shadows as their reality and ascribe forms, reason and life to them. This is the illusion – the shadows from the fire – that is maintained as the 'reality' we should ascribe meaning to. And the illusion of distraction will gain momentum as the cracks in the material system begin to manifest in more obvious ways. People will be increasingly persuaded that everything that is happening – the collapse of financial markets and currencies; increasing political and corporate corruption; interventionist wars; terrorist fears; mounting surveillance; and the loss of civil liberties – is part of the essential and 'natural' growth of social infrastructure in the modern world. Information will be carefully manipulated to present inconvenient truths as convenient lies. The control over the flow and content of information will become essential to the maintenance of power within technologically dependent societies.

Any culture that is moving towards increasing digitization will need to put in place ever-restrictive measures for the effective management of people's social lives, privileges and identities. To a large degree the manufacture of social control is about the management of information. To this extent there will be an increased dependency upon 'data-basing' the individual, with most lifestyle choices (travel, purchases, insurance, health, etc.) being digitally collected and stored. This scenario relies upon various technologies of integrated digital databases; data mining software; biometric security; CCTV cameras; and radio frequency identity (RFID) implants to track objects and people. Already a general array of surveillance mechanisms is in place including the satellite tracking of individual cars, video auto-identification of physical features, monitoring of all electronic communications (including switched-off mobile phones) and data-referencing all credit card transactions. As Bob Dylan sang almost half a century ago, the times they are a-changing. This scenario is a far cry from the early 20th century when most people living in democratic Western countries had an ease of freedom not imaginable today, such as the ability to leave the country, to travel and return without a passport. Yet Western 'democracies' are seemingly moving closer to the strategies of old East Germany's secret police, the Stasi, who operated a phenomenal system of secret spies. It is estimated that this once included one-sixth of the total population of East Germany.

Yet let us not be deceived into thinking that only a very recent 'terror-ist-prone' world is responsible for the high degree of public surveillance. The history of eavesdropping and spying on citizens is as old as civili-zation itself. With modern technology this practice has only become so much more sophisticated. For example, how many of us would be familiar with the global intelligence signals network now commonly referred to as Echelon? This intelligence-sharing (or eavesdropping) network was originally established in 1946 and known as UKUSA. It later incorporated other Western allied powers and has divided the world into specific listening regions: Britain's GCHQ covers Europe (including Russia west of the Ural Mountains) and Africa. Australia's Defence Signals Directorate (DSD) covers South East Asia, the eastern Indian Ocean and the southwest Pacific zones. New Zealand's Government Communications Security Bureau covers the southern Pacific; the US's National Security Agency (NSA) covers both North and South America; and Canada's Communications Security Establishment (CSE) acts as back-up coverage for northern Europe (including northern Russia) and North America. This network is supported by a whole array of hundreds of sophisticated spy satellites (Intelsat) in various low-Earth and higher orbits, including the Mercury, Mentor and Trumpet satellite series.[3]

These satellites capture every phone conversation and electronic com-munication that is sent around the world. The communications are then filtered through a vast array of sorting mechanisms, both machine and human, in order to compile a huge information database. The earthly technologies include the US intelligence base at Menwith Hill in Yorkshire that is a principal US information hub and download link station. Menwith Hill uses supercomputers (including Lockheed Corporation's

SILKWORTH), which processes advanced speech profiling software such as VOICECAST, and uses complex algorithm programs such as MAGISTRAND and PATHFINDER to sort through and arrange the hoards of information gathered. This sensitive information is then shared with the National Security Agency (NSA) in the US. When, in 1975, the late Idaho senator Frank Church investigated the NSA he remarked that if the US ever became a dictatorship the NSA:

> could enable it to impose total tyranny, and there would be no way to fight back … I know the capacity that is there to make tyranny total in America …[4]

Echelon and similar monitoring is in contravention of both Article 12 and Article 19 of the Universal Declaration of Human Rights.

With the advancements in computer technologies it is now possible to implement 24/7 location tracking: the ability to locate, identify, observe and monitor any individual in real time. And many intrusive technologies are being (and will continue to be) rapidly introduced under the auspices of living in a 'post-September 11th world'. The UK Government's Information Commissioner has stated that people in Britain already live in a surveillance society. Britain, at the last count, had more than 5 million CCTV (closed-circuit television) cameras, 1 for every 12 people, which is more cameras than any other country. A 2007 report by the Royal Academy of Engineering (UK) said that travel passes, supermarket loyalty cards and mobile phones could be used to track each person's every move.

These practices of social management and institutional control are the result of activities structured around the 'organizing principle' of modern societies where citizens are being ushered towards vast data-profiling and social cataloguing. On 15 March 2006 the European Union passed Directive 2006/24/EC which made it mandatory for all European Internet Service Providers (ISPs) to hold details on the data traffic of all their customers for at least two years. This includes every website visited, every email sent and every transaction online, for every EU citizen with access to the Internet. With this in mind, let us take a quick glance at the situation today, taking the modern democratic nation of the United Kingdom as our example.

The then UK immigration minister, Liam Byrne, confirmed early in 2007 that the government was considering setting up a database of fingerprints for children aged from 11 to 15. Thousands of UK schools have now been placed into schemes to fingerprint the pupils, and it is estimated that more than one million children (and rising) have already been processed and their biometric data collected.[5] Schoolchildren as young as three years have also been fingerprinted and some of these have been processed covertly and without direct admission to parents. It is also widely known that UK universities regularly keep copies of all emails sent by students from computers situated on campus. It is claimed that educational information is private and not released to other institutions or regulatory bodies. However, the Regulation of Investigatory Powers Act 2000 (RIPA) means that schoolchildren's data can be viewed on the grounds of national security, detecting crime, preventing disorder, public safety, protecting public health, or in the interests of the economic wellbeing of the United Kingdom. In other words, almost on any grounds! In 2007 the *Times* newspaper reported on a leak that the UK government intended to put as many as half a million children annually on a secret biometric database by 2014.

This information creep has partly been implemented through getting people accustomed to being publically monitored, through CCTV cameras, as a form of public safety. Yet CCTV is now a convenient misnomer, as the cameras are anything but 'closed-circuit'. Nowadays, CCTV cameras are more likely to resemble digital webcams as they are digitally networked and can stream footage through nationwide information networks and databases, storing all images digitally and ready for image-recognition software. By the beginning of the 21st century some 3.5 million images were being added each year to the UK database alone. It is now estimated that the UK's Identity and Passport Service has a searchable archive of around 47 million people, more than three-quarters of the known population – and rising. Soon each adult face in the country may be registered on a central national database.

Further, it was recently announced that the UK's Royal Society had been in talks with the National Science Foundation of China (NSFC) to work on a project to develop models for merging human face recognition with gait:

> This joint project will investigate novel algorithms to
> combine facial image identification with both typical and
> abnormal human action and gait patterns in order to
> perform non-intrusive person identification from a distance
> in public space.[6]

Similar new research includes the Celldar project, funded by the British government, which aims to use mobile phone masts to watch individuals and movement in real time by having the mobile phone masts act like radars. The technology works by 'seeing' the shapes made when radio waves emitted by mobile phone masts meet an obstruction, such as walls or trees, which are filtered out by the receiver to construct a picture of moving objects such as cars or people. Previously, radar required expensive fixed equipment; now it can utilize the vast network of already established mobile phone masts to monitor movement as much as hundreds of miles away. Researchers are also said to be working on giving Celldar (a combination of cell phone and radar) 'X-ray vision' capability, effectively seeing through walls and into people's homes. One media report stated that:

> Ministry of Defence officials are hoping to introduce the
> system as soon as resources allow. Police and security
> services are known to be interested in a variety of possible
> surveillance applications. The researchers themselves say the
> system, known as Celldar, is aimed at anti-terrorism defence,
> security and road traffic management.[7]

Are we in need of more road traffic management?

The UK roads are already awash with national cameras utilizing Automatic Number Plate Recognition (ANPR) cameras, with the intention of increasing this to all petrol forecourts, virtually creating a blanket surveillance of every vehicle that uses the roads, including identification of the drivers. On top of this the UK Association of Chief Police Officers (ACPO) wants a 24/7 national vehicle movement database that logs everything moving on UK roads, utilizing ANPR and cameras with OCR (optical character recognition) software, with existing CCTV cameras – overseen from a control centre in London, creating a pervasive monitoring system.

Yet it is not only the surveillance of our movements we have to be concerned about: there is also the unnerving rise of digital identity, dataveillance and digital profiling. The term 'dataveillance' was coined by Roger Clarke in the mid-1980s as a convenient short form for 'data surveillance'. Private database companies have profited from the rising need of industries wishing to benefit from collecting and cross-referencing people's private lifestyle information, not only for monitoring purposes but also for the vast marketing schemes; after all, knowledge is power. Public database profiling is a way of selling information for marketing, using information from online surfing habits ('cookies', spyware, etc.), credit card transactions and store loyalty cards. For example, one data collection service (Metromail) promoted that it was collecting data on 67,000 babies weekly from 3,200 sources in the US. Other services cross-reference medical needs with lifestyle, family, movement and purchases in order to construct a 'digital persona' – a digital profile. Through numerous, and expanding, forms of dataveillance people are being translated from flesh and bone into virtual data-subjects – easy to store, cross-reference and pass around globally. And within the shadows of the fire, our data is indeed being passed around.

Dataveillance is behind the surge in mega-databases emerging both in nations and, economic blocs and in international networks. For example, the UK has plans for a decentralized National Identity Register (NIR) being spread across the national insurance, asylum and passport databases. Europe has the TECS (The Europol Computer System) and the Visa Information System (VIS), as well as the new Schengen travel database, the SIS II, which is open to sharing personal data information with a range of other organizations. Similarly, the US has been working hard to network its state data systems so interstate sharing can be achieved (*see* their earlier attempt: MATRIX – Multistate Anti-TeRorism Information eXchange). For our part we have been increasingly acclimatized to the need for technological infrastructures. Computers and data technology have been designed to be user-friendly in order to pacify people to their presence and use; a type of creep towards a ubiquitous environment of pervasive data-flows.

Information is now being used in such subtle ways without our knowledge of how it affects our lives, our freedoms, our futures. Such intrusions include, but are not limited to, 'loyalty' schemes; person location and tracking; digital signature technology (PKI); Internet tracing and tracking; Digital Rights Management; and biometrics. Some of the latest research includes the issue of microchipping and radio frequency identity (RFID) tagging. For example, the 'Sky-Eye' microchip was originally designed and developed by Israeli researchers for the national intelligence community, but is now being used by wealthy individuals for personal tracking purposes. It is reportedly made from a combination of synthetic and organic fibre so that it uses the human body as its energy source, meaning it can operate indefinitely. When placed under the skin it is said to be invisible to X-ray scans, and can be tracked from satellites in space. Although this particular chip is being taken up by the rich elite who are in fear of kidnapping, similar, affordable technologies are bound to trickle down to the masses. Indeed, there may come a time when the pressure is on for responsible parents to safeguard their children from abduction by similar means.

Also on the rise is the use of RFID tags. Each RFID tag contains an electronic code which could potentially enable every object on Earth to have its own unique ID number. These tags are at present being mainly used in the tracking of goods, and have been used extensively by Wal-Mart (followed by Tesco in the UK). It is therefore only a matter of time before most leading suppliers and retailers employ these chips in their products. There was even a trial by a leading fashion clothes manufacturer to put RFID chips in their garments and to transmit information even when being worn by the consumer. RFID chips are now also commonly placed in new passports as a more effective replacement for the old barcode/swipe method.

The rise of information tagging could conceivably lead to the creation of a global registration system in which not only every physical object but each person is tagged, with the ID becoming activated when in reach of a receiver, which can be embedded seamlessly into the environment – buildings, shops, streetlamps, cars, moving objects, etc. Further, RFID-tagged ID cards could one day be made mandatory with a legal requirement to carry them at all times, thus making it feasibly possible to have real-time location tracking of the population of entire countries which would be placed upon both national and international databases for cross-referencing. As a case in point, India is currently rolling out a nationwide mandatory identity card known as the unique identification (UID) of individuals, as a means of establishing a national UID database. The biometric card will contain all ten fingerprints, an iris scan, as well as a photograph of the person. With a billion-plus population, India now considers it necessary to ensure the identity of beneficiaries for welfare schemes, and to assist poorer citizens to open bank accounts. It is also reported that all children between the ages of 5 and 15 will be included, in a bid to ensure all children get free education. It appears that the digital surrender of identity is a major part of the shadow fire illusion – keeping the population well and truly fastened to the chains of Plato's Cave.

Sociology professor Gary Marx has questioned whether we are not moving towards becoming a maximum security society. Indeed, the old-mind energies cling to the safety of security; needing to feel secure in an increasingly 'insecure' world. Hence, our *shadow fire* underworld is moving stealthily towards not only maximum security but martial societies.

Terrifying Peace – The Rise of Martial Societies

It appears that there is a manoeuvring underway towards an increased militarization of the civil sphere; collapsing the binary notions of 'friend/enemy', 'civil/military'. Our various so-called 'open societies' are fast becoming the playground (i.e. operations field) of the military, in which every citizen is deemed a 'potential terrorist'. In this way a perpetual war can be orchestrated that deems ordinary peacetime to be the battlefield for potential terror. This old-mind strategy seeks to keep the focus upon the need for control and security and, in Plato's analogy, to keep the heads turned towards the wall and away from the fire. There is no better way to construct societies of control than through the notion of a *terrifying peace*. What this expresses is the notion of peace as constituted through the presence – and potential – of terror. In this way, peace does not exist on its own merits but as a state of insecurity in defence against terror.

The UK government, in line with EU statutory law, manifested this *terrifying peace* when using the 'precautionary principle' for suspected terrorists residing in the UK. What this 'precautionary principle' means is that the state can arrest people for what they believe they may do in the future. If the state has a suspicion of future guilty acts it is lawfully able to protect against this by locking away those who may be guilty in the future. The irony here is that once locked away, the suspected person is no longer able to perform what they have been suspected of. This is similar to an old folk story of a wise fool who arrives at the door of the king's castle to be told by the guard that the king's decree is for anyone who tells a lie to be hanged. Then, upon asking for his destination the wise fool replies, 'I am going to be hanged.' 'I don't believe you!' exclaimed the guard, 'you are lying.' 'Very well, then. If I have told a lie, hang me!' 'But if I hang you,' replies the guard, 'then you would have told the truth and I shouldn't have hung you!' 'Exactly,' replies the wise fool, 'this is your definition of truth.'

The paradigm of prevention that the 'precautionary principle' instigates is a dangerous precognitive precedent that is veering dangerously close to the 'thought crime' practices of Orwell's *1984*. It allows the governing powers to imagine the worst with little supporting evidence. What is worse is that politicians in the EU are now using this 'lawful tool' in displays of power, exaggerating fear and instigating a wave of *terrifying peace*. These public constructs are the fantasies of fear and the reliance upon the media projection of fearful images. Such behaviour shows us how the politics of fear operates: it is fear of an imagined future. This fear is the old mind in operation, and can be said to be the final trick on the old mind – keeping it fearful, passive, and thus disempowered towards moving forwards out of this low-energy state.

A perception of permanent war and terrifying peace allows the creeping emergence of martial societies – i.e. societies where military rule and social/civil law have effectively merged. It also allows for the powerful infrastructures of politics, industry and the military to dominate. This 'iron triangle' relationship is now known as the *military-industrial complex* (MIC), as referred to in Chapter One. Such intertwined power structures now permeate most governmental infrastructures and often work above and beyond national governments. These Leviathans of power have cooperated together to shift (or co-opt) the world towards a 'total war' – a permanent war – whereby *terrifying peace* has become the norm rather than the exception. This state of affairs is counterproductive to the energies of conscious evolution and human development.

Such manufactured agendas within our societies serve to create waves of insecurity that reverberate within the human global consciousness. Moreover, the usual response to such 'insecurities' is to develop greater social securities, which further deprive people of their civil liberties and extend the technologies of control that negatively influence the expression of individual consciousness. This is the social construction of fear and learned helplessness which creates greater dependency upon the old energy structures of top-down governmental control. We want to feel safe – we need our governments to protect us from our perceived enemies who wish to destroy our way of life. We thus ask for powerful state protection – yet it always comes at a price. Part of this price is our subjugation, and the handing over of our authority to others – to external dependencies. Yet just this act of expecting others to be responsible for us has a powerful psychological effect of disempowering us. Not only do so many people hand over their physical responsibilities and power, but also, perhaps more importantly, they give away and relinquish their spiritual, inner power. Again, this is the final trick on the old mind – a willing compliance to the old energies and a distraction away from the finer, more subtle energies that are attempting to penetrate our understanding and awareness (as I explain in later chapters). Much of this illusory distraction can be placed under the heading of F.E.A.R. = False Evidence Appearing Real.

This agenda of FEAR is attempting to establish a 'perpetual war for perpetual peace' that is without end. Inside this web of deceit, played out by the military-industrial complex, is an ever-greater stranglehold on human consciousness and the development of our empathic nature. The presence of fear, insecurity, conflict and similar distractions are the older, heavier energies that hold back human physical and spiritual evolution. If we fear the future, are caught perpetually within the shadows of Plato's Cave, we limit our own possibilities. We also drastically weaken ourselves – mentally, spiritually and emotionally.

It is our responsibility as a sentient race of spiritual beings to win this 'war of minds' and to begin shifting away from the heavier old-mind energies of fear, control and exploitation. We need to remind ourselves that rather than living in a world of threats and insecurities we actually exist in a world of opportunities and transformations. We should all be making a conscious, willing choice for breakthrough, transformation and evolution.

In line with this book's hypothesis, the increasing shift towards martial societies, in which the notion of *terrifying peace* becomes the norm, represents the dark part in our transitional period. The real fear, however, lies in the hearts of those who hold material power (whether political or economic) and who are worried about losing this stranglehold of power. It is as if they are attempting to keep a building from collapsing by adding more and more rings of scaffolding around the structure. Our societies, likewise, are being increasingly fenced by over-regulating laws, surveillance, monitoring, restrictions, invasions into personal privacy and the loss of civil liberties. At the same time the global economic situation is teetering on the verge of collapse, putting many people out of work and out of homes, reliant upon food vouchers, shelters and medical assistance. The veil of illusion is close to being lifted on our global financial systems, to reveal their duplicity and unworkable schemes. Not only people but nations are going broke.

Austerity measures have hit some countries quite badly, with 2010 having been a hard year for Iceland, Greece and Ireland especially. Greece's austerity measures in 2010 led to some high-profile civil protests, demonstrations and strikes. On 29 September 2010 several major European nations experienced well-organized national protests and strikes. Spain, for example, had a national strike day to protest over austerity measures where the whole nation effectively closed and came to a standstill. As well as large protests in Athens tens of thousands of people from around Europe marched across Brussels in a protest against spending cuts by some EU governments. October 2010 saw a series of major protests and demonstrations in France as people challenged and opposed the government's planned pension reforms. All workers at the 12 fuel-producing French refineries went on strike for days, and many of the major fuel depots were blockaded to stop supplies from leaving (again, the weak spot being a nation's energy). France was badly affected in terms of flights, rail services, hospitals, schools and all road transport. In October 2010 the International Labour Organization (ILO), a UN agency, published its annual 'World of Work' report where it stated that social unrest had already been reported in at least 25 countries.

Further, the ILO warned of growing social unrest because of fears that global employment will now not recover until at least 2015 because of the growing economic and social depression. In November 2010 more than 100,000 people yet again marched through Dublin's streets in protest over the international bailout and four years of austerity ahead.

Following on from this disruptive year, 2011 began with an unexpected explosion of protests and rioting in North African Muslim territories, which then spread rapidly to some Arabian Gulf nations. Whilst some of these protests were over corrupt regimes, it also involved spiralling food costs, which are affecting the poorer regions as staple commodities are hit by inflation. The unrest began in Tunisia during December 2010– January 2011 in what has now been termed the Tunisian revolution, or Jasmine revolution. The demonstrations and riots were reported to have started as protests against unemployment, food inflation, corruption and freedom of speech. Nationwide protests succeeded in ousting the incumbent regime. This catalysed protests in neighbouring Algeria in January 2011, where a wave of riots erupted all over the country protesting against similar injustices. The riots were notoriously marked by a series of self-immolations in front of government buildings. Most notably the wave of North African protests moved swiftly to Egypt where on 25 January 2011 a series of ongoing street demonstrations, marches, rallies, acts of civil disobedience, riots and violent clashes erupted. The protests began with tens of thousands marching in Cairo and a string of other cities in Egypt, demonstrating against a mixture of social, political, legal and economic injustices. Hundreds of thousands of demonstrators rallied in Cairo's Tahrir Square for weeks until finally hearing the news that incumbent President Hosni Mubarak had resigned as leader after 30 years of rule. The protest wave continued to roll on, forming protest movements in such regions as Bahrain, Yemen, Saudi Arabia, Morocco and Jordan, and a bloody civil war in Libya.

Yet as our social, political and economic edifice shows further signs of cracking and decay, those in power in the Western nations especially will seek to increase their regulatory control. The edifice of illusion cannot be allowed to fall: or rather, those of us chained in Plato's Cave cannot be permitted to turn our heads and view the source of the shadows upon the wall – the real fire. The final trick upon the old mind is to keep it focused on the illusion of the old 'reality' (the shadow fire) whilst the world around starts to tear apart at the seams. Distractions will be provided to keep the old mind occupied: these will include increased fear and insecurity, media stories that focus on negativity, financial worries, credit debts, global climate politicking and general ongoing propaganda campaigns for continued public passivity. However, this darkened period is, as I have explained, the trial of our passing.

The opening quote of this chapter from Taoist philosopher Huanchu Daoren outlined very nicely how adversity is, in fact, a medicine that we can use to refine our conduct. Moments of adversity are thus the catalysts for our growth, our maturity as persons, as nations and as a species. As Huanchu Daoren rightly says, it is the pleasant situations that will in fact tear us apart, partly through our unawareness. So in this period of darkening, lower energies are becoming more manifest, not because they are gaining ascendency but because of the very opposite – they are waning. It is, in effect, the years of the last gasp for the once dominant material power structures. The cycle of peak gross materialism is now on the descendent and finer, more subtle energies of human conscious-ness are beginning their ascendancy. It is for this very reason, I propose, that there is such open and visible material conflict in the world today: material power structures are now openly fighting for their final gasps of air. Such old-energy power structures are attempting to hold back new incoming and ascending conscious energies.

A new era is on the rise. We are currently in the gestation of a new cycle; a cycle of rising consciousness and material awareness, as the next chapter begins to explain.

CHAPTER SIX

End of an Era:

A New Cycle in Gestation

An important scientific innovation rarely makes its way
by gradually winning over and converting its opponents ...
what does happen is that its opponents gradually die out and
that the growing generation is familiarized with the idea
from the beginning.

Max Planck

It would not be too much to say that myth is the secret opening
through which the inexhaustible energies of the cosmos pour
into human cultural manifestation.

Joseph Campbell

The future belongs to those who give the next generation
reason for hope.

Pierre Teilhard de Chardin

It seems that we have arrived here, at Chapter Six, with the title *End of an Era*, a much more positive offering than the previous two chapters which spoke of the dark night and being caught in Plato's Cave. So, having come this far, why now the sudden shift? The shift in focus and emphasis is to show that what was described in the preceding chapters was in fact the last-ditch attempts (a dying gasp) to retain control over a rising consciousness within humanity; and which will eventually fail. Why? Because, as this chapter will discuss, humanity is very likely now passing through a grand historical and cosmic cycle whereby we are now ascending once again away from times of 'darker' gross materialism towards what has been referred to in our mythology as the Golden Age – a period of finer energies and heightened consciousness. Let's begin this journey by going back once again to the words of Plato ...

Plato wrote that humanity could only know the 'real' world in the form of memories; by what he termed *anamnesis*, meaning the recovery of buried memories, both individual and collective. Plato insisted that all thought was recollection, and that humankind generally existed within a state of collective amnesia, having only fragments of recollection as reference points for reality. That is, humanity had lost (or fallen) from an earlier state of heightened being and now had only traces of this memory in their collective psyche as a reminder. In this paradigm it is further suggested that humanity passes through constant cycles that descend from higher ages to progressively lower ages, and then ascend back to higher ages, as recorded by the Hindu Yugas. This means that collective images and myths reappear in our minds, in our histories, as grand archetypes that dwell as close to us as our own systems of thought, as signifiers of memory to assist humanity not in the creation of imaginative worlds but rather in re-creating our recollections of such realms/states of bygone times. In other words, remembrances of what we believe is our mythic lost Golden Age – a 'Paradise' – and the nature of grand cycles of the ages.

It has been suggested that humanity resonates closely with the concept of Paradise because our ancestors once dwelt in such a state and time, and thus we carry within our collective consciousness vestiges of remembrance; a deep sense that we once belonged to something 'higher', and to which we may one day return. Within our interior selves lies the hope of returning to something once 'lost' – a *Paradise lost*. This notion has been expressed in allegorical form in many tales, such as in the parable of the pearl of great price, and this one, 'The Precious Jewel', adapted from Eastern sources:

> In a remote realm of perfection, there was a just monarch who had a wife and a wonderful son and daughter. They all lived together in happiness.

> One day the father called his children before him and said: 'The time has come, as it does for all. You are to go down, an infinite distance, to another land. You shall seek and find and bring back a precious Jewel.'

> The travellers were conducted in disguise to a strange land, whose inhabitants almost all lived a dark existence. Such was the effect of this place that the two lost touch with each other, wandering as if asleep. From time to time they saw phantoms, similitudes of their country and of the Jewel, but such was their condition that these things only increased the depth of their reveries, which they now began to take as reality.

> When news of his children's plight reached the king, he sent word by a trusted servant, a wise man: 'Remember your mission, awaken from your dream, and remain together.'

> With this message they roused themselves, and with the help of their rescuing guide they dared the monstrous perils which surrounded the Jewel, and by its magic aid returned to their realm of light, there to remain in increased happiness for evermore.[1]

This allegory/parable, amongst others similar, reveals that a latent message lies hidden deep within our interior self, and acts as an umbilical of remembrance keeping us in touch with a forgotten ancient history. Mythological research, such as that undertaken by Joseph Campbell and Mircea Eliade, has shown that one story in particular threads its way through nearly all traditions and myths – the story of a lost idyllic golden age and the hero's journey to restore the world to its former glory and high state: a tale of loss and the need for heroic restoration. It is also a journey to reconnect ourselves with a sense of the sacred, to cosmological systems that embed humanity within a sense of the universal, a dimension of meaning, where the human psyche merges into the significant whole.

Many myths recovered from the past, and from indigenous tribes, reveal a worldview of our ancients that accepted all things as part of a living and conscious cosmos, connected with an energy that spread through all, giving life and animation. As mythological researcher Richard Heinberg wrote:

> I feel compelled toward the view that our cultural memories of a Golden Age of harmony are the residue of a once-universal understanding of the spiritual dimension of human consciousness, and are at the same time memories of how contact with that dimension has been almost completely severed.[2]

The contact may appear almost severed, yet traces of it have remained in records scattered through various domains. Ancient writings, not only myths, talk of this once Golden Age. The Roman poet Ovid wrote of a time when:

> the birds in safety winged their way through the air and the hare fearlessly wandered through the fields … There were no snares, and none feared treachery, but all was full of peace.[3]

Likewise, the *Annals* by 1st-century Roman historian Tacitus describe a time when:

> most ancient human beings lived with no evil desires, without guilt or crime, and therefore without penalties or compulsions. Nor was there any need of rewards, since by the prompting of their own nature they followed righteous ways. Since nothing contrary to morals was desired, nothing was forbidden through fear.[4]

And as I shall discuss shortly, the Yuga ages of Hindu philosophy outline very clearly the nature and time scale of this rise and fall of Golden Ages–Dark Ages.

This once bygone state that the stories and myths refer to as the Golden Age – or Paradise – can also be regarded as a metaphor for an evolved state of consciousness as well as a highly evolved state of civilization. Humankind's state is that of having fallen into the grip of gross matter, and of having left behind a finer awareness of subtle energies. We have, as all great religious traditions commonly state, entered into a realm of separation from a 'divine' source. The anthropologist Mircea Eliade, in his *The Sacred and the Profane,* writes that every historical culture has regarded the human condition as being under a temporary spell of unnatural limitation and separateness. Further, that our world now contains symbols and signs that serve to jolt human consciousness into some degree of reawakened awareness and remembrance, much as in the tale of the 'Precious Jewel' told above. Eliade reminds us that in so-called 'primitive' societies the act of understanding the symbol can help to succeed in 'living the universal'. Similarly, mythologist Joseph Campbell describes how the aim of ancient spiritual practices, tribal myths and shamanic teachings is to assist in recovering a lost mode of awareness.

It is easy to conclude that the myth of Paradise (or of a Golden Age) represents an innate and universal longing, deep within us, for a state of tranquillity but from which we are separated. Metaphorically it could merely indicate a state of inner being that is naturally balanced and harmonious. Perhaps there have been historical ages in which human beings shared a state of oneness or union with all life and their environment, and that this peak of civilization was indeed lost. Cultural historian Riane Eisler, for example, has uncovered much evidence of past cultures/ civilizations that were not male dominant, violent and hierarchic, and where peace and prosperity reigned for long periods.[5] Such matriarchal cultures could indeed have represented a metaphorical Golden Age.

The Hopi legend of the 'First People' talks of a time in the ancient past when people 'felt as one and understood one another without talking', as if suggesting a form of collective telepathy. This legend describes a time when humans on the planet manifested a form of suprasensory perception, and where dialogue often occurred between various entities. Anthropologist Roger Wescott writes that:

> Moreover, most mythic traditions concur in asserting that, in the Golden Age, human beings associated easily and often with beings that were discarnate or only intermittently incarnate, ranging from awesome cosmic deities to playful local spirits.[6]

Eliade, likewise, noted in his research that ancient myths spoke of a friendship between animals and humans, with knowledge even of their language. Eliade speculates that the shamanic imagery and/or visions of human transformation into an animal may be a metaphorical account of re-establishing a connection that was lost 'at the dawn of time'. According to Eliade, the shaman goes into a transcendental state in order to 'abolish the present human condition', which is now regarded as a resultant state from the 'Fall', and to re-enter into the condition of 'primordial man' as was the natural state during the Golden Age.[7] Mythologist Richard Heinberg considers whether:

> ... Paradise may be seen as serving a specific function, as a *design for living* embedded in the circuitry of human consciousness. All biological organisms, including human beings, contain elements of design ... Perhaps we also contain within us a neurological or psychic program for the optimal design of social and spiritual relations between ourselves, the Cosmos, and Nature – a design of telepathic oneness and interspecies communion that represents the goal toward which our individual and collective experience would naturally tend to unfold.[8]

Heinberg is suggesting here that memories of Paradise/the Golden Age may not only refer to a physical reality or time but also serve as a trigger function to catalyse human neurological and psychic functioning into continued evolutionary growth. The memory, then, is not only as a remembrance of things past (as Proust would say) but also a 'design' wired into us as perhaps a social and spiritual guide during 'dark ages', between peaks and towards the next ascending Golden Age. This, whilst speculative, does present an attractive and appealing hypothesis that, whilst it cannot be proven, can at least be considered. However, at the present time humanity still exists in a state of separation – the so-called 'Fall'.

Various religious, spiritual and indigenous traditions all refer to this rupture, or 'Fall' – from a higher state of awareness, behaviour and morals, descending into greed, egoism, fear and selfishness. It is a state where the focus is almost all upon gross materialism, rational science and 'dirty' energies (coal, wood, oil, etc.). It is also sometimes indicated that this lower state of humanity is the cause of Earth cataclysms – geological, climatic, etc. – that not only wipe out huge numbers of people but also create a psychological trauma within the collective human psyche. Gnostic, Hindu and Buddhist traditions talk of humanity forgetting its true purpose; of how distraction of, and attraction to, the physical world produces a continued state of separation. Teutonic Norse myths state that a renewal of the world would only come after great destruction in which a period of chaos and disorder would arise that would see humans commit many degrading and tragic acts. As discussed in Chapter Three, there are numerous accounts in ancient and sacred texts that depict the theme of cyclic destruction and renewal; from biblical accounts, Hindu scriptures and Tibetan narratives. Similarly, there are various indigenous accounts, such as from the Mayan and Hopi histories, that align their myths to the 26,000-year precession of the equinox (the time it takes for the tilt of the Earth to make a complete passage to its original astronomical position in the zodiac). Yet they are not alone.

It has been found that there are many ancient myths that contain references to celestial cycles and their impact upon human civilization. According to the book *Hamlet's Mill*, a work of comparative mythology, there are over 200 myths/folk stories from over 30 ancient cultures that refer to the 'Great Year' – the precession of the equinoxes.[9] Marking the passage of the 'Great Year' was important to many past cultures, as if this timing – or rather calendar – was marking a significant cycle. Laurie Pratt, a researcher into the Hindu Yuga cycles, notes that:

> We must grant, therefore, that man can have no more
> accurate universal measuring-stick for the passage of time

than that afforded by the position of the fixed stars in relation to the yearly equinoctial place of the Sun.[10]

The grand cycles of the Yugas may indeed have something to teach us about the rise and fall of epochs, civilizations and the consciousness of humanity. After all, as T S Eliot so eloquently reminded us:

> We shall not cease from exploration
>
> And the end of all our exploring
>
> Will be to arrive where we started
>
> And know the place for the first time.
>
> from *Four Quartets*, 'Little Gidding'

The Rise and Fall of Ages

Ancient myth and folklore from around the world speak of the Great Year and refer to a long-ago Golden Age as part of a grand cosmic cycle of growth and decay. Archaeological records are forever being updated to reveal new evidence of the decline and collapse of civilizations throughout the ancient world. This trend in decline peaked recently in the early Middle Ages, a time of contraction where long-distance travel and trade almost ceased overnight. This near-anarchic period of tribalism, warlords and serfs is commonly referred to as the Dark Ages, *circa* AD500. Then, almost a thousand years later – as if on cue – the wheel begins to turn again and a new impetus emerges, an energetic surge in knowledge, scientific discovery and artistic expression that was the Renaissance period. Is there a pattern here, some kind of cyclic trend? Many ancient myths and teachings think there is; and one of the most explicit teachings on this cyclic trend is in the Hindu Yugas.

In Hindu philosophy the Yugas refer to a grand epoch that is divided into four ages: the Satya Yuga (Golden Age), Treta Yuga (Silver Age), Dwapara Yuga (Bronze Age) and Kali Yuga (Iron Age). Hindu cosmology tells us that the universe is created and destroyed each full day of Brahma (lasting up to eight billion years). In this time the cycles of creation and destruction repeat, like passing seasons, shifting from periods of greater growth (springtime) to times of decline and hibernation (winter). Like the seasons on Earth, both Nature and the consciousness of humanity goes through changes. It is thus said that the grand Yuga cycles affect the phases of life on the planet (growth–decline) and the subsequent capacities of the human psyche. A complete Yuga cycle passes from a high period of growth (Golden Age) to a period of decline (Dark Age) and back again. This grand cycle of time is said to be correlated, or caused, by the solar system's motion through interstellar space – specifically its motion around another binary star.

Now the subject of our solar system being a binary star system is a controversial one, and has been debated for decades by astronomers. At the same time the cause of the Earth's precession has not been fully agreed upon by modern astronomers, some claiming it is due to a slow change in direction of the Earth's axis caused by the gravitational forces of the Sun and Moon (as put forward by Newton), whilst others believe that it is caused by the motion of the Sun in space along its own orbit.[11] However, many ancient teachings have made reference to the fact that our own sun does have a binary star, of greater magnitude, around which it has an orbit, bringing the solar system with it. This idea of a grand central star around which our solar system revolves has been considered by many ancients to be Alcyone, the brightest star of the Pleiades. To the Babylonians it was Temennu ('The Foundation Stone'); the Arabs had two names for it – Kimah (the 'Immortal Seal') and Al Wasat ('The Central One'); and it was Amba ('The Mother') of the Hindus. Its present name of Alcyone was derived from a Greek word signifying 'peace'. There is a mention in the Bible of the Pleiades constellation that contains Alcyone where the Lord asked Job: 'Where wast thou when I laid the foundations of the earth? … Canst thou bind the sweet influences of Pleiades?' (Job 38:4–31).

According to Hunbatz Men, a Mayan daykeeper and elder, the ancient Mayans constructed their calendars to reflect this orbital revolution around Alcyone:

> Of the many calendars of the ancient Maya, behind them all was the calendar of the great cycle of 26,000 years – the time it takes for our Sun to complete a single revolution around Alcyone, the central star of the Pleiades, with all our galaxy's orbiting planets accompanying it.[12]

Hunbatz Men reveals that the ancient Mayans regarded the Pleiades system as being the home and origin of human consciousness, and that the cycles of the ebb and flow of consciousness were built into their social, cultural and religious systems, through correspondence with the movement of the Pleiades star system.

Another indicator to this orbital movement comes from German writer/astronomer Paul Otto Hesse who published in his *Der Jüngste Tag* (*The Last Day*) how our planetary system forms part of the system of suns that belong to the Pleiades system, and that our sun occupies the seventh orbit which revolves in a 24,000-year orbit. Further, that this orbit is divided into 2 periods of 12,000 years each, of which 10,000 years are of 'darkness' and 2,000 years are of 'light'. Hesse claims that humanity has now entered the beginnings of the 2,000-year period of 'light'.

However, another controversial subject still in contention regards the exact dating/timing of the Yuga cycles themselves. According to the Laws of Manu, one of the earliest known texts describing the Yugas, the length is:

> Satya Yuga – 4,800 years
> Treta Yuga – 3,600 years
> Dwapara Yuga – 2,400 years
> Kali Yuga – 1,200 years

This makes for a total of 12,000 years to complete one arc of the cycle (declining from the Golden Age to the Iron Age). In order to complete one full cycle (back from the Iron Age to the Golden Age) another 12,000 years is required, making a grand total of 24,000 years. However, this is still not the 26,000 years of the precession of the equinoxes noted today. Yet the ancient astronomers, we learn, had calculated the rate of the Earth's precession slightly differently, to 50" yearly. Modern science now puts the present rate of precession at 50.1" yearly (or 1°0" in 72 years) making it not 24,000, but 25,920 years for the vernal equinox to make one whole circle of the zodiac. Hence, one great cycle of the Yugas can now be clearly correlated as equal to the Great Year precession.

There is still some debate as to the correct duration of the Yugas as more recent, and popular, interpretations measure the years in terms of the demigods (1 year of the demigods is equal to 360 human years), making the Yugas much longer. For example, the 4,800 years of the Satya Yuga would now be 4,800 x 360 which equals 1,728,000 years. Since the highly respected 19th/20th-century Indian yogi Swami Sri Yukteswar Giri (teacher of Paramahansa Yogananda) agrees with the shorter duration, as written in his *The Holy Science*, correlating with the earliest known texts of the Laws of Manu, I am inclined to agree with the traditionalists on this dating. So in which Yuga are we currently? The obvious one might be the Kali Yuga – the Iron Age – to which many commentators readily, or hastily, concur. However, this may not be the case. Again, it is a matter of number-crunching to find the exact dating.

In *The Holy Science*, Sri Yukteswar wrote that during the latter years of the Dwapara era (about 700BC):

> Maharaja Yudhisthira, noticing the appearance of the dark
> Kali Yuga, made over his throne to his grandson [and] ...
> together with all of his wise men ... retired to the Himalaya
> Mountains ... Thus there was none in the court ... who could
> understand the principle of correctly accounting the ages of
> the several Yugas.[13]

This was because, Sri Yukteswar tells us, nobody wanted to announce the bad news of the beginning of the ascending Kali Yuga, so they kept adding years to the Dwapara date. Therefore, when the last year of the 2,400-year period of Dwapara Yuga passed away, and the first year of the 1,200-year Kali Yuga Dark Age had arrived, the latter was numbered as the year 2401 instead of year 1 of Kali Yuga. In AD498, when the 1,200-year period of Kali Yuga of the descending arc had been completed, and the first year of Kali Yuga of the ascending arc began, the latter was designated, in the Hindu almanacs, as the year 3601 instead of year 1 of Kali Yuga of the ascending arc.[14]

With this new understanding of the dating of the Yuga ages, the present full cycle has been calculated as:

> Satya Yuga – Golden Age of humanity – starts 11,502BC
> Treta Yuga – Silver Age – 6702BC to 3102BC
> Dwapara Yuga – Bronze Age – 3102BC to 702BC
> Kali Yuga of the descending arc – Iron Age – 702BC to AD498

> (the peak of the early Middle Ages – the Dark Ages, after the
> fall of Rome)
> Kali Yuga of the ascending arc – AD498 to AD1698
> Dwapara Yuga – ascending Bronze Age – AD1698 to AD4098
> Treta Yuga – ascending Silver Age – AD4098 to AD7698
> Satya Yuga – the next Golden Age – will commence in AD7698

In terms of attributes the Yugas generally highlight the rise and fall of great civilizations, as well as the ebb and flow in the morality, ethics and the quality of consciousness in humankind. During the descending arc, not only do civilizations become more materially based but there is also a loss of truth, wisdom, sincerity and integrity; as if saintliness turns into decadence. It is said that in the Golden Age of Satya Yuga, humanity comprehends the source of universal divinity and how the universe is sustained; has complete wisdom, oneness, purity, intelligence, and works with the finest energies of the cosmos. In Treta Yuga, the Silver Age, humanity has lost its peak of oneness yet still works with an extensive knowledge and power over universal energies (such as magnetism) and cosmic forces, and constructs harmonious and peaceful cities and civilizations. In Dwapara Yuga, the Bronze Age, humanity retains a comprehension of some of the finer forces and more subtle energies of the cosmos, and various forces of attraction and repulsion, and understands that all matter, all atomic form, is nothing other than the manifestation of energy and vibratory forces. Finally, in Kali Yuga, the Iron Age, humankind's knowledge and power is restricted to the world of gross matter, and focused primarily upon material concerns.

According to Yukteswar, each ascending age enhances humanity's mental faculties and clarity of understanding, which includes knowledge of the finer forces at work within the cosmos. This begins with a rudimentary understanding of electrical forces. Yukteswar writes that:

> About AD1600, William Gilbert discovered magnetic forces
> and observed the presence of electricity in all material
> substances. In 1609 Kepler discovered important laws
> of astronomy, and Galileo produced a telescope. In 1621
> Drebbel of Holland invented the microscope. About 1670

Newton discovered the law of gravitation. In 1700 Thomas
Savery made use of a steam engine in raising water. Twenty
years later Stephen Gray discovered the action of electricity
on the human body.[15]

In the second decade of the 21st century we are now several centuries
into the ascending arc of Dwapara Yuga (which began in 1698) so should
therefore be discovering that energy underlies matter, and working with
even finer sub-material forces. Indeed, the advent of quantum mechanics
in the early part of the 20th century has led to a revolution in how we
understand universal forces – right on cue. However, are the Yugas really
a serious way of understanding human history? After all, we are not
taught about them during our history lessons in school.

Despite this absence of conventional data on the cyclic nature of
history there are clues, allegories, signs and revelations in various diverse
sacred scriptures. These include the Bible; the Vedas of the Hindus; the
Books of Thoth/Hermes of the Egyptians; the Zend-Avesta of Zoroaster;
the Kabbalistic Zohar of the Hebrews; the Woluspa of the ancient
Scandinavians; the Popol Vuh of the ancient Mexicans; the Tanjur of
the Tibetans; and the mystical Hymns of Orpheus. In the Book of the
Wisdom of Solomon it is written:

> The thing that hath been, it is that which shall be; and that
> which is done is that which shall be done; and there is no
> new thing under the sun.
>
> Is there anything whereof it may be said, See, this is new? It
> hath been already of old time, which was before us.
>
> There is no remembrance of former things; neither shall
> there be any remembrance of things that are to come with
> those that shall come after.
>
> Ecclesiastes 1:9–11

Also, famously, Plato reveals in his *Timaeus* that the Egyptians held oral
records of past bygone civilizations:

Thereupon one of the priests, who was of a very great age, said … you Hellenes are never anything but children, and there is not an old man among you … there is no old opinion handed down among you by ancient tradition, nor any science which is hoary with age. And I will tell you why. There have been, and will be again, many destructions of mankind arising out of many causes; the greatest have been brought about by the agencies of fire and water … and so you have to begin all over again like children, and know nothing of what happened in ancient times, either among us or among yourselves.

N.B. *The infamous texts from Plato's* Timaeus and Critias *contain references to the lost civilization of Atlantis.*

* * *

Archaeological research may reject the cyclic theory of civilizations, yet, as a relatively young science, it has in effect only scraped the surface of human history with the majority of available knowledge left untouched and still, literally speaking, under the ground. It is likely that many unknown ancient civilizations also lie inaccessible under the oceans of the world, sunk and hidden through millennia of geophysical upheaval and cataclysms. Examples include the recent discovery of a civilization 5,000 years older than the Indus Valley culture, found in the Gulf of Khambhat (formerly known as the Gulf of Cambay) in the Arabian Sea off the west coast of the India. Also, there are the underwater structures including a pyramid, wide terraces, ramps and steps that have been found in Japanese waters off the island of Yonaguni near Okinawa. There have been similar recent discoveries that have filled books of what is now termed 'alternative history' and which is largely shunned and ridiculed by mainstream traditional scholars.

It may just be that our mainstream 'academic' knowledge is lacking in its absence of the cyclical law that could represent a framework for the rise and fall of civilizations. Instead, our mainstream theories prefer to believe that a primitive humanity emerged from a Palaeolithic Age and entered a Neolithic or New Stone Age of rudimentary agriculture and into the first faint beginnings of human culture about 15000BC. In other words, the history of civilization is linear, a straight path from hunter-gatherers to the industrialists of today, rather than the alternative that:

> ... follows a circular (rather, a spiral) course, with upward and downward half-circles which blend into each other as naturally and inevitably as day follows night, and season succeeds season. Scholars grant that a cycle of growth and decadence is evident in the history of all past empires and cultures, but they have not yet perceived that the trend of civilization as a whole follows a similar cycle.[16]

In this theory the descending arc of the cycle will witness the gradual loss of immense knowledge and heritage of the previous great epochs through descending millennia, scattered and strewn into fragments, considered anomalies, until the known historical achievements of humankind are nothing other than the material structures built with 'sticks and stones' during the final descending Iron Age. It could well be that past records and traces of once-great civilizations have vanished so completely that modern scholars will never admit the possibility of their ever existing.

Even the remnants of past civilizations that we do know something about cannot be considered primitive just because they 'came before'. This is especially so when even today architects say they cannot replicate the exact precision of the building of the Egyptian pyramids – even with the most modern technology. Let us consider also the remnants found at different places around the world: the grandiose Hindu ruins of Ellora in the Dekkan; the Mexican Chichen-Itza in Yucatan; and the grand ruins of Copan in Honduras, amongst many others. The cyclic theory of ascent–descent begins to make more sense when we consider that the lowest point of the cycle was said to have been reached in AD498, at exactly the same time that much of the world was plunged into the near-barbarism that accompanied the fall of the Roman Empire and the break-up of western lands into tribal regions. This theory of cycles in human civilization accounts for the lack of continuity in the progress of humankind, and provides a pattern for why it appears that socio-cultural evolution seems to abound in start-stop leaps rather than in a clear developmental linear fashion. Let us now take a brief look at this historical pattern.

Into the Ascending Arc of History

Humanity entered what has been designated the darkest, densest and most unenlightened period of history in the year 702BC – the beginning of the Kali Yuga (Iron Age) of the descending arc. This period roughly corresponds with the founding of ancient Rome (the precursor to the Roman Republic, and later the Roman Empire) and the start of a more or less fair chronological historical record. It is a record of the rise and fall of mighty empires, of the destruction of human knowledge, and of the dominance of wars, invasions and strife. Whilst I do not claim here to give an accurate historical overview (a whole volume would be required), a brief outline of just a few events may serve to give a general flavour of the epoch.

We can begin by noting how the Kali Yuga saw the collapse of the great Assyrian Empire (in its Neo-Assyrian phase) with the fall of Nineveh before the conquering Medes, Babylonians and Persians in 612BC. Assyria was then ruled by the Chaldean civilization of ancient Babylon, until that too was ruled by the Achaemenid Empire (also known as the Persian Empire) with its power centred in Mesopotamia. The great Persian Empire was then invaded by Alexander the Great and subsequently collapsed. Around the same time we also saw the final decline of the once great Egyptian dynasties, as the Late Period of Egypt began with the 26th Dynasty (672BC to 525BC) and ended with the 30th Dynasty (380BC to 343BC) and its final dwindling until Egypt finally fell under Greek rule when Alexander the Great conquered the country in 332BC. The great days of Greece, however, were over by the 2nd century BC and in 30BC, after the death of Cleopatra VII, the Roman Empire finally declared that Egypt was to be a Roman province and ruled by a selected prefect of Rome.

By this time the Roman Empire had already asserted its geographical dominance with the capture of Carthage in 146BC, an important and famous Mediterranean city and seaport; Carthage was to become the Roman Empire's third most important city. In the same year the Romans also destroyed and captured the Greek city of Corinth, another strategic ancient city-state. The era of the Roman Empire finally ended in AD476 when a revolt, led by the Germanic general Odoacer forced the abdication of the last of the Western Roman Emperors. Europe in the 5th century saw itself break up into various tribal warring factions, as Attila the Hun and his army of Eurasian nomads laid waste to much of Europe and created the Hunnic Empire. Fighting ensued over Europe between the Huns, the Goths (Visigoths and Ostrogoths) and the Vandals. Around the same time India was invaded by the Indo-Scythians who founded the Kushan dynasty over all northern India. The Hephthalites, known as the 'White Huns' later came to rule parts of India through the 5th and 6th centuries AD, inflicting much atrocity and cruelties upon the people.

This period of invasion upon invasion and the rise and fall of subsequent empires gave the descending Kali Yuga Iron Age a flavour of violence, greed and material dominance. It is perhaps little wonder, then, that the Christ figure of Jesus of Nazareth appeared during this period as a timely reminder of the inner kingdom that lay within – the lost jewel. However, this is not the place for a discussion on Christianity. Suffice to say that humanity suffered much in order to reach the ascending arc of the Kali Yuga, the period from AD498 to 1698. The scene now begins to shift to Western Europe and to the Americas.

The ascending arc of the Great Year broke with the past and started a new journey for humanity; an upward spiral of civilization and human evolution that is said will culminate in the year 12498. However, this first period of the Iron Age saw a fragmented and divided populace. By the 10th century the population of Europe comprised a scattering of European and Asiatic nomadic blood and tribal allegiances: Huns, Goths, Vandals, Alans, Franks, Teutons, Lombards, Czechs, Burgundians, Magyars, Bulgars, Slavs, Norsemen, Ephthalites, Indo-Scythians, Finns, Arabs, Turks, Avars, Angles, Saxons, Jutes, Picts and Scots. These tribes had almost all been migratory peoples, at once invading and settling, century by century, in Europe, Africa and Asia. These races inter-married with the peoples whose lands they conquered, and over the course of centuries evolved into our present-day races. These seemingly chaotic tribal states and regions slowly began to give way to a new class of governance, as tribal kings declared themselves 'divine rulers', and their populations became their subjects. These early European centuries gave rise to the Age of Feudalism – a socio-political system of rigid class structure that served a purpose within times of great chaos, insecurity and uncertainty.

Out of this new socio-political system of rule emerged the Crusades at the end of the 11th century, continuing until the final years of the 13th century. Whilst these series of religious wars may seem to be a dark period in history for many people, it succeeded in opening a channel to Europe through which much new knowledge and influence from the Muslim world could penetrate and impact the stagnating West. The degree to which the Arabs disseminated great learning and sciences to the West has now been well documented. For example, the oldest university in the world, Al-Azhar, was established in Cairo in AD970, and influenced the later European universities in the 11th and 12th centuries (Bologna, Paris, Oxford, etc.). Arabic knowledge included mathematics, physics, chemistry, medicine, pharmacy and the use of anaesthetics. The introduction of the so-called Arabic numerals, brought from India, greatly stimulated European learning. It is also said that the concept of hospitals came from the *Bimaristans* (places of the sick) first established by the Seljuk Turkish ruler of Damascus and the Mamluks of Cairo, and brought to the West through the Crusades. The first critical historical study – the *Muqaddimah* – was made in the 14th century by Ibn Khaldun. The first book to be printed in England – *The Dictes and Sayings of the Philosophers* – was a translation from an Arabic work.[17] Further, Arabic translations of Aristotle and other Greeks were introduced into Western thinking in the 15th century through Spain.

The great revival of learning in Europe can be said to have begun in the 15th century with the introduction of the printing press and paper manufacture (paper was first brought to Europe from China by the Arabs). Europe was once again introduced to the old classical culture, the thought of ancient Greece and Rome, of Babylon and Egypt. European classical literature of the likes of Dante and Chaucer – and later Shakespeare and Goethe – is now seen to have been influenced by Arabic sources. The Renaissance was a flowering of European thought and culture (as was discussed in Chapter One) and occurred at the crux of the ascending arc of the next Yuga – the Dwapara Yuga (Bronze Age).

The Dwapara Yuga or the Bronze Age of the ascending arc began, according to our time references, in 1698. In the past four centuries of Dwapara Yuga the world has, by and large, made greater strides forwards in knowledge and discovery than in all the 24 centuries (comprising two Kali Yugas) that preceded the modern period. Knowledge in the world is now expanding exponentially and discoveries and inventions have transformed the world. As humankind has left the Iron Age, we are seeing a gradual move away from the structural materials of iron and steel towards the use of lighter, and finer, materials. We have literally triumphed over the Iron Age of the previous Kali Yuga cycles. The Industrial Revolution was the peak of these material infrastructures that opened up the expansion in transportation and urban growth. The Dwapara Age that began in 1698 is marked by an understanding of what Sri Yukteswar termed 'fine matter forces'; i.e. advances in the understanding and use of forces that are more subtle and less physical, such as electrical and atomic forces. As humanity progresses along this ascending cycle we are set to increase our understanding of the forces and energies of the universe that will perhaps lead to new discoveries in the use of magnetic forces and bio/nano technologies. Indeed, we are already well into the age of electricity and its finer (more etheric?) qualities: the Internet, cyberspace, avatars, teleconferencing and near-instantaneous global communications. This is indicative of our need to rise above the heavier energetic elements of coal and oil (finite fossil fuels) towards more subtle energies that may comprise magnetic, quantum, or even the infamous 'free energy' sources.

According to Mayan Elder Carlos Barrios, the world of the Fifth Sun (our present ascending age) is associated with energy, and with the development of a new awareness and relationship with energies. It could be that humanity is thus entering a period of discovering new aspects of energy and how to harness the energies and forces associated with not only our developing technologies but also our increased knowledge of quantum, magnetic and electrical universal forces. In other words, the mind of humanity and its capacity for understanding are also attuned to the grand cycles of time.

The Cyclic Mind of Humanity

Today we have much more knowledge about how human brainwave frequencies operate and their relationship to external influences and impacts. For example, in the early 1950s German physicist Dr W O

Schumann calculated that global electromagnetic resonances were present in the cavity formed by the Earth surface and the ionosphere. Schumann set the lowest-frequency (with highest-intensity) mode at approximately 7.83Hz, which is in the alpha brainwave range, and found that the Earth's surface, the ionosphere and the atmosphere form what could be seen as a complete planetary electrical circuit. This planetary circuitry acts as a 'waveguide' that handles the continuous flow of EM waves, and is now known as the Schumann Resonance (SR). In fact, it was this atmospheric circuitry of global EM resonances that Nikola Tesla speculated, in 1905, could be utilized for the creation of worldwide wireless energy transmission.

These SR frequencies are important since all living biological systems are known to function within electromagnetic field interactions. In fact, EM fields are what connect living structures to resonant energy patterns (or morphic fields[18]). The SR cavity formed between the ionosphere and the Earth produces oscillations capable of resonating and 'phase-locking' with brainwaves, since the human brain is also an EM receiver and transmitter. EEG measurements have found that the brain has the following four frequency bands:

> delta (up to 4Hz)
> theta (4–7Hz)
> alpha (8–12Hz)
> beta (12–30Hz)

The Earth's SR waves have been observed by experiment to oscillate at several frequencies that are very close to the brain's frequency bands; and even closer when a person is in deep meditation.[19] In particular states, a resonance is possible between the energy field of the human being and the planet. In such a state of resonance it is speculated that a mutual 'information-sharing' energy field is created. This is hardly surprising since the human body (both physically and 'energetically') evolved over eons of geological time as part of Earth's own evolution. The human species is thus a product of the Earth's environment, and must have built up an energetic relationship to surrounding atmospheric EM oscillations. As Earth is surrounded by an ionosphere (a layer of electrically charged particles), natural fluctuations in frequency thus impact upon the energy field within and around the human body. It is reasonable to assert, therefore, that the frequencies of the Earth's naturally occurring EM waves have shaped the development of human brainwave signals.

If the frequencies of human brainwaves evolved in response to Earth's own wavelengths then it is very likely that variations in the Earth's oscillations will result in reactive changes in the human body and mind. Such changes could be categorized as behavioural and mental changes. For example, it could be that incidences linked to the classic states of 'lunacy' (often accredited to the Moon's influence) could arise from a variation in atmospheric EM frequencies in conjunction with Moon/planetary forces. In fact, there was one study that analysed the correlation between the incidence of ionospheric disturbance and the rate of admission to the Heathcote Hospital (Perth, Western Australia) over a three-year period. Results indicated that when an ionospheric disturbance occurred then the admission rate changed. The report's authors give the probability factor of the association being random in the order of 2000:1 against.[20]

The fact that energies which circulate in the Earth impact and influence the human mind and body should not be regarded as mystical or esoteric. At all times our physical bodies act in a similar fashion to lightning rods grounding (or 'earthing') energy. The well-documented human biofield thus binds us closely to the ionospheric and EM fields of planet Earth. As in a physical energetic circuit, the human body is closely interwoven with the Earth's fluctuating energy fields, which to some degree helps to regulate our body's internal clocks and circadian rhythms. We also need to remember that Earth is likewise affected by solar and stellar activity. According to physicist and Nobel Laureate Professor Hannes Alfvén:

> The conditions in the ionosphere and the magnetosphere
> of the earth are influenced by the electromagnetic state in
> interplanetary space, which in turn is affected by the Sun.
> There are a number of solar electromagnetic phenomena
> … sunspots, prominences, solar flares, etc. Other stars'
> electromagnetic phenomena are of importance, most
> conspicuously in the magnetic variable stars.[21]

Recent speculations on the Earth's precession of the equinox have, as stated earlier, pointed towards our solar system having a binary star.

Again referring to Sri Yukteswar in his book *The Holy Science,* when 'the sun in its revolution round its dual comes to the place nearest to this grand center ... the mental virtue, becomes so much developed that man can easily comprehend all, even the mysteries of Spirit'.[22] What this suggests is that there may be some form of great stellar force (perhaps an electromagnetic pulse or field) that affects the Earth as it draws closer to its binary star as part of the cyclic Great Year (precession of the equinox). Whilst this hypothesis is still speculative it does illustrate how the spiral/cycles coincide with the rise and fall of civilizations and the life of humanity on Earth.[23] And our sciences, too, are indicating that the human mind is under the influence of fluctuating EM energies that have both solar and interstellar origins, as was noted by Professor Hannes Alfven above.

Similarly, the electromagnetic field theory of consciousness, proposed by Susan Pockett and Johnjoe McFadden, says that the electromagnetic field generated by the brain (as measurable by electrocorticography) is the actual medium for the experience of human consciousness (more on this in later chapters). The Cemi (conscious electromagnetic informa-tion) Field Theory suggests, in essence, that consciousness is related to the EM fields that the body produces, especially those produced by the brain. This new and startling science of consciousness links up with other research (such as that by physician Frances Nixon) to demonstrate that not only do humans have a personal EM field but also that it appears to be connected to the EM field of the Earth. (*See* also the research of Dr Robert O Becker in his book *The Body Electric.*) This also clearly ties in with the information we are receiving about the energy interactions with the Earth's Schumann Resonance.

To recap, there is now increasing evidence that stellar sources in the cosmos generate huge magnetic and EM waves/pulses affecting the ionic and magnetic atmosphere of the Earth; further, that these forces can have a marked effect upon the biological and mental functioning of humanity. It is thus reasonable to speculate that the cyclic passing of the Great Year (as defined by the Yuga epochs) may in fact be a blueprint for describing the rise and fall of energies that are involved in the evolution of human civilizations and conscious being. After all, the cycles of celestial orbits are remarkably reliable and constant over human historical time.

As Walter Cruttenden, a researcher on the binary star theory, remarks:

> Think of the power of drops of water to cut through stone;
> then think of the very long duration of the huge magnetic
> and electromagnetic pulses generated by distant stellar
> sources, wave after wave permeating our world. There is a
> possibility that they could prove at least as powerful over
> the long term than any experiment we can generate in a
> laboratory in the short term.[24]

As the stellar winds blow, so to speak, human awareness increases in its knowledge of 'finer forces'. As our civilization moves further into this ascending Dwapara Yuga (Bronze Age) we may find a greater emphasis and acceptance of ever subtler forces and fields, such as the human bio-field and consciousness.

In the following chapters I will examine what I consider to be developments in the rising tide of human consciousness; to conclude with a look at our new and coming generations. To begin with, the next chapter takes a look at the emerging interplay of humanity's individual and collective empathic mind.

PART III

Emergence

CHAPTER SEVEN

Birthing the Empathic Mind:

A Revolution Towards Critical Mass

There is nothing in a caterpillar that tells you it's going to be a butterfly.

R Buckminster Fuller

The past of the human mind is written in every achievement of civilization, from the pyramids through the plays of Shakespeare and the theory of relativity to the ball-point pen and the H-bomb. Its future – if it is to have one – will be written in its ever increasing utilization of its potentialities and in its achievement of control over itself.

George H Estabrooks

An individual person has an integrity, a quality, a being and an existence; two people acting in a harmonious and complementary fashion produce an extra factor and a number of people working and thinking and feeling and offering themselves together, and each consciously involving their essential being, are capable of producing a thing of amazing beauty.

Omar Ali Shah

The previous chapter spent a good deal of time laying out the argument for a cyclic version of history, with a time scale based upon the precession of the equinox, referred to as the Great Year. I discussed how the Great Year plays a significant role in many of our world myths, tales and teachings. Some people might be quick to dismiss this as little more than a long-standing wonder and affiliation for the stars, as is natural for the human gaze. I am more inclined, however, to accept that there is something more than mere stargazing operating here; that myths are the carriers of significant information. I am more disposed to the view that:

> It seems that when cultures rise and fall, their arts and
> their literatures do likewise. But there is something which
> has a higher factor of survival. Fables outlive fact. Legends
> penetrate where logic perishes. Folklore, myth, and legend
> transcend the fluctuations of the historical process. It is as
> though a myth carries such a penetrating energy that it can
> leap the gap between cultures – a carrier-wave that unites the
> ceaseless and separate generations.[1]

Leaping the generations of our fragmented historical record was very important for many myth-making cultures – why? It may well have been that they had something to tell future generations. To inform those civilizations coming afterwards that nothing lasts forever, and that the cyclic nature of rise and fall was an inevitability one should prepare for rather than dismiss or deny. Major authorities on the Yugas, despite dating contradictions, have placed our present world at the early part of the ascending arc of the Dwapara Yuga – the Bronze Age. Yet if this is the case, then why do things look so bad?

There is no denying that from one perspective the 20th century looked like a veritable Age of Anxiety. Taking only a brief look at some of the events that afflicted life in the last century of the previous millennium we have World War I (1914–18); the Bolshevik Revolution (October Revolution) of 1917; the Great Depression in the US and the infamous 1929 stock market crash that affected financial markets worldwide. Soon after this came the rise of Communism and Fascism across Europe, with Stalin's 'Great Purge' of the 1930s and the eventual beginnings of

World War II (1939–45). This horrific war manifested many faces of human terror, including the Nazi concentration camps and the atomic bombing of Hiroshima and Nagasaki. Shortly after this time the Korean War (1950–3) started what was in effect a proxy war between Communist China (with Russian assistance) and the US. This spiralled into the 'Communist' threat and the Cold War, including such incidents as the Bay of Pigs, the Cuban missile crisis, McCarthyism and the threat of nuclear annihilation. This ongoing Cold War tension between 'Democracy vs Communism' led into the Vietnam War (1955–75) and the proxy wars in Afghanistan during the 1980s. During this time the world also saw the Yom Kippur war (October 1973); the Balkan/Yugoslav wars (1991–5); the Rwandan genocide (1994), as well as the ongoing civil wars in South Africa. There has been ongoing conflict between Israel and Palestine, with tensions also between Lebanon, Hizbullah and various rival factions for Middle East peace and control.

As parts of the world were dealing with the new infection that was labelled AIDS (Acquired Immune Deficiency Syndrome), the globalization project (sometimes referred to as global imperialism or neo-colonialism) reached across the world through various agencies, notably the WTO (World Trade Organization established in 1995); and the World Bank and the IMF (both established in 1945 as a result of the Bretton Woods agreement). The 1990s witnessed the crash of both the Russian and Asian 'tiger economies', as well as the First Gulf War (1990–1).

These incidents are but a few of the many complex, greater or lesser, national or international, events that permeated the 20th century. Even in the first decade of the 21st century the world has seen the 11 September 2001 attacks on US soil, another war in both Iraq and Afghanistan, the subsequent global 'War on Terror', and the continuous devastation that nature inflicts upon the planet's inhabitants. It is thus reasonable to see how the last 100 years have been an Age of Anxiety, resulting in numerous psychological symptoms, including anxiety, apathy, inertia, paranoia, denial, escapism, introversion, violence, addiction, insomnia, fatigue, listlessness, stress, frustration and fear.

Yet this is only one part of the great transformation occurring in world affairs. These negative, physical, destructive events are indeed the most visible, the most traumatic, and to which we are unwittingly drawn through the actions of politics and world affairs. At the same time a huge wave of transformative movements has been building over the last few centuries; developments that indeed fall within the scope of an ascending age of consciousness. In the following chapters I wish to focus on these transformative movements and events that mark the potential upward curve, or forward development, of human civilization and, perhaps more importantly, of the growth in human consciousness.

I must stress that in these few pages it is only possible to lightly touch upon the vastness of transformative change that has been moving through our cultures and world consciousness. A whole encyclopaedia would be needed to do justice to these developments, so I apologize in advance for the brevity of the next few pages. Saying this, I will attempt to dip a toe into the great waters of change ...[2]

An Age of Radical Seeking

A new type of consciousness began to emerge after the Industrial Revolution; one that had been affected by the electrical energies that were lighting up an era of rapid growth. Just as the rise of the telegraph gave a metaphoric model of how the human nervous system worked, so too did the new technologies of the Second Industrial Revolution – the telephone, radar, cinema, automobile and aeroplane – create a new foundation for the reorientation of consciousness. A new perception of the dimensions of space and time began to birth a psychological consciousness; a consciousness that wanted to look beyond the borders and horizons of the physical frontier. The end of the 19th century was also a significant period in the rise of spiritualism and mediums, general interest in esoteric matters, and the public emergence of occult movements.

Just to give a broad overview, the 1870s onwards saw a peak in the growth of spiritualism in English-speaking countries. Interest was rife in communicating with the dead, contacting the afterlife, and believing in information from the astral plane. By 1897 it was said that spiritualism had more than eight million followers in the US and Europe, with state and national conventions, lecture tours and summer camps held on a regular basis. By 1880, there were about three dozen monthly spiritualist periodicals published around the world; and in 1882 The Society for

Psychical Research (SPR) was established in the UK. A few years later, in 1901, the Spiritualists' National Union (SNU) was founded in the UK and remains one of the largest spiritualist groups in the world. By 1914 the Society for Psychical Research had 320 registered Spiritualist Societies in Britain.

At the time that interest in spiritualism was peaking, the Theosophical Society was established in New York City by Helena Blavatsky, Henry Olcott and William Judge in 1875. Theosophy heralded a revival in Western occultism and in perennial wisdom. It was also a forerunner to later movements that sought to bring Eastern teachings and traditions to a Western audience. Theosophy has had a large impact upon Western mysticism as it brought forth many personages who later found their own individual channels for teaching, most notably Annie Besant, Alice Bailey, Krishnamurti and Rudolf Steiner (who went on to establish the Anthroposophical Society). By the end of the 19th century, spirits were well and truly out of the closet.[3]

The same period of the late 19th and early 20th centuries also saw the founding of The Hermetic Order of the Golden Dawn, with its first temple in the UK (London) in 1888. By the mid 1890s the Golden Dawn was gaining popularity both in the UK and later in Germany especially. Well-known members included Irish poet W B Yeats; authors Arthur Machen and Evelyn Underhill; and infamous occultist Aleister Crowley. In a similar vein the spiritual teacher and mystic G I Gurdjieff was spreading his ideas from Moscow to Paris, from New York to London, aided by the teachings of former pupils P D Ouspensky and J G Bennett.

In 1920 Paramahansa Yogananda arrived in the US and established the Self-Realization Fellowship the same year and introduced thousands of Westerners to the art of meditation and yoga. In 1946 Yogananda published the phenomenally successful *Autobiography of a Yogi* which has sold millions of copies worldwide. Other personages gathering devotees and spreading teachings throughout the western hemisphere at this time include Sri Aurobindo; Hazrat Inayat Khan; and Sri Meher Baba, amongst others. Now the floodgates were open and a whole range of mystical, occult and oriental teachings began to emerge within Western society, as well as creating bridges to Eastern ashrams and religious centres.

So, at this time there emerged a great wave of influence that turned people's thinking towards a more interiorized, as well as a more transcendental, state. It was a shift from the physical towards a belief in, and an exposure to, non-physical realms. Coming as it did at a time of on-going industrialization and material expansion, one must wonder if the timing is pure accident. Yet the 'inward turn' was not only happening in the occult sphere. The shift towards a more intuitive reasoning was marked by the rise of the American Transcendentalism movement in New England (US) in the first half of the 19th century, with notable figures such as Ralph Waldo Emerson, Henry David Thoreau, Walt Whitman and Margaret Fuller. This movement reacted against religious dogma and over-intellectualism and sought to find truths through direct inner experience; that is, the transcendentalists aimed for trusting an internal 'knowing' and experience of events rather than through the medium of external manifestations.

This line of enquiry was further enhanced when in 1901 Canadian psychiatrist Richard Bucke published his now famous work *Cosmic Consciousness: A Study in the Evolution of the Human Mind*. A year later in 1902 Harvard psychologist William James published his series of lectures in the book *The Varieties of Religious Experience: A Study in Human Nature*. These ideas were beginning to circulate amongst an educated public at the same time that psychoanalysis, developed in Vienna in the 1890s by Sigmund Freud, was also percolating into mainstream circles. The early part of the 20th century was a period when the 'collective unconscious' was becoming a conscious part of the collective mind. The theories of Freud, Jung, Reich and other psychoanalysts were changing how people regarded human behaviour and parameters of human thinking. Early childhood impacts, experiences, repressions and sexuality were all now being unearthed as contributing to contours of the human mind. What happened 'out there' was recognized as being a manifestation of what was going on inside a person's mind.

These developments coincided with the rise of the motion pictures as a cultural phenomenon; a way of projecting ideas onto the external screen. Philosophy too was taking on new ideas about the creative vitality within the human, nature's forming of wholes greater than the sum of their parts, and the nature of flow within the universe: Henri Bergson's

Creative Evolution was published in 1907 (in English 1911); Jan Smuts's book *Holism and Evolution* in 1926; and Alfred North Whitehead's *Process and Reality* in 1929. Yet perhaps the most revolutionary change in human thinking came about in the realm of physics; specifically the emergence of quantum mechanics.

The early decades of the 20th century saw a revolution in physics, from Einstein's publication of his general theory of relativity in 1915, providing the standard theory on our laws of gravity, to the dual state of particles (photons) in 1926, and Heisenberg's 'Uncertainty Principle' in 1927. The people behind these new discoveries are now almost household names: Niels Bohr, Werner Heisenberg, Max Planck, Erwin Schrödinger, John von Neumann, Paul Dirac, Wolfgang Pauli and others. By 1927 the field of quantum physics was reaching a wider acceptance amongst the scientific establishment. And in 1957 physicist Hugh Everett presented his 'Many Worlds Theory' that postulated an infinity of parallel universes whereby the universe splits every time a quantum system makes a choice, and there are billions of quantum events taking place within each ounce of matter every second. In this model there could be another universe where the dinosaurs continued to evolve – perhaps they evolved high intelligence and now write books on evolution! Quantum physics then finally presented to the world the concepts of particle–wave duality, non-locality, observer interference and wave collapse. Suddenly, the world was not as fixed, durable, or mechanical as previously thought. It was now seen as an unpredictable, uncertain, energetic sea of chance: God did, it seem, play dice after all.

Information became the keyword for the middle of the 20th century, with cybernetics (Wiener), Communication Theory (Shannon) and early computing (von Neumann and Turing) all emerging with rapidity. This new information revolution was capped by the eventual breakthrough discovery, in 1953, of the molecular double helix structure of DNA (Crick and Watson). The human mind was now processing information at a faster speed than at any time in known history; and most of these new developments concerned the *interior gaze*. The 20th century became a time for asking and answering such questions as: What lies beyond life? What is behind matter? What lies behind our conscious thoughts? What lies behind all biological life? The thrust for human meaning, the age of a radical seeking had been born, and it manifested most clearly through the revolutionary second-half of the 20th century.

The half a century from the 1950s to the end of the millennium began with a human howl for substance and inner searching. The poet Allen Ginsberg portrayed this inner rage with his famous poem 'Howl':

> I saw the best minds of my generation destroyed
> by madness, starving hysterical naked,
> dragging themselves through the negro streets at
> dawn looking for an angry fix,
> angelheaded hipsters burning for the ancient
> heavenly connection
> to the starry dynamo in the machinery of night.

The search for the heavenly connection came through a sporadic surge for experimentalism, for opening new horizons, sometimes creatively, other times throwing caution to the wind. In some instances it manifested as a hedonistic mix of intoxication, exuberance and illumination, as in the Beat Generation and the creative expressions of Jack Kerouac, Allen Ginsberg and William Burroughs. Other times it was channelled through the new growth of interest in Buddhism and ecology as through the work of Alan Watts, D T Suzuki and Gary Snyder. A Western counter-culture was now emerging through the newfound popularity of Eastern teachings (Buddhism, Taoism, Sufism, etc.) and the experimental play-fulness of mind-altering processes. The zeitgeist of the age can be seen through the psychologist and counterculture guru Timothy Leary's famous dictum: *Turn On, Tune In, Drop Out.*

Significantly, during this period of experimental cultural expression a new form of psychological consciousness was being explored. Through psychoanalysis and the theories of Freud, who had exposed sexuality and notions of self-esteem and the inferiority complex to the public stage, the 1950s and 1960s opened up new areas of self-evaluation. People were increasingly exploring their own feelings, self-reflection and the interior gaze. Timothy Leary was right to suggest that the new era had shifted to 'the politics of the nervous system'. Likewise, Theodore Roszak, in *The Making of a Counter Culture* (1968), noted that sociology had given way to psychology and that the trip was now inward, making everything open to question.

The inward trip during the 1960s and 1970s was popularized by the experimentation with psychoactive fungi, largely given exposure in the US by the ethnobotany of Robert Gordon Wasson. This later materialized into experimentation with the once-legal drug LSD (lysergic acid diethylamide) that was initially synthesized by Albert Hofmann and popularized by the antics of Timothy Leary, Ken Kesey and the Merry Pranksters, amongst many others. In the 1970s the anthropological research and writings of Terence and Dennis McKenna were gaining a wider readership in their sober assessment of the role of psychedelic drugs in society. This search for non-ordinary states of consciousness also led to many Westerners seeking out a shamanic training. Perhaps most popular during the late 1960s and through the 1970s were the various books of Carlos Castaneda, which described the author's apprenticeship with the shaman known as Don Juan.

The market place was open for experimenting with human potential, as was evidenced by the popularity of the Esalen Institute, founded in California in 1962, that offered workshops on such subjects as meditation, Gestalt, yoga, ecology, psychology, spirituality and holotropic breath work. Transpersonal psychology became a defined field with the publication of the *Journal of Transpersonal Psychology*; notable names in this field included Abraham Maslow and Stanislav Grof; and later Ken Wilber, Charles Tart, Stanley Krippner, Claudio Naranjo and Oscar Ichazo.

Interest in transpersonal issues, of interior realms and metaphysics opened the door to a dramatic surge in forms of spiritual belief quickly labelled as 'New Age'. These included life after death, past lives, angels, auras, channelling, divination, crystals, I-Ching, spiritual healing, prayer circles, holism, organic foods, spirit guides, etc. Sacred sexuality too became a focus with people connecting with Tantric sex, Taoist sexual practices and Native American sacred sex traditions. There was also a surge of interest in the ancient esoteric areas of alchemy, Hermeticism, the Kabbalah and Gnosticism. On 16–17 August 1987, the Harmonic Convergence gathering took place which brought many people together to celebrate the planetary alignment occurring and to facilitate the shift towards a new era.

Planet Earth was now in full focus, especially after the *Apollo 11* Moon landing on 20 July 1969. The first photos of Earth taken from space seemed to galvanize people's ecological awareness, alongside Rachel Carson's 1962 environmental classic *Silent Spring*. The ecology movement was spurred by other such notables as Gregory Bateson, E F Schumacher, Arne Naess and Thomas Berry. In 1970 the US Environmental Protection Agency was established and the world held its first Earth Day. In 1971 Greenpeace was founded; and in 1972 the UN Environment Program was set up. The 1960s and 1970s represented a period of tremendous change in thinking and attitudes, with the support of feminism, sexual liberation, civil rights, CND and freedom of expression. Despite the atrocities of the Vietnam War and the assassination of John F Kennedy, people were still turning on and tuning in to a new energy of change. Large-scale gatherings, such as the music festivals of Woodstock and the Isle of Wight, offered a place for community that celebrated a form of neo-tribalism and self-expression. These events later influenced Burning Man, Glastonbury and other large-scale gatherings now worldwide. The power of change brought about the eventual collapse of the Soviet Union and the fall of the Berlin Wall in 1989/90.

By the 1990s the most popular poet in the US was the Persian Sufi Jalalludin Rumi; holography and the holographic universe was a new popular paradigm; the left-right working of the brain hemispheres was a popular subject; the Internet was revolutionizing communications; and notions such as the noosphere, Global Brain and collective consciousness were almost commonplace. What a revolution of human thought in such a short span of human history! In between we saw a flurry of artistic and literary movements including, in no particular order: Cubism, Expressionism, Surrealism, Dada, Modernism, the Frankfurt School, stream of consciousness, and many more that would require several books to recount. A phase of immense cultural, mental and psychological growth has occurred in the last 150 years.

The new scientific paradigm has come a long way since Newton's clockwork universe. Consider that the scientific contributions to human knowledge include: quantum physics, quantum biology/biophysics, holography (holographic universe and holographic brain), string theory (multiverses and extra-dimensions), systems theory, systems philosophy, self-organization, non-equilibrium systems, chaos and complexity theory, implicate order, morphic resonance and many more. Science established the Genome Project, nanotechnology engineering and quantum computing. It even produced the first successful genetic cloning, of Dolly the sheep, in Scotland in 1997. Cyberspace is the new shared domain that exists beyond conventional notions of time and space, and virtual communities play around with digital identities. Despite the dangers of these new technologies,[4] an acceleration of possibilities marked the end of the 20th century and the beginning of the new millennium.

The Great Acceleration

The second half of the 20th century saw a rapid acceleration in almost all spheres of life. Some of this 'acceleration' has occurred in our environmental systems, and to detrimental effect. We only have to look at biodiversity loss, deforestation, the chemicals we are throwing into the ground and the atmosphere, ocean acidification, global freshwater decline and topsoil depletion to see some of the effects of recent human enterprise. With the simultaneous growth in human populations and erratic geological conditions this could lead us to change from using the term 'The Age of Anxiety' (as the 20th century has been called) to 'The Age of Disequilibrium'. However, an acceleration of chaotic energies also has no alternative but to force a species mind-change on a global and perhaps interior level. The changes I have only touched upon briefly suggest a greater shift towards individual autonomy; a deepened sense of self and psychological reflection; an increased perception of inner and outer realities; and a heightened recognition of the sensory nature of human experience. In other words, there has been an astounding growth in the psychological evolution of the human self.

The manner in which we communicate reflects our own internal processes. It may be that the rise in global communication technologies (Internet and mobile phones) reflects a new form of participatory consciousness amongst people. This new model is a distributed one; in other words, it connects people horizontally in a more egalitarian way rather than through hierarchical structures. It also catalyses people into being more active through their participation. No longer are we the passive audience, as in earlier electrical revolutions of radio, then television: the new model is YouTube, Facebook, Twitter, blogging and text messaging. The dialogue is now more active; people are onstage and orchestrating their own connections; managing their own forms of voice and self-expression. At the turn of the century, as the 1990s tipped into the third millennium, the social-civil body of the planet began to stretch its tentacles.

Social networks have matured tremendously over the past decade; the list of global Non-Profit Organizations (NPOs) grows longer with each passing year. These innovative networks are the forums for visionary thinkers; concepts spread virally through the electronic nervous system of the planet as once-fringe ideas go global. A new civil body is being constructed by the distributed contributions of individuals in every conceivable physical location. Talks are broadcast regularly – such as in the TEDTalks series of innovative lectures – and social collectives form, activate, influence and stimulate alternative thinking and ideas. A more mature form of collective social intelligence is beginning to manifest in various parts of the globe, as the key element of the Internet 'isn't the consumption of information or interactive services but participation in a social process of collective intelligence …'[5]

This new networked model of civil society represents a burgeoning collective intelligence. It is an intelligence that is arising out of our increasing interrelatedness, and one that is being exposed to a global world of contradictory realities and multicultural perspectives. As Pierre Teilhard de Chardin correctly stated:

> The Age of Nations is past. The task before us now, if we
> would not perish, is to shake off our ancient prejudices, and
> to build the Earth.[6]

This non-hierarchical bottom-up format may be the working model for the future and, like the Internet, can be built to withstand shocks, attacks and breakages: we re-route, disperse and re-join at a later point in the network. This is the peer-to-peer collaborative model – a way of greater individualization within a shared, complex, diverse yet unified field of interactions. This networked unity may be a new model to make the old one obsolete. Buckminster Fuller nailed the point exactly when he said:

> You never change things by fighting the existing reality.
> To change something, build a new model that makes the
> existing model obsolete.

Externally we seem to be a vast, distant and separated collection of people, yet the reality may be the opposite: a dense, intimate, closely entwined species of various races, individual yet sharing a nonlocal sense of being. And with the rapid rise of physical global travel and tourism to complement our virtual global communications, the world has extended its nervous system to expose millions of people to each other, different cultures and circumstances. Younger generations of people worldwide are growing up with a new expression of consciousness; the 20th century's exploration of the psyche, mixed with technologies of communication and connection, herald a more reflexive mode of thought. People today are comfortable in expressing themselves with strangers; they explore and express their inner thoughts, feelings, emotions and ideas with hundreds of unknown persons online, from various cultural backgrounds. More and more daily interactions are empathic as we react and share news, stories and emotional impacts from sources around the world.

Empathy is one of the core values by which we create and sustain social life. Exposure to impacts outside of our own local and narrow environments helps us to learn tolerance, and to live with experiences that are richer and more complex, full of ambiguities, multiple realities and shared perceptions. It is a way of constructing more social capital in our world. It is a model that was used in ancient communities where cultural capital preceded commercial capital; when cultural relations were primary and came before commercial relations and focused on the social benefit rather than the profit. We see this happening in modern variations today such as open source software (e.g. Linux), or in collaborative tools such as Wikipedia, when a global commons for sharing can work above the individual thrust for profit and commercial gain. And we have also seen it in active operation in the form of 'smart mobs'.

The term 'smart mobs' was coined by cultural critic Howard Rheingold to refer to mobile social networks that organize their activities via mobile phones, usually through text messaging. According to Rheingold, these mobile networks are the new 'social revolution' in that they are shifting social practices through connecting like-minded people together into collective action at short notice. Such networks are constantly on the move, constantly communicating, and forever able to 'swarm' within a matter of minutes if physically able. As a case in point, mobile text messaging in Manila, the Philippines, was a major contributor in ending the presidency of incumbent Joseph Estrada. A text message of 'Go 2EDSA, Wear blck' was sent around and, within the first hour, tens of thousands of Filipinos descended upon Epifanio de los Santos Avenue (known as Edsa). Over a four-day period more than a million people showed up in an effort to oust Estrada.[7]

The well-known anti-WTO protests in Seattle in 1999 – often referred to as 'The Battle of Seattle' – coordinated crowds of protestors through phones, laptop emails and texting. These anti-WTO protest movements were modelling themselves in the nature of distributed, self-organizing networks. Although their interests varied within the overall movement, they came together in their protests to create an action greater than the sum of their parts.

A more recent example is that of the 'Occupy Wall Street' movement in New York City (based in Zuccotti Park on Wall Street) that began on 17 September 2011 and within a few weeks spread to over 70 major cities and over 600 communities in the US. October 15th 2011 also saw an international 'Occupy' day that involved similar protests in over 900 cities worldwide. All of these protests used the new forms of social media – the Internet, mobile phones, online social networks, etc. – to organize their 'smart mob' gatherings. Now in the age of Twitter, Facebook and YouTube, people-centred content is more than ever active in promoting people-power dissent and action across the globe, from the 'Arab Spring' of the Middle East to the angst of Middle England. We are no longer joined by blood ties alone but by larger, sometimes global, affinities.

We sometimes forget that humans cannot live by food alone; we are in need of nurture, affection and shared interests. This fact has now been clearly established by psychologists who have worked on maternal-separation and social-isolation experiments. They clearly demonstrate the importance of care-giving and companionship in social and cognitive development. A growing number of psychologists have argued that a child depends on deepening relationships with other people in order to develop a sense of selfhood and self-awareness.[8] This corroborates what neuroscience has discovered with 'mirror neurons' about how we also share sensory impacts. A 'mirror neuron' is a brain neuron that is activated ('fires') when a living being (such as humans, primates and other mammals) observes the action of another. In other words, if an individual watches another person eat an apple, then the exact same brain neurons will fire in the person observing the action as if they themselves were performing the act. Such neuron behaviour has been found in humans to operate in the premotor cortex and inferior parietal cortex. In a series of experiments a group of people were hooked up for brain scans (fMRI) and watched other people; their somatosensory cortex was activated by observing the others being touched at that moment.

This phenomenon of 'mirror neurons' was first discovered by a research team in Italy in the 1990s when studying the neuronal activity of macaque monkeys. This discovery has led many notable neuroscientists to declare that mirror neurons are important for learning processes (imitation) as well as language acquisition. In more modern general terms we might also say that this capacity is what ties a person in sympathy and empathy to another's situation. It may also explain why people become so emotionally attached to events on television, and even cry in response to watching someone crying on the screen. In this way we are emotionally *entangled* through a mirroring of neuronal firing in the brain. If we expand this understanding to take in worldwide events through global communications and networks of connection we can say that people are increasing not only their empathic relationships with each other but also their *entanglement at a distance*. New developments in psychology, cognitive science and neuroscience are laying the groundwork for a wholesale reappraisal of human consciousness. This is what I mean about the 'great acceleration'. The human race is not only accelerating in terms of its information retrieval/storage and its science/knowledge base, but also in its empathic entanglement: the rising web of a planetary nervous system. Or, as writer Doris Lessing liked to refer to it, the rising of the Substance-Of-We-Feeling (SOWF).

During this accelerating phase of our socio-cultural and inner evolution we are asked to expand and develop our cognitive, emotional and perceptual faculties. Harvard professor of psychology Howard

Gardner has outlined in his book *Five Minds for the Future* what he considers to be the five separate but related combinations of cognitive abilities that are needed to 'thrive in the world during eras to come' and which we should develop for the future. Gardner's five minds, or rather mindsets, are paraphrased here as:

1   To master important subjects rather than simply knowing about them. To stay up to date with the subject and to know how to work steadily over time to improve skill and understanding.

2   To be able to integrate large quantities of multidisciplinary facts and apply them to one's work.

3   To pose new questions, developing new solutions to existing questions, stretching disciplines and genres in new directions, or building new disciplines.

4   To be open to understanding and appreciating the perspectives and experiences of those who are different from the individual.

5   To do one's work in an ethical way that reflects responsibilities to others and society; to reflect on the nature of one's work and the needs and desires of the society in which one lives.[9]

Gardner also refers to a type of 'existential intelligence', what he calls a 'heightened capacity of appreciation and attention to the cosmological enigmas that define the human condition – an exceptional awareness of the metaphysical, ontological and epistemological mysteries that have been a perennial concern for people of all cultures'.[10] The psychological impacts we experience will be primary in developing the perceptions necessary for the future. We are today exposed to each other in ways without precedent. The children being born as part of the new millennium (sometimes referred to as the 'Millennials') are growing up embedded within virtual social networks that transcend space and time, as well as cultures, national boundaries and local ideologies. The younger generations are accustomed to send and receive information in a way that may also help to nourish local networks – and not, importantly, to replace them.

This may account for the increasing numbers of young people in developed nations becoming involved in community and social projects and NGOs; taking a year out to help in another culture abroad, to learn and experience, and to offer assistance. Volunteering amongst the young, despite what appears to be the contrary, is on the increase. Young people are even sacrificing their lives for peace and justice, as evidenced by the actions and subsequent death of Rachel Corrie in occupied Palestine. It is not only a call for equality – it is a loud call for tolerance and justice. These are signs of an emerging relational consciousness, a service-to-others (STO) as opposed to service-to-self (STS).

Another growing movement is the 'Roots of Empathy' programme – educating young schoolchildren about emotional needs and relations. Founder Mary Gordon writes:

> The Roots of Empathy classroom is creating citizens of the world – children who are developing empathic ethics and a sense of social responsibility that takes the position that we all share the same lifeboat. These are the children who will build a more caring, peaceful and civil society, child by child.[11]

The great acceleration (or New Planetary Era?) is moving further towards a planetary consciousness that is collective and shared: a model of greater connectivity and global communication (horizontal), with closer intimacy, with Earth customs and cosmic perspective (vertical).

It is my firm understanding that humanity is currently passing through times that will catalyse both psychological and physical changes. As the earlier chapters discussed, we are on the cusp of many older energy systems breaking down. Yet many people have been sensing this for some time now, as events in the second half of the 20th century have indicated. Also, within developed nations there has, over the past few decades, been a significant shift of values in that more and more people are seeking a quality of life that has moved away from materialism and towards meaning and happiness; towards simplifying their lifestyles (even before the recent economic crashes). So far, a good quality of life for too many people has been provided by raiding the world's finite energy sources and co-opting other nations' resources. However, being forced to downsize can be a good thing, turning people's emphasis away from external status and material possessions to a focus on what is local and meaningful – relations, local resources, working with one's self and the needs of others. Any form of inconvenience, or even hardship, needs to be taken as a beneficial interiorizing process; a way to develop self-reflexive consciousness. Sometimes in order to gain we must first experience what it is to lose something. Troubled times can lead to an extension and/or manifestation of empathic consciousness, as we realize the interconnectedness of our worsening situation – just like the war 'bunker' mentality during World War II, a coming together of the people in times of need.

It is also important to remember that for the new energies manifesting in our times, the old model of technology will not work. As I described in Chapter Two, the old technological mind of control, bureaucracy and organization, which has led to our present surveillance world (Chapter Five), will no longer serve us. Our technologies not only need to be more fluid, as in emerging social media that is free to access (e.g. YouTube) and social networks free of censorship, but also more egalitarian and democratic. Technology that aims to dominate will not be able to work with the new energies of consciousness that will manifest over the coming years.

These conscious energies will include a rising protest from people for more transparency and justice in our national and international systems. There will be many more social protests and strikes on the horizon if these systems do not begin to better serve egalitarian and ethical human interests. Further, as the social transition goes through many years of change (remember that these cycles are long, and are not offering immediate relief) the world may first have to pass through a period of fragmentation due to energy depletion in the future and/or technological infrastructure problems. A new form of integral consciousness is less likely to embrace a corporate global techno-industrial future, despite what some thinkers argue. However, even though there may be initial periods of fragmentation this will not diminish a collectively evolving empathic mind that will inform a greater awareness for working together;

community-building; shared values and ethics; and working towards remodelling how the world operates.

It will not be 'business as usual' as most future forecasters seem to predict; many forecasters simply offer a linear view that is just a more 'planetary' version of today's world. This view does not take into account 'system jumps'; the tipping points, or rather phase transitions, that characterize the fluctuations of growth. The future may well be a more mindful, spiritually aware and ecologically-integral period, yet it may first also be a more chaotic, fragmented and disturbed global picture as the people of the world – and the world's systems – learn to reassemble themselves into a radical new form of existence in line with the resources available to us.

This period of transformation of life on Earth is likely to include heightened impulses for radical social change and cultural renovation; alongside new discoveries in science, energy and our knowledge of the cosmos. There will manifest an increased drive for human betterment that will be marked through intensified activism for social, political and ecological change; and for changes in the balance of global power. Large demographic shifts and the active presence of many cross-cultural movements will release much concentrated energy for psychological and physical change. Planet Earth is entering a sustained period for monumental change, requiring humanity not only to draw on all its physical and psychic resources of creativity and vision, but also to shift into capacities that could ultimately serve to be extremely liberating for the self.

Reaching Critical Mass

It is certainly no small claim to say that the 3rd millennium will stimulate and nurture a new form of human consciousness. To paraphrase the famous saying of J B S Haldane, the future of humanity may not be only queerer than we suppose, but queerer than we can suppose. And as Terence McKenna once said, we need to take out our conclusions from being central to our culture and replace them by a sense of the mysterious. The future may open up a greater sense of the mysterious than we have anticipated. Some of this mystery may surround the greater capacities inherent within the human, as I shall discuss in the following chapters. To help us arrive where we are already heading we will have to question, and perhaps discard, many of our belief systems. Rather, we should put the role of direct experience in place of enforced belief systems that are self-limiting functions. It limits our vision to have beliefs when the universe is stranger than we can suppose and is thus continually overriding our beliefs, making them limiting factors if we cling to them.

Experience must be made primary; therefore the language of the self must be primary. We need a new language, and in order to have a new language we need a new sense of reality. Rather than consuming ideological visions we need to be the creators of them – to send them out. Let our visions and creativity breed and mutate like viruses in proactive and beneficial ways. Terence McKenna used to urge his listeners to 'Live as far into the future as you can live'; reminding them also that energy is now rushing into our reality like into 'the realm of the densely packed'.

The opportunity is here for change and betterment like never before in our recent history. This means that the responsibility is also here; and these two factors may never be present again at exactly the right moment when they are so badly needed. What the human species may now be witnessing, on the cusp of this critical mass, is the rise of intuition, empathy, greater connectivity to the world and to people, and a sense of 'knowing' about what each given situation demands. Being nurtured within each person is a growing sense of the greater cosmic whole: the realization that humanity exists and evolves within a universe of intelligence and meaning. This can serve to impart within humanity a more profound, and acknowledged, spiritual impulse.

After all, we are already on the way to where we are heading. One can see clearly that Bob Dylan was right when he sang 'There's something happening … but you don't know what it is. Do you, Mr Jones?'[12]

CHAPTER EIGHT

A Creative Cosmos:
Re-Aligning with a Living Universe

What stood out for me in the early stages was the interconnectedness of everything to form a seamless whole. The entire universe is an undivided, totally unified, organic phenomenon. I saw various breakthroughs ... as but the early phases of the scientific discovery of this wholeness. I knew that these discoveries would continue to mount until it would become impossible for us not to recognize the universe for what it was – a unified organism of extraordinary design reflecting a massive Creative Intelligence.

Christopher Bache

The dreams of magic may one day be the waking realities of science.

Sir James Frazer

Humans have their duties as do the plants, the stones, and the darkness.

Rose von Thater-Braan

There is an old fable about a young fish which, upon hearing of the wise old sage fish that lives upriver, decided one day to swim upriver to seek out this wise one. After much hard swimming against the current, and after what seemed like such a long time for the young fish, he eventually arrives at the cleft in the rock where he sees the wise fish. Exhausted, panting, yet eager to converse, the young fish approaches the wise one expectantly. 'Yes,' says the wise one, 'what is the question that you have so desperately come here to ask?' 'Well,' begins the young fish, 'I've had this burning question on my mind for so long. I really need to know ... what's this thing that is called "water"?'

We are all of us surrounded each moment with the mystery, the energies, the tools for our own future living, just as the young fish in the above tale. We are already, and always have been, immersed in the 'waters' of our existence, so to speak. And this existence is not a solitary, isolated life on a stony rock hurtling through a chemically active yet 'dead' universe, as our science would perhaps lead us to believe. As was discussed in Chapter Six, it is very likely that we have entered what has been termed as the rising arc of the Dwapara Yuga, the Bronze Age; and in this cycle of development humanity retains a comprehension of some of the finer forces and more subtle energies of the cosmos. This includes a progressive understanding of the various forces of attraction and repulsion, leading to recognition that all matter, all atomic form, is nothing other than the manifestation of energy and vibratory forces.

In fact, we have in some ways already arrived at this stage with the latest discoveries of quantum mechanics, string theory and the model of a holographic universe. Despite arriving here in 'theory', and despite many of our scientists having utilized these findings in some of their latest investigations, this recognition has not yet seeped into mass public consciousness. It is a relatively few people on this planet who genuinely understand and accept (or 'get it') that all physical life is a secondary manifestation from a primary source of energy. Since thought-waves and consciousness are themselves forms of energy, then it can be logically deducted (if not intuitively sensed) that consciousness is a primary source of all life. This shift – or leap – from a material basis of life to a universal foundation of energies and consciousness may itself represent this ongoing transition of understanding towards the 'finer energies' that

Yukteswar referred to as part of the Dwapara Yuga cycle. If this is indeed the case, as I believe it is and for which this book argues, then humanity is on the cusp of a paradigm shift from a dead to a living, creative universe.

Entangled within a Creative Cosmos

It is high time that humanity's dominant belief systems, and scientific dogma, moved away from its dreadfully reductionist and anthropocentric view of the universe. From this stance the general consensus is that we have been lucky to have found ourselves in a 'just-right' universe that was accidentally created by chance. Yet according to the calculations of mathematical physicist Roger Penrose, the probability of coming across such a universe, fine-tuned to life, by random selection is 1 in $10^{10^{123}}$. There would be more certainty that a living universal intelligence existed than this! Physicist Bernard Haisch asks, in response to this extreme probability, whether it would be so strange after all to consider the existence of a transcendental agency or intelligence at work? Yet, as Haisch himself admits, whilst the calculations certainly suggest this alternative such a hypothesis is outside of empirical study.

So how did we humans, or rather our universe, arrive at such luck? Well, the scientific rationalists have come up with the 'infinite universe' theory which suggests that instead of just one, there must be an infinite number of other universes, in other dimensions, so that by the law of probability one has to be just right, purely by chance! The corollary is that there is an infinite number of dead universes out there (somewhere) so why shouldn't one of them just randomly happen to have the exact fine-tuned gaseous mix required for what we have come to regard as 'life'? Thus, human self-consciousness is a fluke that just happened to occur because our trillion-plus starry universe ended up supporting the complex growth of neurochemical evolution – now isn't that a radical idea![1] According to evolutionary biologist Elisabet Sahtouris:

> We stand at a critical time in human history where the 'self-evident' axiomatic 'truth' of a depressingly meaningless mechanical universe running down by entropy, magically giving rise to biological creatures doomed to endless

competitive struggle to get what they can while they can, is no longer defensible.[2]

Whilst a mechanical universe may no longer be feasible, in Sahtouris's words, it still remains the dominant worldview. At least the scientific community is shifting to see a bigger picture beyond the 'solitary universe' thinking; and some are now even framing universes in terms of birthing organisms. Science writer John Gribbin sees the universe as just one component within a huge array of other universes; what he views as a self-reproducing system connected by space 'tunnels' that join a 'baby' universe to its 'parent'. In this anthropomorphic view Gribbin explains that those universes that leave the most 'offspring' are the successful ones. Still, the dead universe theory – as opposed to the living universe one – assumes that all life was organized by random processes thanks to a spewing out of chemical debris from a massive explosion several billion years ago. Well, if that's the meaning of life, it doesn't leave us much to go on.

But what's so wrong with the 'living universe' theory? It puts forward the notion that the universe, our cosmos, is a continuous flow-through of energy. Within a living universe the whole underlying energetic order is recreated and sustained at each moment, rather than being a lifeless, random mass. Such a shift in perception of the meaning of our cosmos would have profound implications for our understanding of the significance of human life. As social scientist Duane Elgin remarks:

> In a dead universe, consumerism makes sense; in a living universe, simplicity makes sense. If the universe is unconscious and dead at its foundations, then each of us is the product of blind chance among materialistic forces. It is only fitting that we the living exploit on our own behalf that which is not alive. If the universe is lifeless, it has no larger purpose or meaning, and neither does human existence ... However, if we consider the universe to be alive, then we have an inherent connection to a deep, fundamental and penetrating intelligence. Every action in a living universe carries meaning, responsibility, and consequences. It shifts our way of perceiving the significance of life. We are then imbued with an evolutionary purpose.[3]

Surely, then, we need to consider ourselves as more than accidents of physics and chemistry? As humanity advances not only in its scientific discoveries of 'finer energies', but also as our species develops its innate capacities and organs of intuition, empathy and new patterns of thinking, the realization may finally dawn on us that there is no inconsistency in viewing our cosmos as a living, energetic environment. And in this way our species, in stepping further along its evolutionary journey, will see that the cosmos not only continuously sustains us but that we are all intimately related to everything that exists. After nearly 4 billion years of evolution upon Earth, humans may finally regard themselves as agents of co-creation within an active creative cosmos.

It is interesting to note on this discussion of a living universe that Nobel Prize scientist Francis Crick, who co-discovered the DNA sequence, could not understand how even a single assembled protein could have emerged by chance. Crick calculated the odds of this happening as just 1 chance in 10^{260}: this is an immeasurable sum when we consider that all the atoms in the entire visible universe have been calculated to amount 'only' to 10^{80}. Both Francis Crick and astronomer Fred Hoyle believed that life was already too complex when it first appeared on Earth and thus must have originated elsewhere first. Hoyle is now infamous for stating, somewhat controversially amongst his peers, that for complex life to have originated by chance is statistically the same odds as a hurricane blowing through a scrap yard and producing a Boeing 747. He promoted a general Panspermia hypothesis which says that life exists throughout the universe and is distributed by bacteria being present on passing/crashing meteoroids, asteroids and planetoids.

Similarly, Crick in his book *Life Itself: Its Origin and Nature* put forward the hypothesis that since it was highly unlikely that complex bacteria on Earth arose by random chance it was therefore more likely to have arrived at Earth by what is known as 'Directed Panspermia'. That is, the seeds of life, the early bacterial forms of DNA, may have been purposely spread by an advanced extraterrestrial civilization; either because this civilization was facing extinction, or as a means for terraforming planets perhaps for later colonization. Crick concludes this hypothesis by stating that DNA is 'not of this Earth'. It may be interesting to note also at this point that there have been allegations that Crick used LSD to help decipher/visualize the patterned structure of DNA. According to a newspaper article in 2004 an associate, who had met Francis Crick at Cambridge, was told by him that 'some Cambridge academics used LSD in tiny amounts as a thinking tool, to liberate them from preconceptions and let their genius wander freely to new ideas'.[4] Crick then went on to tell him that he had perceived the double-helix shape whilst on LSD. As an addendum to this, researchers from Boston University and Harvard Medical School in the mid 1990s examined 37 DNA sequences to see if they contained a patterned form of organized language that would comply to known laws (specifically Zipf's Law or Shannon's Information Theory). Whilst they discovered that the coded sequences of DNA did not follow any of these patterns, the 97 per cent un-coded sequences, or 'junk DNA', did indeed plot 'communicable patterns' as if they could carry coded messages.[5]

There is indeed still much to learn in terms of the 'hidden languages' of our creative environment; it is a positive foreshadowing that many disciplines – psychology, philosophy, theology etc. – are now gradually beginning to shift in perspective, in terms of viewing ourselves as part of a dynamic, living universe. This is surely an indication of the changing times, of the recognition that humanity's evolution requires more than an endless struggle within a dead universe. The notion of having existence within a mechanical blind universe, which neither acknowledges nor cares about the role and function of life, may once have been a useful paradigm, yet now must surely be cast aside as an outworn dogma. It no longer makes sense to perpetuate this separatist, isolationist perspective in an era where our very significance and survival implores us to adopt an integral and ecological view of physical and conscious life. We need to recognize that looking to the future means that we, collectively, have to shift away from the limitations of our assumptions.

It may be that at present our individual imaginations are constrained by the boundaries of our collective psyche; however, this collective psyche is now changing and evolving. As it once dawned on the early sea-faring explorers that the world could not be flat, so now is the realization beginning to grow within people's minds that the universe of which we are a part is not in fact dead, but full of vibrant life and conscious energy. Our latest scientific terms are now starting to reflect this realization, as words such as quantum vacuum, zero-point energy, creative energy and quantum consciousness are now beginning to infiltrate our literature, media and speech. The possibility of life existing within an energetic universe appears more probable with each new discovery and tweak in our paradigms of human thought. The fact that our blueprint – DNA – could have potentially arrived from elsewhere in the universe is another pause for thought.

If we pursue this line of enquiry then we must, sooner rather than later, come to the question of whether there exists conscious intelligence within such a living universe. Further, can transpersonal states of consciousness form a connection, or bridge, with such other conscious realms? Whilst to some people this may sound too far-fetched, I would offer the suggestion that the transpersonal dimension of consciousness has been known for millennia amongst various traditions, regardless of the fact that it has been largely denied and dismissed by our rational sciences.

The Primacy of Consciousness

The rational view that we are an isolated sentient species, even perhaps alone in the vastness of a chemically gaseous universe, is a relatively recent worldview and dominant paradigm. When the idea of communing with other 'intelligences' is brought up, many people automatically think of shamans and tribal rituals that the modern world has labelled as 'primitive'. Yet despite our very recent modern criticisms, and against rational logic, elements of almost every society that has existed since the appearance of modern humans has exhibited some form of belief in the existence of beings and intelligences in other realms. And despite the seeming differences in outward forms the central uniting factor is a fundamental connection to inherent 'irrational beliefs' in the supernatural; that is, in the non-material forces that penetrate the veil into our everyday realities. As historical researcher Graham Hancock notes:

> Belief in the supernatural – whether manifested through spiritual beings thought to have been born in human form, or through revelations to particular humans – has been responsible for social, political, economic and cultural developments 'of monumental significance in the history of mankind'.[6]

This relationship to supernatural forces goes back even as far as the rock paintings of therianthropes (shape-shifters from human to animal form) that date back 35,000 years, and are speculated to be the early origins of human religious traditions. The symbolic paintings and drawings on cave walls and traces of ancient rituals which appear throughout the Palaeolithic era display a 'primitive' people in touch with the unseen realm, with a creative world beyond that of the human, and a transcendental space which modern humans, in effect, have never stopped attempting to access. In recognition of this, noted anthropologist David Lewis-Williams has built a theory, after extensive investigations, which explains how the people of the Upper Palaeolithic era harnessed altered states of consciousness to fashion their society, and also used such imagery as a means of establishing and defining social relationships.[7]

Notably, anthropologist Weston La Barre has stated that:

> All our knowledge of the supernatural derives de facto from
> the statements made by religious visionaries and ecstatics,
> i.e. prophets and shamans ... Priests only administrate the
> ecclesia established on this supernatural basis ...[8]

In spite of the tens of thousands of years that separate modern humanity from its ancestral cave-dwellers, the notion of entering into a more dynamic and creative union with the larger cosmos has been, it appears, a hard-wired aspect of our deeper selves. Throughout the millennia those persons more able to access this capacity, such as shamans, mystics and prophets, have often done so for the benefit of their communities, and to bring knowledge and aid to the human family (whether local or on a wider global scale). To many who negotiate these realms, and maintain these capacities, the notion that the wider cosmos is a living, intelligent realm is second nature. It is also fair to say that virtually all human beings have the capacity to access these latent abilities; many people are already doing so without actually realizing it, or casting it off as coincidence, fluke, good luck, or weird anomaly. However, in this modern age of radical seeking (*see* previous chapter), there has been a great increase in the number of people reaching the understanding that the universe can be connected to, and aligned with human intentions. Again referring to Hancock he notes that:

> Once we have entered a state of consciousness that has
> been altered deeply enough – itself a universal neurological
> capacity of the human race – it seems that everyone,
> everywhere, experiences visions containing very much the
> same combinations of patterns and shapes.[9]

What this seems to suggest is that the human brain (our neurological
capacity) may function as an antenna into the finer realms that form a
part of the larger creative cosmos. Swiss scientist Albert Hofmann, best
known as the first person to synthesize LSD and to learn of its psychedelic
effects, wrote in his autobiography *LSD: My Problem Child*:

> Since the endless variety and diversity of the universe
> correspond to infinitely many different wavelengths,
> depending on the adjustment of the receiver, many different
> realities ... can become conscious ... to shift the wavelength
> setting of the receiving 'self', and thereby to evoke alterations
> in reality consciousness.[10]

In a previous book, *The Struggle for Your Mind,* I noted how the human
nervous system operated on a synchronous quantum field level and thus
could operate as a receiver of finer energies. In a similar manner it has
been suggested by many thinkers that the brain is also likely to function
as a biochemical and bioelectric receiver that, directly or indirectly, may
be 'tuned into' a variety of wavelengths not normally accessible to our
consciousness. This could be one of the primary reasons for the great
emphasis in wisdom traditions on fostering an altered state of consciousness through such practices as fasting, deprivation and meditation (as
practised by the early ascetics); sweat lodges; exhaustive ritual dancing/
spinning in circles; and prolonged chanting and prostration, etc.
Humanity has been experimenting with countless methods to induce
an alternate state of consciousness for millennia, as if inherent within
the deeper self there is a remnant, a trace, of an ability to transcend to a
finer state of being that has now become lost to us.

Yet modern rational science has remained blind to this, or considers
it a fringe, esoteric irrational belief system. Naturally, such a course of
investigation does not lend itself to 'rational', scientific proof. To take
Rupert Sheldrake's metaphor, it is like taking apart a television set to

investigate each part, such as the transistor, the tube etc., yet not being able to understand how the programmes are received or where they come from. In other words, it is the elephant in the dark scenario whereby the individual parts are investigated, pulled apart and scrutinized, yet the overall integral significance and functioning is completely lost.

This integral vision has thus, so far, often been the domain of the few, and the bridge to integrate the spiritual/non-physical with the everyday world has been tenuous in many cases. Often this connecting bridge has been manifested through direct personal revelation, which in past cases such as the Gnostics, Cathars, mystics and seers etc., was vehemently stamped out by religious authorities (as in the infamous Inquisition). Yet as our world gradually moves into an era of finer, subtler energies we are likely to find that the future stage will be based more on consciousness: the sciences of consciousness, the vision, creativity and evolution of consciousness, and the notion that consciousness is primary. Consciousness researcher Dr Strassman has noted that:

> By revolutionizing our understanding of spirit realms,
> hopefully our understanding of the physical/material
> realms would evolve – into more ethical, co-operative and
> beneficent practices.[11]

Dr Strassman views consciousness as an inherent part of the universe such that any theory or science which does not recognize this will never be a complete description of humanity's place in the larger cosmic picture. Further, Dr Strassman contends that a creative and dynamic communion with transpersonal realms of experience may help humanity to recognize and understand the situation we are currently facing here on Earth:

> Establishing – with a sober, altruistic intent – reliable and
> generally available means of contact with these different
> levels of existence may help us alleviate some of the pressing
> issues we are facing on this planet in this time-space
> continuum. It even may be that the information and
> resources we gather in these noncorporeal realms are more
> important to our survival – and ultimately our evolution –
> than that which we obtain via strictly physical means.[12]

We have seen in the previous chapter that the radical seeking and experimentation of the 1960s, with altered states of consciousness especially, have helped to prepare the way for a generation more in tune with transpersonal concepts and values. It may well be that 'the actual experience that extra-sensory states exist may be the foundation for a future which contains extra-sensory experience as a widespread attribute'.[13] It is important that we embrace ideas *now*, so that they may become acceptable mental currency in advance of their actualization.

Such actualization would create new strata of meaning within our human lives to counteract the growing forces of psychological and social isolation, anxiety, stress, depression and other similar states of dis-ease that afflict materialistic societies, too heavily dependent upon a pharmaceutical lifestyle. The now redundant view that the physical life we have on Earth is the only life we have has been the driver of a physically abusive and hedonistic way of living that embraces rampant consumerism (retail therapy?), violence, sexual gratifications, chemical-infested food, drastic pollution and the severe desecration of our natural resources. It is a paradox that our extended conscious awareness has yet to fully acknowledge a cosmic heritage that has consciousness at its core.

The denial of the primacy of consciousness has been a prime factor behind humanity abusing the Earth and all her bounteous gifts as nothing more than a useful commodity to utilize as we see fit. This denial is systemic throughout our species and adds to our increasing inhumanity. It degrades the quality of our deepest thoughts, emotions, actions and inner states. It could ultimately also be our collective undoing if we, as a sentient species, remain unable to confirm any sense of meaning, wonder, dynamic creativity and living intelligence beyond our material agents and forces. If the truth of the primacy of consciousness were to be reasserted, and accepted on a wide scale within the hearts and minds of humanity, human life would become qualitatively different and many of the obstacles facing our world today would be removed.

Human self-consciousness is a recent evolutionary endowment, relatively speaking, and as yet we seem unable to grasp the full extent of its capacities and possibilities. It is as if we haven't yet learnt how to think properly, still inundated as we are with the 'old mind'. We haven't yet engaged in a collective perceptual shift; however, the time is getting nearer when such a critical mass will be reached since a majority is not required. A mental mutation is already underway within our human societies, almost in a fractal sense. By this I mean each element of our diverse lives around the globe, although outwardly different, contains the same inner aspects that respond similarly to impacts and influences, be they mental or emotional. Humanity manifests more commonality than difference; like a fractal geometric design, if a small part of humanity is magnified into focus it still resembles the whole. As renowned Persian poet Rumi stated:

> Let the drop of water that is you become a hundred mighty seas. But do not think that the drop alone becomes the Ocean. The Ocean, too, becomes the drop.

At the same time that our global networks of communication are interconnecting us in new, varied and fascinating ways, spreading empathy and commonality, the new sciences of consciousness are slowly beginning to recognize how we are non-physically connected through many subtle and indirect interactions (e.g. *see* 'mirror neurons' from the previous chapter). Cultural historian and environmentalist Thomas Berry observed that the universe is not a collection of objects but rather a *communion of subjects*. Likewise, we are coming around to viewing the fact that 'a community, people working together with their hearts and minds in alignment around a shared intention of the highest integrity, creates an amplified field of intentionality, like a laser beam of coherent consciousness ...'[14] Such sparks of a new 'coherent consciousness', a new perceptual paradigm, are breaking through around the world in diverse and unexpected ways, from both our elders as well as our younger generations (more on this in the next chapter).

Canadian psychiatrist Richard Bucke, in his *Cosmic Consciousness*, anticipated that this state of consciousness would gradually be experienced by more and more people until a 'critical mass' would unfold, shifting our collective human thinking onto a new trajectory. This *phase-shift* would mark the transition from a material 'dead universe' into the understanding that our planet, with its native species, is an inherent part of a much more vast, living, creative cosmos. As such, this new paradigm would bring with it the recognition that what we do here on

Earth reflects back onto the larger canvas of life above and beyond our one planet. This new consciousness, as Bucke intimated, may seem far away yet in reality may require nothing more than the slimmest of shifts, as William James noted:

> … our normal waking consciousness, rational consciousness as we call it, is but one special type of consciousness, whilst all about it, parted from it by the filmiest of screens, there lie potential forms of consciousness very different. We may go through life without suspecting their existence; but apply the requisite stimulus and, at a touch, they are there in all their completeness … No account of the universe in its totality can be final which leaves these other forms of consciousness quite disregarded.[15]

Many other philosophers, especially those who were experimenting with transpersonal states of perception during the 20th century, began to perceive the strata of human consciousness and the narrow range that defined modern humanity's viewpoint. Aldous Huxley, for example, once referred to our current limits of thought as 'a measly trickle of the kind of consciousness which will help us to stay alive on the surface of this particular planet'.[16] Yet at the same time Huxley recognized that individuals could shift this 'trickle' of consciousness into a more receptive state, either through deliberate spiritual exercises, psychological mechanisms such as hypnosis, or by means of drugs. These 'temporary by-passes', as he called them, would allow glimpses of the bigger picture of reality. Similarly, Graham Hancock, whom I referred to earlier, believes that it is highly probable that around 2 per cent of the human population has the type of brain chemistry in 'just the right state of flux' that would allow them periodic glimpses into visions and an altered transpersonal state of consciousness without the need for drugs or other means of deliberate stimulus.

What this tells us is that there are alternative states of consciousness to which access appears to be inherent within the human being; only that a deliberate set of stimuli is often required in order to catalyse this shift. However, there is also a possible slim minority of individuals who are able to access these states, perhaps unknowingly, and at sporadic times. Some of these transpersonal shifts may also account for the presence of paranormal (psi) abilities and phenomena such as extra-sensory perception and psycho-kinesis that are prevalent throughout many cultures, both modern and the more tribal-based. The Huxley/James/Hoffman school of thought would concur that alternate realities do indeed exist (perhaps at an alternate level of vibration?) and can be accessed when our 'receiving apparatus' – our brains and nervous systems – are altered in their chemical composition, wiring or vibration, either naturally or by artificial means.

It may also be speculated that if we take the cyclic Yuga Ages as a template, then our current rising Dwapara Age (Bronze Age) reflects the fact that our solar system is in a different part of its orbit around our binary star. Thus, our solar system is now entering a phase that reflects differing gravitational and electromagnetic forces. It could therefore be feasible to suggest that humanity's dawning awareness of the finer, subtler energies of our universe will coincide with a shift in the mental faculties of our species. Our new sciences that investigate the quantum nature of the universe may be an initial step in this direction. So too may be the reported increase of people's beliefs in the transpersonal properties of human consciousness.

The New Psychophysics

If our mental faculties are due for a tune-up then this will turn out to be a momentous shift upon our human evolutionary journey that is still so relatively recent. Since our origin as humans reaches back only a few million years (according to current scientific knowledge), then it is estimated that we have experienced only 200,000 generations. This is a short span of time when compared to the earliest known bacterial forms of life, which have gone through 10 trillion generations; horses – 27 million generations; and elephants – an estimated 10 million. Further, according to the skeletal remains of prehistoric human beings there appears to have been no observable change in human anatomy for at least 100,000 years. We have, however, made great progress upon our cultural, social and neurological evolutionary path. It is almost certain that we would find huge differences if we compared a brain's neural structure from today's modern society with that of a person's brain from even 50,000 years ago. The cultural-social conditions, survival requirements, and everyday experiences all converge to influence and shape the neurological condition of our human brains. We are, to put it bluntly, at the whim of shifting energy and information flows. And under these conditions our neurons fire in different areas of our brains, thus forming diverse groups and specific connections. As neurologists like to say – neurons that fire together, wire together!

Our modern sciences have made great strides in unfolding the mystery of consciousness and human neurological functioning. We have analysed the way we think, feel and behave to a point where we are very clinical about this. Thus, evolution for us is as much a psychical and psychological adaptation as it is physical. As cultural historian Lewis Mumford once stated:

> If 'Be Yourself' is nature's first injunction, 'Transform
> Yourself' was her second – even as 'Transcend Yourself'
> seems, at least up to now, to be her final imperative.[17]

The notion of 'transcending ourselves' is very much a part of the evolutionary trajectory of humankind. That this is so can perhaps be seen from the ageless perennial wisdom traditions; the shamanic rituals; the earliest recorded otherworldly creatures on ancient cave walls; as well as the ongoing presence in human societies of the inherent search for meaning and the yearning for self-revelation. As some validation of this it has recently been discovered that the Chauvet-Pont-d'Arc Cave in southern France is full of painted monsters, 400 metres below the surface, where a mixture of carbon dioxide and radon gas leads to hallucinations. In these cave chambers the wall paintings become so strange and 'otherworldly' that scientists now think that heading down to the chamber may have formed part of a ritual for prehistoric man. These rituals may in fact be one of the earliest known examples of using substances (in this case the natural mixture of carbon dioxide and radon gas) to induce altered states of consciousness: in other words, a shamanistic experience.

As I have suggested throughout this book, humanity may now be in need of a new collective worldview; one that sheds the way of 'old mind' thinking and replaces it with a perceptual paradigm that is more relevant to today's changing world. This transition is metaphorically described as resembling a collective planetary near-death experience; a rite of passage or underworld journey, where the 'hero' emerges with new perceptual faculties gained from the 'dark' experiences of the journey (*see* Chapter Three). In this sense it is worth remembering that humans are *wired for change*. The latest research in the quantum sciences, including biophysics, throws new light upon the workings of the human mind/brain and consciousness, as well as the human nervous system and our DNA.

We can think of the brain as a collection of nerve cells that operate much like a multilayered frequency receptor. Due to initial conditionings, early on in life (such as experiences and external impacts) each receptor becomes wired to perceive a particular wave frequency. As the brain's receptors tune in to a particular pattern of waves a 'pattern recognition' response is received by the brain and interpreted according to the perceptions allotted to the frequency. In other words, the act of *tuning in* involves picking up familiar frequency patterns out of the ocean of frequencies that surround us constantly. By tuning to the same patterns again and again we are reinforcing a particular perception of reality which is, more often than not, shared because of our local cultural environment. We are thus tuning into a shared, or consensus, reality pattern unconsciously and forming our perceptions continually from this. Unfamiliar patterns often get ignored since they do not fall within our receptor remit.

Perception is thus dynamically created, moment by moment, as the brain constantly scans the bands of frequencies that surround us. However, if this pattern-recognition behaviour does not evolve over time, our perceptual development is in danger of stalling. The result is that we become fixed – or trapped – within a particular reality. This is why human development requires that we move through various paradigm shifts in order to evolve our collective thinking/perceptual patterns. In other words, our development rests upon simultaneous psychical processes as well as biological.

However, materialistic science has dominated our way of thinking to the point where we are taught to dismiss subjective and intuitive impulses and experiences. Yet it has now become an evolutionary necessity that our dominant reliance upon material pursuits be balanced with an increase in consciousness research that supports the significant role of a 'shared' or 'extended' mind. Part of this breakthrough is coming through the research into how our human minds are affected by electromagnetic fields, as was briefly touched upon in Chapter Six.

The existence of an electromagnetic (EM) field associated with the brain was known as far back as 1875, when the English physiologist Richard Caton made electrical recordings from the brain surface of dogs and rabbits. Then the breakthrough and beginning of modern EM-field theories in biology began to emerge from 1970 onwards, with reports coming out on the ground-breaking work of Soviet bioelectromagnetics researchers. This research was amongst the first to posit the outline for an EM-field theory of living organisms and their relationships to the environment. These days the theory of the electromagnetic field of consciousness is more popular amongst researchers; one of the principle proponents of this theory today is Johnjoe McFadden.

The current theories suggest that the electromagnetic field generated by the brain is the actual carrier of conscious experience. McFadden proposes that the 'fields generated by one hundred billion neurones must overlap and superimpose, to generate an extraordinarily complex EM-field inside our brain'.[18] In this way an EM field is created from the neuronal electrical activity in the brain, and this EM field will, in turn, amend neural electrical activity. Thoughts and images in our minds might be induced not by the firing of specific neuronal patterns but rather from the effects of a complex EM-field wave. That is, each neurone contributing to the thought or image will generate its own EM field, each of these superimposing to form the overall complex wave that becomes the final thought or image inside our minds.

As if to validate this, further consciousness research has shown that a person's conscious experience correlates with the synchrony of neuronal firing rather than with the number of neurons firing. This aspect of the synchronous firing of neurons is thus argued by its proponents to greatly amplify the influence of the brain's EM field; just as a team of people working harmoniously together on a project would be more efficient than each working as a non-communicative individual.

In this EM-field theory of human consciousness McFadden proposes that the information from the brain's neurons is integrated to form a *conscious electromagnetic information field* in the brain. This has now been termed the *cemi* theory of human consciousness. One of the advantages of this theory is that it may help to account for a range of human psychic – psi – experiences, since it postulates the presence of an extended mind field, as I discuss later in the chapter. It also suggests that an individual's attention and awareness can help to focus a synchronous firing of multiple neurons rather than the firing of individual neurons. Since neurons firing together generate a stronger EM field, practices that encourage this neuronal coherence will provide for a more balanced mental state. This may go some way in explaining why many religious, spiritual and holistic traditions encourage group meditation as a way of stimulating group consciousness and connection.

It has also been shown that practised meditators can achieve an extremely high level of cross-hemispheric synchronization. Similarly, people who mediate together have been discovered to synchronize their brain activity. Through the use of EEG brain scanning it has been found that brainwave activity is synchronized amongst the participants of the group. Likewise, families may, according to some psychotherapists, possess a common unconscious and shared emotional field; such as the established research proving brainwave correlations between the brains of identical twins. It can perhaps be speculated here that this is a result of resonance occurring between the various EM fields of human consciousness.

We can only hope that the brain's conscious EM field is vigorous and sufficiently resistant to external impacts since the modern world is now hugely awash with the electromagnetic fields from our ubiquitous technologies. For example, according to the research of Robert O Becker 'the human species has changed its electromagnetic background more than any other aspect of its environment ... the density of radio waves around us now is 100 million or 200 million times the natural level reaching us from the sun'.[19] Becker has no doubt that the greatest polluting element in the Earth's environment during our present era is the rapid growth in electromagnetic fields. The fast rise in mobile phone usage worldwide has contributed significantly to our exposure to EM energy above and beyond our normal limits. Some mobile phones operate in the megahertz range, others in the gigahertz range, which is billions of cycles per second. This means that the EM radiation is oscillating at extremely rapid frequencies. However, the issue of EM radiation is still under debate and remains a controversial subject.[20]

It is interesting that McFadden views life and consciousness as quantum phenomena, and that the interactions between our EM fields and matter can be described by the theory of quantum electrodynamics (QED). Here we may now be speculating on the coherence between EM fields and quantum fields, which I shall discuss further in the next chapter. We will leave McFadden's ideas here with his enigmatic remark that 'great ideas are not pulled out of the air; but out of the quantum multiverse'.[21]

However, the trail neither stops nor begins here; to get a fuller picture we need to take a look at what was being discovered in terms of brain research in the 1970s – and this picture brings us to the pioneering work of Karl Pribram. Pribram's holonomic brain theory of perception and memory, first proposed in 1971, has also helped to contribute to the modern field theory of human consciousness. Pribram's theory proposes that information received by the brain is enfolded by 'Fourier-like transformations', and since Fourier processes are the basis of holography the information is thus stored in the form of holographic interference patterns, i.e. coherent EM fields. Basically, holographic processes enable an information field (generally in the form of light) to be reconstructed once the original source of its information is no longer present. Further, since holography operates as a field, each part of the hologram contains the whole. In terms of the brain, Pribram proposed that memories can be accessed from different areas since each part of the brain contains the whole, in a holographic manner. In this way the holographic nature of the brain can store a huge amount of information. This would indeed be a very efficient way of storing information when we consider that eminent mathematician John von Neumann calculated that during an average lifetime of 70 years we accumulate some 280 trillion bits of information. In this way Pribram proposes that coherent holographic fields mediate between consciousness and neurological processes.

Together with physicist David Bohm, Pribram later merged his model with Bohm's more general 'holographic theory of reality', which then suggested that reality may itself be organized in a holographic way. Thus, the external physical world we perceive would be a second-order manifestation of the more fundamental holographic 'implicate order' which forms the basis for the universe's fundamental unbroken wholeness. A few years later John Eccles, a Nobel prize-winning neurophysiologist, postulated that consciousness has in fact an existence independent of the brain, and that the 'self' interacts with the body and the external physical world using the brain as an instrument. Then in 1984 the physicist Henry Margenau suggested that the mind may exist as a type of non-material field, analogous to quantum probability fields.[22] What this has led to is the acknowledgement that there are varied respected researchers now basing their hypotheses on the notion that consciousness may have a field-like nature.

For example, the new field of quantum neurodynamics is based on the hypothesis that brain processes are to be understood on the basis of quantum field theory. Experimental data has now been published from various credible sources supporting quantum processes in the brain, as well as evidence for the presence of quantum holography.[23] There are even popular science books on the market today which have introduced many new readers to the interesting and eye-opening ideas of existence within a holographic reality, such as Michael Talbot's highly readable *The Holographic Universe*.

With all these new discoveries in our physical and biological sciences we are gleaning more and more information that describes how, rather than existing as separate units like islands dotted on the ocean, living organisms are in fact swathed in energy fields and waves of penetrating information flows that immerse our senses, more as if we were drops within an ocean. It is fair to say that there is a renaissance underway in human understanding, and each new finding has, at its core, a common feature: they each confirm that humanity is an intrinsic, dynamic and participating player within a creative living universe. Our old Cartesian separateness is no longer valid as a working model as it goes against the very ecological core that forms the fundamental foundation of all cosmic life – the notion of reciprocal maintenance.

This realization of our hidden connections has been percolating through the corridors of human science as well as through our popular consciousness over the last few decades.[24] This represents, in the words of Fritjof Capra, the *turning point* of human cultural evolution.[25] In fact, since the 1920s many developmental biologists have proposed that biological organization depends on fields, whether they are called biological fields, developmental fields, or organizing fields. However, whilst many of these field theories recognized that, for example, all cells inherit fields of organization, they couldn't explain the organization itself. That is, until UK biochemist Rupert Sheldrake proposed a novel interpretation of how biological morphogenetic fields may operate. Morphogenetic fields refer to groups of cells that respond to specific signals in order to develop particular biological structures, such as organs. Sheldrake now proposed that these signals acted as evolving patterns of biological information that were transmitted nonlocally through what he terms *morphic resonance*.

When Sheldrake proposed this hypothesis in his book *A New Science of Life: The Hypothesis of Morphic Resonance* in 1981 there were outcries from the academic community, some of whom accused Sheldrake of pseudoscience and of deliberately mixing magic with science. Now that this fury has largely abated more people are beginning to see the validity in Sheldrake's claims and have begun to test this hypothesis. The notion of morphic resonance helps to explain how different animal species have evolved from their ancestors in a way that is more adaptive and quicker than orthodox accounts of Darwinian evolution. Morphic resonance describes how a species collective memory is transmitted, or rather inherited, by later generations through nonlocal field transference, with each individual drawing upon and contributing to the collective memory of the species. In this way there is no need for the vast amount of past species memories to be stored inside the brain. This form of self-organization offers a more dynamic picture of the ongoing two-way interactions between living organisms and their environment. Further, this process of dynamic feedback may not only be restricted to biological evolution, suggests Sheldrake, but may also play a role in 'physical, chemical, cosmic, social, mental and cultural evolution'.[26]

Morphic fields can thus be described as patterns of organized information that exist external to the brain; i.e. as non-visible energy fields. These non-visible fields store consecutive generations of biological information that can be accessed by living creatures that share the same ancestry; each particular species can 'lock-in' to their particular biological patterns that are part of this nonlocally organized information. The idea of morphic fields that underlie nonlocal transmission of evolutionary patterns, gives us a whole new way of perceiving the relations, communication and actions between living beings – including humans. As Sheldrake has gone on to explain, the species morphic fields help to connect together the individual, or group, members even when they are many miles apart, and provides a means – a channel of communication – through which organisms can stay in touch at a distance. In effect Sheldrake is postulating a theory for the extended mind when he says that mental activity is not actually confined to the insides of our heads. Thus, not only thoughts and emotions but also our intentions and our acts of attention have influence in the external world around us. Whilst this may sound a little 'too much' for some people Sheldrake notes that we are already familiar with this idea of extended fields:

> ... for example magnetic fields extend beyond the surfaces of magnets; the earth's gravitational field extends far beyond the surface of the earth, keeping the moon in its orbit; and the fields of a cell phone stretch out far beyond the phone itself. Likewise the fields of our minds extend far beyond our brains.[27]

The hypothesis that the fields of our minds extend far beyond our brains can also account for such anomalous phenomena as telepathy. On this subject Sheldrake has performed thousands of experiments, with humans as well as animals,[28] and concludes that these occurrences are not paranormal since telepathy, and similarly the sense of being stared at, are both common happenings. Whilst they may seem 'paranormal' to those of a rational Cartesian mindset, such psychic phenomena may in fact be manifestations of an inherent capacity of the human brain.

One way to think of this is to consider that most of human knowledge rests upon anomalies, as each discovery often replaces one that came before it. According to Thomas Kuhn's theory of paradigm shifts, a new paradigm of thought comes into being when a sufficient number of anomalies have arisen which cannot be explained within the current accepted view. Hence, the paradigm 'shifts' and incorporates the previous sets of anomalies into the accepted consensus knowledge base.[29] As the number of so-called 'paranormal' events begins to accumulate as valid occurrences within the mainstream, it may be that extended theories of mind, such as proposed by the likes of Sheldrake, will begin to be considered more seriously by the orthodox scientific establishment.

Referring back to the earlier discussion of our present Yuga cycle (our Dwapara Yuga or the Bronze Age of the ascending arc), we are moving into the era where humanity will gain knowledge on the finer energies of the cosmos. These finer, subtler energies may very well include awareness of how information/organizing fields (both electromagnetic and quantum) contribute to nonlocal effects and phenomena of the extended mind. Let us not forget that to our own ancestors only a couple of hundred years ago the modern television, with its nonlocal transference of images and sounds, must have seemed like an act of magic. As Arthur C Clarke's third law states: 'Any sufficiently advanced technology is indistinguishable from magic.'

And yet we don't even need to rely on advanced technology to infer 'magical' workings – the phenomenon of our own inherent magic is around us all the time (if only we knew how to 'see' it). For example, Sir Laurens van der Post in his book *The Lost World of the Kalahari*, describes how local bushmen had telepathic communication far beyond the range of sensory communication, sometimes knowing about a hunt up to 50 miles away and thus when to prepare for the hunters' return. In order to research such phenomena Sheldrake has created a database which, as of 2003, had 312 actual cases of human premonition, precognitions or presentiments; 76 per cent of which were warnings to individuals about dangers, disasters, or deaths. Similarly, a national survey in the US in 1990 resulted in 75 per cent of people saying they had had at least one kind of paranormal experience, and 25 per cent had telepathic experiences.[30] Perhaps the most succinct popular modern summary and analysis of such phenomena to date is Dean Radin's book *The Conscious Universe*.[31] The positive side of this is that such discoveries can be liberating:

> ... the recognition that our minds extend beyond our brains
> liberates us. We are no longer imprisoned within the narrow
> compass of our skulls, our minds separated and isolated
> from each other. We are no longer alienated from our bodies,
> alienated from our environment, and alienated from other
> species. We are interconnected.[32]

It may well be that much of what passes as 'unexplained phenomena' is actually connected, directly or indirectly, with information that is being transferred through nonlocal energy fields. The shelves in book shops (and virtual shelves online) are full of volumes having been written, either by laypersons or scientists, discussing experiments on remote viewing, ESP, telepathy, clairvoyance, precognition, etc. It is also now more commonly recognized that many police and intelligence agencies throughout the world routinely use 'psychics' to assist in criminal and information-gathering cases – and often with success. Also, much of the modern research on communication 'at-a-distance', often referred to as remote viewing, began in the early 1970s at the Stanford Research Institute (SRI) by the physicists Hal Puthoff and Russell Targ, which incidentally was largely funded by the CIA. Such is the nature of 'exposure creep', a great deal of information on this subject is now a part of popular culture, and is even being taught in public workshops. Also part of popular books are the discourses on the power of the extended mind to effect healing at a distance, researched and analysed by medically trained practitioners such as Larry Dossey and Charles Tart.

Unbeknown to the world a great deal of paranormal research was conducted in the USSR during the Cold War, surprising and alarming the Western governments when this information finally became public. It was reported that at one Russian conference a Dr Sergeyev remarked that, according to his research, the most favourable time for psychic activity to occur is when there are magnetic disturbances of the Earth caused by sunspot activity.[33] On a similar note, Russian physiologist Dr Leonid Vasiliev, who headed the Soviet Union's first parapsychology laboratory in Leningrad, commented that 'Discovery of the energy behind psi will be comparable to the discovery of atomic energy'.[34] Or, as another person put it – 'Human society today is faced with the dilemma of a breakdown or a breakthrough in human consciousness to match the breakthrough in science and technology'.[35]

Now we are more than half a century beyond these days of early investigations, and very quickly moving into a new era of quantum research – literally taking humanity on a journey into the very heart of how the universe works. Yet are we quite ready for this?

As I have attempted to propose in earlier chapters of this book, the modern technological flows of information and communication may be helping to get people accustomed to intimate and meaningful relations-at-a-distance, stimulating empathic relations in global contexts. With this in 'mind' it would appear that humanity may indeed be more prepared than we think to begin shifting towards a nonlocal field/wave paradigm of energetic connections. It may well be that Carl Jung's proposition of a 'collective unconscious' nearly a century ago was the forerunner to preparing the human mind to conceive of a deeper, fundamental field-like unitary reality underlying life in a creative cosmos.

CHAPTER NINE

Field of Dreams:
Participating in a New Mindful Reality

Human beings and all living things are a coalescence of energy in a field of energy connected to every other thing in the world. This pulsating energy field is the central engine of our being and our consciousness ... At its most fundamental this new science answers questions that have perplexed scientists for hundreds of years.

Lynne McTaggart

Humanity has just entered what is probably the greatest transformation it has ever known ... Something is happening in the structure of human consciousness. It is another species of life that is just beginning.

Pierre Teilhard de Chardin

In the previous chapter I explored the notion that human life is a dynamic part of a living, creative cosmos. As such, evolution and consciousness are not to be considered as linear processes that occur within a vacuum, but are scales of development that have their counterparts within a universe that is conscious-orientated. That is, consciousness is primary within what we can perceive as a materially visible cosmic order. It is appearing increasingly probable that biological life and consciousness both co-exist within nonlocal fields of energy. Further, our latest scientific discoveries and technological innovations are helping to prepare humanity for the realization that meaningful relations can operate at-a-distance; and energetic connections manifest through nonlocal fields of information transference and exchange. With this in mind I would like to continue this journey, and to take you, the reader, further down the rabbit-hole of conscious enquiry.

As we delve further into the study of biophysics and biofields (as introduced in the previous chapter) we find that some of the latest research reveals that a form of *quantum coherence* operates within living biological systems through what are known as biological excitations and biophoton emission. In this context 'coherence' refers to wave patterns that converge harmoniously. A popular example of this is the laser (Light Amplification by Stimulated Emission of Radiation) whereby the multiple waves of amplified light are directed in a narrow beam in *coherence* that results in a condensed and greatly empowered energy. This means that metabolic energy is stored as a form of electromechanical and electromagnetic excitations. It is these coherent excitations that are considered responsible for generating and maintaining long-range order via the transformation of energy and very weak electromagnetic signals. After nearly 20 years of experimental research, Fritz-Albert Popp put forward the hypothesis that biophotons are emitted from a coherent electrodynamic field within the living system.[1] What this describes is that each living cell is giving off, or resonating, a biophoton field of coherent energy. If each cell is emitting this field then the whole living system is, in effect, a resonating field – a ubiquitous nonlocal field. And since it is by the means of biophotons that the living system communicates, then there is near instantaneous inter-communication throughout. This, claims Popp, is the basis for coherent biological organization – referred to as quantum coherence.

This discovery led Popp to state that the capacity for evolution rests not on aggressive struggle and rivalry but on the capacity for communication and cooperation. In this sense the in-built capacity for species evolution is not based on the individual but rather on living systems that are interlinked within a coherent whole:

> Living systems are thus neither the subjects alone, nor objects isolated, but both subjects and objects in a mutually communicating universe of meaning ... Just as the cells in an organism take on different tasks for the whole, different populations enfold information not only for themselves, but for all other organisms, expanding the consciousness of the whole, while at the same time becoming more and more aware of this collective consciousness.[2]

This implies that all biological organisms continuously emit radiations of light that form a field of coherence and communication. Coherence, it appears, is the byword for living systems.

Researchers at the Californian HeartMath Institute have been investigating cardiac coherence through exposure to specific emotions. It has been found that when a person experiences positive feelings like love, care, appreciation and joy, their electrocardiograph becomes coherent. On the other hand, when exposed to negative emotions like anger, worry, or hostility, the electrocardiograph shows incoherent patterns. The phenomenon of biological coherence has been speculated to be the factor behind the transfer of healing energies between people.

In one experiment two people (one healer/sender and one patient/receiver) were separated at a distance, as well as being electromagnetically shielded by Faraday cages. Under these conditions it was found that a synchronization of the brainwaves occurred between healer and patient at the specific moments when 'healing energy' was sent. Likewise, research undertaken in more than 25 studies has shown that the brainwaves of all 4 brain areas synchronize and become more coherent during meditation, even in people inexperienced in meditation. Further, according to scientific researcher Marco Bischof:

> ... studies by biophoton researchers have demonstrated that
> the coherence increase of the EEG in meditation is correlated
> to a corresponding increase of the coherence of biophoton
> emission from the body of the subjects ... meditation not
> only makes the brain waves more coherent, but also increases
> the coherence of the biophoton field of the whole organism.[3]

The biophoton field of the human (the human biofield) is said to consist of numerous partial fields that superpose in multiple ways, and that the overall state of the biofield is constituted by their various interactions. It has also been postulated that the biophoton field forms the basis of memory and regulates biochemical and morphogenetic processes.[4] The various degrees of coherence might also be a factor between different degrees of consciousness that are manifested, or at least the degree of a living being's state of awareness.

These relatively new developments in biophysics have also discovered that all biological organisms are constituted by a liquid crystalline medium; and that DNA is a liquid crystal lattice-type structure (which some refer to as a liquid crystal gel) whereby body cells are involved in a *holographic* instantaneous communication via the biophoton field. Moreover, biophysics has discovered that living organisms are permeated by quantum wave forms. Biophysicist Mae-Wan Ho informs us that:

> ... the visible body just happens to be where the wave
> function of the organism is most dense. Invisible quantum
> waves are spreading out from each of us and permeating
> into all other organisms. At the same time, each of us has
> the waves of every other organism entangled within our own
> make-up ... We are participants in the creation drama that
> is constantly unfolding. We are constantly co-creating and
> re-creating ourselves and other organisms in the universe.[5]

This incredible new information actually positions each living being within a nonlocal quantum field consisting of wave interferences (where bodies meet). The liquid crystalline structure within living systems is also responsible for the direct current (DC) electrodynamic field that permeates the entire body of all animals. It has also been noted that the DC field has a mode of semiconduction that is much faster than the nervous system.[6] Human consciousness, we are told, is not only in a 'wave-interference' relationship with other mind-fields, but also is constantly transmitting and receiving information. This new understanding of the human quantum/informational field also gives credibility to the existence of extrasensory perceptions (ESP) and related abilities, that was referred to in the previous chapter. Our bodies as well as our brains appear to function like receivers/de-coders within an information energy field that is constantly in flux. As clinical psychiatrist Daniel Siegel notes:

> The neural networks throughout the interior of the body, including those surrounding the hollow organs, such as the intestines and the heart, send complex sensory input to the skull-based brain ... Such input from the body forms a vital source of intuition and powerfully influences our reasoning and the way we create meaning in our lives.[7]

This further tells us that the body forms an extended mind, or informational neural field, with the brain as the receiver and interpreter of the signals. According to Siegel, the human mind is a 'relational and embodied process that regulates the flow of energy and information'.[8]

Given that DNA is a liquid crystal lattice-type structure which emits biophotons, this leads to a new understanding that it may in fact have properties that give rise to a quantum field. In light of these recent findings we may begin to refer to DNA as being *quantum DNA*. That is, DNA not only operates in a linear fashion to encode genetic information and protein building, but also emits a nonlocal energy field. It is within this field that instantaneous communication can occur through a coherent pattern of waves at the quantum level. This suggests that the 97 per cent of human DNA that is not involved in protein building is active within a quantum state. It may well be that increased manifestations of field-like, nonlocal forms of intuition and knowing (what may be termed speculatively as *quantum consciousness*) will come from part-activation of the portion of DNA that so far has baffled our scientists with its function.

Such a potential activation of our 'quantum DNA' may likely be related to a future state of human consciousness, and has until now remained dormant in response to human consciousness not being sufficiently prepared for its manifestation. This field 'life-force' may be similar to the pervasive 'pranic energy' which, as Gopi Krishna states, forms the impulse for evolutionary growth in the human nervous system:

> ... an ever-present possibility, existing in all human beings by virtue of the evolutionary process still at work in the race, tending to create a condition of the brain and nervous system that can enable one to transcend the existing boundaries of the mind and acquire a state of consciousness far above that which is the normal heritage of mankind at present.[9]

This transcendental stage of consciousness, depicted above as being a part of our natural evolutionary heritage, is connected with the human brain and nervous system. We now know that we have a DNA quantum field activated within our bodies. Some biophysicists are already discussing whether quantum processes may not be a common denominator for all living processes. As such, a quantum informational field throughout the human body will determine the coherence of our biofields. This makes one wonder to what degree human consciousness would be affected by various external impacts (environmental, cultural and cosmic), especially in relation to fluctuations in the electromagnetic frequencies caused from terrestrial, solar and cosmic sources.

The possibility of a scientific validation of the existence of nonlocal fields of consciousness would place greater emphasis upon recognizing a form of collective or group consciousness within humanity. With this in mind we would do well to return to those practices, recommended for centuries by spiritual traditions and teachers, that would enhance such states: that is, meditation, reflection, watchfulness and mindfulness, etc. Einstein was famous as a daydreamer throughout his life and he often claimed that the greatest inspiration came to him when in such states. Enhanced connectivity between humanity may thus be served by each of us paying more attention to our inner states and striving for harmony and balance in our lives.

A vast range of materials exist to help in enhancing these inner (or 'quantum') states, and can be found within many traditions, whether from the major religions (Christian, Islamic, Judaic, Sikh); or from other streams of wisdom such as Buddhism, Taoism, Sufism and similar meditative practices. There are also many written materials that have the function to stimulate right-hemisphere activity. This is the case with many Sufic stories (such as the Mulla Nasrudin tales), as well as famous stories from the *Thousand and One Nights*, and poems from Jalalludin Rumi (which are now best-sellers in the West).

Within such states many people have recorded experiencing very profound connections with what has generally been termed the collective consciousness. Philosopher Ervin Laszlo refers to this collective information field as the *Akashic Field*.[10] There is now reason to speculate that this so-called nonlocal Akashic Field is in fact a part of our shared (and overlapping) quantum fields of consciousness. Modern science has for a long time considered the human brain as the centre of consciousness; yet this belongs to the materialistic and linear thinking that consciousness is a product of complex matter. The brain is indeed our most complex neurological arrangement, consisting of the most intricate network of synapses. Yet it is more likely that the brain functions as a receiver and transcriber of electrical signals that are emitted from the body's biofields. In this way the trillions of parts of our human DNA act as a coherent quantum field to regulate every part of our body in each simultaneous moment.

The human body is thus a resonating quantum field that could be the repository for human consciousness. Our reality is therefore provided by the work of the brain that transcribes signals into perceptions, yet it is the DNA which is a living intelligence. This idea of DNA being a living intelligence is not new to many indigenous wisdom traditions. For example, as anthropologist Jeremy Narby pointed out, shamans who undergo trance states often seem to be communicating with DNA as a means of acquiring knowledge about plants, healing and spirit worlds.[11] Subsequently, Narby explored how Nature is also imbued with this form of living intelligence which acts as survival patterns to enable evolutionary growth.[12] Shamans, intuitives, and others who are able to tap into this living intelligence find a 'design' or blueprint behind all physical structures, which points to a quantum field of living intelligence that acts as an evolutionary impulse within all living systems.

These findings hold the potential for a radical re-writing not only of modern science but also of how modern cultures operate. For example, the social environment in Western societies largely ignores the harmonious development of the left–right working of the brain, opting instead to focus more on a left-brain rational functioning that operates as mechanical, linear, competitive and narrow. The abstract right-brain, with its magical world of creative visionary thinking, has been mostly sidelined throughout our recent history, as documented by Iain McGilchrist in his excellent scholarly book *The Master and His Emissary: The Divided Brain and the Making of the Western World*. Yet much of human right-brain activity was the source for indigenous wisdom, shamanic practices, and similar traditions that Western materialistic thought has sought to ignore over the years. Often our own intellectual training conditions us to think of such 'magical practices' as primitive, barbaric, and worthy of little more than Western colonialism or re-education. Yet those of us in the 'civilized' West, with our left-hemisphere dominated brain, live in the everyday world of material things and separate objects. The world would seem a very different place if we were to recognize it as a nonlocal field of energetic connections.

A Participatory Field-View of Reality

Recent decades have seen an advance in the ecological view of living systems, and the interconnectedness and interaction between humans, nature and environment. However, this new paradigm of thought should not be restricted to the material level, but needs to be extended also to embrace the nonmaterial levels of the human psyche and consciousness. I have attempted to explore in this book how, in recent decades, the world of the inner self has opened up; how it has been explored through transpersonal sciences, self-realization and individual self-actualization, and how the inner realm of human consciousness is no longer separated from us as a prohibited space somewhere inside our heads. Through our various cultures we are developing the language, the skills and nuances to sense and articulate our personal, revelatory experiences. The once shamanic realm of contact with non-material energies is gradually being externalized into a physical reality of altered perceptual paradigms.

Even our new scientific discoveries are explaining and validating nonlocal realities of connection and energetic entanglement. As discussed in Chapter Seven, the notion of mirror neurons and empathy is the forerunner to understanding the fundamental interrelationships of sentient beings. And now we are learning that extended fields of conscious information and communication exist between individuals and groups as a medium of coherence that may further entangle humanity into a collective 'grand family'. As Sarah Hrdy writes in *Mothers and Others*:

> Were it not for the peculiar combination of empathy and mind reading we would not have evolved to be humans at all ... Without the capacity to put ourselves cognitively and emotionally in someone else's shoes ... Homo sapiens would never have evolved at all.[13]

From infancy, to adolescence, and to adulthood, the distinction between inside and outside, objective and subjective, has always been a transient, undefined boundary – only that socio-cultural conditioning has sought to crystallize these fluctuating borders. However, today there are increasing numbers of people who are beginning to perceive the presence of subtle energy fields, whether around their bodies, around the bodies of others, or in the environment. The interest in metaphysical subjects these days has exploded, with a new language and mindset emerging to deal with these increasingly common phenomena. It is now becoming acceptable to speak in terms of reiki, chi, pranic energy, and even in terms of quantum energy. Not only are many cultures and societies learning to deal with a new wave of technological social networks – with Facebook, Twitter and YouTube – but also with an increase in energetic awareness of human connections and an extended mind.

In a sense, humanity is learning how to be a more interactive collective family. Never before in our known history of the species have we come to a point where we are sailing in the same ship, afflicted by the same concerns, and affected similarly by a range of global impacts. When a poor harvest affects the growing areas in China, Australia and the US, for example, the world food distribution networks reverberate across all nations. When a virus pandemic spreads out from a crowded poultry market somewhere in South Asia, it affects all nations without reserve, grinding transport hubs to a slow crawl. This realization is now dawning on the peoples of the world: that we are already a part of the field fabric of a collective family.

This realization is being keenly felt, too, by the younger generations: generations that are growing up accustomed to having a network of hundreds, perhaps thousands, of virtual friends across the globe; sharing intimacy and empathizing easily with an international social group of like-minded souls. This younger generation is manifesting, whether conscious of it or not, a nonlocal-field level of relationships. It is almost like a state of resonance that supports the person as a differentiated individual whilst at the same time reaching out into linked networks that become part of a diversified whole. It is a form that mimics the quantum state of the particle and the wave: each person is clearly isolated from another by physical space, yet is at the same time very much entangled in a conscious space of connectivity and communication. In other words, each is participating in a field-view of reality; a reality that creates an extended set of responsibilities as one's thoughts and actions can reverberate much further afield. In this worldview:

> ... the substantiality of the world almost vanishes while relationships become central: locality, individuality and separateness are less important than nonlocality, wholeness and connectedness. The picture shifts from an 'objective worldview' of a world composed of separate objects seen only from the outside and interacting mechanistically by their surfaces, to a field worldview where there are no separate objects and no clear boundaries. The new worldview is a 'participative worldview', as it constitutes also a shift from viewing the world from the outside to experiencing everything from the inside: therefore with the field view the psychic aspect of reality is becoming predominant, because the experiencing subject posits itself not anymore outside the world, but becomes part of it.[14]

The human individual has the capacity to be consciously aware of the effect of thoughts and actions upon others: to consider their reactions, to reflect upon their thoughts, and to decide whether to behave differently. In other words, each person has the ability to develop consciously, and with awareness, from each interaction with both the external and internal experiences. Sociologists have, up until now, been largely focused on human identity as characterized by individualization, especially so in 'modern/postmodern' society, where each person appears to be categorized as acting with autonomy, with a self-fashioning, service-to-self attitude. Yet this is a myopic vision on two counts: on one hand it neglects that humans are social animals and instinctively seek groupings and attachments; and on the other it fails to recognize that the nature of human consciousness also undergoes change along with socio-cultural revolutions. It may be very likely that a form of consciousness will emerge, at first on the periphery, perhaps with the younger generations, that will then seep into the core of all our future societies.

Social scientist Duane Elgin has mapped out what he considers to represent the shifting states of human consciousness over historical epochs. He notes these to be:

1   Contracted consciousness (early humans)
2   Sensing consciousness (hunter-gatherers)
3   Feeling consciousness (agrarian era)
4   Thinking consciousness (scientific-industrial era)
5   Observing consciousness (communications era)
6   Compassionate consciousness (bonding era)
7   Flow consciousness (surpassing era)

Using this scale it would appear that global humanity is now shifting from the communications era (observing consciousness) into the bonding era (compassionate consciousness). We could perhaps also re-title the bonding era to become the community era and see this as representing increased empathy. This transition from exhibiting an observing consciousness towards manifesting a compassionate consciousness would represent the move from the 'old-mind' energies towards the 'new-mind' energies that were discussed in the earlier chapters (*see* Part Two) and which signified the *rite of passage* or *global initiation* that were referred to.

Likewise, the surpassing era could be renamed as the new energy era and represent not only the rise of nonlocal field awareness but also symbolize scientific developments into new era energy forms and an increased understanding of the subtle forces of the universe. This era of *flow consciousness* would fit well with the next evolution of human consciousness that appears to be showing elements of a transpersonal-integral nature.

None of these states, however, are completely separate from each other; rather, they overlap and merge as one era fades and converges into the next, the new coming in initially at the periphery until it reaches a tipping point where it becomes the new paradigm. Already, flow consciousness is slowly percolating into our perceptual paradigms as more and more people embrace and instinctively trust non-material information. The dominant materialist worldview is under increased scrutiny as more people awaken to the possibility that their intuitive glimpses – dreams, visions, premonitions, etc. – are trusted sources of information that originate from alternative senses. Through seeking practices that were once considered metaphysical (or even strange), such as spiritual practices, yoga, meditation, psychotherapy, transpersonal therapy, bio-feedback and altered states of consciousness, people are accessing a once-hidden, or rather neglected, realm of senses and self-knowing.

As more people realize that the subtle realm of extrasensory information is not a figment of fantasy or delusion, but in fact has a scientific foundation, these states of consciousness will become more widely accepted, credible and sought. Also, we may find that our orthodox social institutions will begin to incorporate them into the status quo of consensus reality and experience. However, such a transition will not be immediate; as philosopher Ervin Laszlo says:

> The consciousness of individuals can transform instantly, through a sudden insight or revelatory experience, but the consciousness of the species is likely to take time to spread in society. There are people today who live with a traditional or a medieval consciousness, and a few with the consciousness of Stone Age tribes. In the same way there will be humans in the next generation who will achieve transpersonal consciousness, while others, the great majority at first, will persist in the ego-bound consciousness that characterized most of the 20th century. In time, however, a more evolved consciousness is likely to spread over all the

continents. It will spread by a form of contagion. An evolved
mind is 'infectious', it affects less evolved minds … A more
evolved consciousness will motivate people to develop
their own consciousness, it will transform humanity's
collective unconscious. Unless we produce a major societal
or ecological catastrophe, most of our species will eventually
graduate to transpersonal consciousness, and the next step in
the evolution of human consciousness will be achieved.[15]

Whilst the transition may not appear to unfold suddenly to us, within
evolutionary terms it will be a revolution. And participating in this
unfolding consciousness revolution will be both a personal growth
imperative as well as a collective human responsibility.

As humanity enters a time of social and cultural change, of altered
perceptions and challenges to our worldview, we are almost certainly
going to be coerced into altered modes of consciousness. In other words,
in order to readapt and to survive the breakdowns of the old mind/old
energy (discussed in Chapters Four and Five), our collective worldview
will need to shift to an ecological nonlocal and more intuitive mode.
This shift, as described by the Yuga cycles, will mark a developmental
understanding about both the physical laws of subtle energy as well
as the growing capacities of non-material energies of human comprehension, connection and communion. In the words of psychiatrist Ede
Frecska[16], this involves a shift towards a more direct-intuitive-nonlocal
mode of perception. According to Frecska's investigations he notes that
humankind throughout history has spent great reserves of energy in
trying to alter states of consciousness, and that human culture is characterized by the existence of institutionalized procedures for altering
consciousness, suggesting that such activities are a near-universal characteristic of human culture.[17] In a survey by Erika Bourguignon of
488 societies it was found that 437 of them had one or more culturally
patterned forms of altered states of consciousness.

However, what I am proposing is that with the influx of new magnetic
and cosmic energies entering the Earth, caused by the Earth's orbital
position upon the spiral of the Yuga cycle (*see* Chapter Six), humanity
may be undergoing a natural form of consciousness mutation within

an evolutionary pattern. This new influx of energies is likely to impact upon all fields – Earth's magnetic field, the human electromagnetic and biofields, and the quantum fields emitted by the DNA of all living beings. Frecska notes that:

> If nonlocal data enters our sensory cortex we are likely to project this into our perceptual field in the form of visions and/or apparitions … our physical body, and our ego, acts as an anchoring point for perceptual-cognitive-symbolic processing. Rationality and physical science regulates information from the perceptual-cognitive-symbolic mode; we can say that what is called mysticism, or paranormal, operates on the direct-intuitive-nonlocal mode – this latter mode, however, correlates with the quantum entanglement aspect of quantum physics.[18]

Whilst these two modes of the cognitive and the intuitive may operate simultaneously, and have been known as the subjective and objective modes of knowledge, our modern societies have largely prioritized the objective interpretation and dismissed the subjective as the imaginative realm. This 'imaginative' realm of subjective experience is most active when we are children, although quickly diminishes as our social institutions and peer conditioning intervene to install a consensus social reality. Yet the direct-intuitive-nonlocal mode of perception is an evolutionary trait that is still with us, and which may be beginning to manifest in the new generations of intuitive children. How we process information, how we perceive ourselves within the bigger picture – i.e. as part of a living or dead universe – will always underlie and inform the state of our culture.

It is possible that the nonlocal connections between our species will be one of the aspects that will become more dominant in the years ahead; just as the Internet is a physical representation of these nonlocal ties and relations. The direct-intuitive-nonlocal mode (as Frecska calls it) will surely be a more effective means of comprehension and understanding as it bypasses the sensory organs that act as interpretive filters. Also, the direct-intuitive-nonlocal mode operates outside of linguistic barriers, which may explain why many altered state experiences have offered similar results. Whether in the similarity of hybrid creatures found in cave drawings from around the world,[19] from the experiences of subjects under dimethyltryptamine (DMT),[20] or from the various accounts of shamanic journeys into the non-material realm,[21] the subjective mode has depicted quite a consistent universal picture and experience.

Many traditional rituals and wisdom traditions actually function to break down the ordinary consensus cognition; the use of specific sounds/rhythms (drumming, chanting), fasting, frenzied dancing, etc., may work to stress the cognitive and rational mode of perception to the point that, unable to cope or 'control' the situation, an alternate state of consciousness comes to the fore. Clinical psychiatrist Dr Rick Strassman proposes that in such states the brain releases certain amounts of naturally present DMT which stimulates the direct-intuitive-nonlocal mode.[22] Similarly, Frecska hypothesizes that shamans are able to enter the nonlocal state and, by mastering nonlocal connections, interpret the information they absorb and bring it back to the local rational world. What was once considered to be the realm of the supernatural can now be seen as the nonlocal field universe. Shamans, and similar practitioners, were those people who first learnt how to utilize human capacity for entering, through systemic procedure, nonlocal fields of information and connection, and to bring this knowledge back to a local reality.

Graham Hancock believes that 'all human beings have the capacity to be shamans and that in some societies the proportion of men and women in the population who exercise this capacity may be quite large'.[23] The nonlocal field perception of reality is now being experienced by more and more people, from all walks of life, who are accessing an altered state of consciousness, whether it be from a prescribed ritual, religious/spiritual exercises, or spontaneous bursts of intuition and insight. Some of these experiences have been categorized as 'extraordinary encounters', and have been noted to affect a person's inner state as well as physiology.

I described in Chapter Three how psychologists Kenneth Ring and Margot Grey had both conducted studies on people who reported near-death experiences. It was found that they often returned from the experience with a changed worldview, one that embraced the living universe concept and the primacy of consciousness. Ring's study groups almost all tended to agree that their experiences reflected a purposive intelligence and that they were part of an accelerating evolutionary current that is driving humanity towards higher consciousness. Both Ring and Grey concluded that such encounters into the nonlocal realm appeared to offer a gateway to a 'radical, biologically based transformation of the human personality'.[24]

Ring and Grey believe that having an extraordinary experience with a nonlocal connectedness actually impacted the human nervous system, possibly releasing transformative energy, or at least in some form affecting the biological system of the individual. They view people who have experienced the nonlocal realm, whether through the near-death experience or other methods, as being the forerunners of a new species of humanity. Both agree that the real significance of such nonlocal encounters may actually be in their 'evolutionary implications for humanity'. Ring, who has studied the near-death experience for nearly 40 years, has concluded that encounters with a nonlocal reality appear to accelerate a *psychophysical* transformation, and that such encounters may well herald what he calls the *shamanizing of modern humanity*; that is, helping to develop humanity's latent capacities for a direct, intuitive mode of perception.[25]

The participatory field-view of reality reflects an intuitive mode of perception that somehow penetrates into a nonlocal field of connection, communication and comprehension. As discussed, this understanding is now being validated by the latest findings in the quantum sciences, notably quantum mechanics and biophysics. The information now being obtained about the characteristics and behaviour of biophotons, and of quantum coherence within living systems, reinforces a holographic picture of nonlocal reality. Leading physicists are now speculating that quantum computation lies at the heart of most physical processes, as mentioned in Chapter Eight. Roger Penrose and Stuart Hameroff propose a model of consciousness that is attributed to quantum computation in cytoskeletal proteins organized into a network of microtubules within the brain's neurons. This organization creates a nonlocal field with the cytoskeletal matrix serving as an antenna. Anthropologist and shamanic practitioner Hank Wesselman notes in this regard that:

> Recent changes to quantum theory and current discoveries
> in neurobiology reveal that the brain organizes information

holographically and functions like a massively parallel quantum computer, with the microtubules in the neurons of the brain being the likely quantum hologram receptors.

It has been suggested that the quantum hologram is the wave portion of the wave-particle duality for macroscale objects. It has also been proposed that the quantum hologram may tie the phenomenal universe of quantum, micro, macro, and cosmic-sized phenomena together, and that the quantum hologram may be the mechanism through which nature learns. This knowledge implies that the quantum hologram may be the basis for all perception, including psychic awareness.[26]

This suggests that the brain can function in resonance with the whole universe through nonlocal information-energy fields and thus provides the missing link between objective science and subjective experience. As Frecska puts it: 'Nonlocality is to the physicist what interconnectedness is to the mystic, quantum hologram is the foundation through which to understand virtually all paranormal phenomena.'[27] In other words, when the human brain interacts with local aspects of the universe through a cognitive-linear perception, we form what we know as our consensus view of reality. Yet when our brains, for whatever reasons, suddenly (or gradually) enter into a direct nonlocal interaction with the universe's energy fields, then we have a unique perception of non-ordinary states of consciousness.

These forays into direct nonlocal consciousness used to be the domain of experienced practitioners (shamans, mystics, psychics) who may have undergone rigorous and lengthy training. Our 'everyday consciousness' of the local view of the universe is largely unprepared for the realms of non-ordinary reality. In our present era, and in Western civilization especially, the nonlocal mode of perception (subjective experience) has not been encouraged, or even recognized, and so has atrophied and become the province of the esoteric sciences. It may be because the local cognitive view of reality allows for an increased sense of individualism, favoured by the ego, and as such is the sphere of power, money, competition and greed. The nonlocal view of reality, however, embraces cooperation, connection, correspondence and collective comprehension.

And it seems that we are already witnessing the emergence of this new feature of human consciousness.

Imaginal Worlds, New Generations

The notion of the energetic field view of reality, underlined by quantum processes, could be a step towards the next stage in human evolution – the evolutionary development of quantum consciousness that is the basis for the collective mind of the human species. Various mystics and consciousness researchers have alluded to this by a variety of names; they range from cosmic consciousness, superconsciousness, transpersonal consciousness, integral consciousness, and more. All these descriptions share a common theme; namely, the rise of intuition, empathy, greater connectivity to the world and to people, and a sense of 'knowing' about what each given situation demands. Further, the emergence of a form of *quantum consciousness* would likely instil within each person a sense of the greater cosmic whole; the realization that humanity exists and evolves within a universe of intelligence and meaning, a living universe. This would serve to impart within humanity a more profound, and acknowledged, spiritual impulse.

In this book I have put forward the idea that our solar system, which of course includes Earth, may be part of a larger orbit around a binary star that corresponds to larger epochs of time, specifically periods of relapse and regeneration. As the solar orbit enters a cycle of regeneration there are stronger cosmic forces (gravitational, magnetic, plasma, etc.) that could all in some way result in increased wave patterns (vibrations) entering into the quantum DNA field and catalysing a shift in the consciousness of humanity. If such a vibratory shift is a potential means of catalysing quantum consciousness, this could then lead to increased intuitive faculties and extrasensory phenomena not only becoming an implicate part of our lives but also opening up access to greater creativity and inventive capacities for participating and designing our way ahead in the world. The rise of these attributes within a small percentage of people, initially, could eventually lead to a critical mass that would tip human consciousness into a new perceptual paradigm and worldview.

Forms and intimations of these new consciousness patterns are already emerging in the world, but as yet they have not become a part of mainstream research. Such evolutionary 'mutational' agents include visionaries, mystics, artists, psychics, intuitives, spiritual teachers, and what have been termed the new 'Indigo Children'. As Dr Richard Bucke stated in his work *Cosmic Consciousness* the early signs of this new evolutionary development have been appearing within humankind for some time:

> The simple truth is, that there has lived on the earth,
> 'appearing at intervals', for thousands of years among
> ordinary men, the first faint beginnings of another race …
> This new race is in the act of being born from us, and in the
> near future it will occupy and possess the earth.[28]

This suggests that there have been attempts, or social movements, to help prepare the 'mental soil' for a new consciousness to slowly seed and grow. On the whole, social/cultural/material forces are slow to react to the need for an evolving paradigm of human consciousness. Yet this is nothing new, as throughout recorded history many individuals who have felt an awareness of the need to seed an evolutionary impulse into social life have been caught up in revolutionary events or been involved in social-cultural upheavals. These events and human efforts may indicate, according to Gopi Krishna, a stirring of the human evolutionary impulse:

> I can safely assert that the progress made by mankind in
> any direction, from the subhuman level to the present, has
> been far less due to man's own efforts than to the activity of
> the evolutionary forces at work within him. Every incentive
> to invention, discovery, aesthetics, and the development
> of improved social and political organizations invariably
> comes from within, from the depths of his consciousness by
> the grace of … the superintelligent Evolutionary Force in
> human beings.[29]

Perhaps it can be speculated here that in order for continued cultural and species growth there are particular periods of human history wherein humanity becomes ready, or in need of, the activation of particular faculties or evolutionary traits. It may be that during this transition period towards an understanding of the finer, more subtle energies of the cosmos (to paraphrase Sri Yukteswar), humanity will adapt, or be forced to develop, new creative and inspired aspects of consciousness. However, as in all paradigm shifts, old energies inevitably must give way to the new, and it may only be a matter of time before new generations move into evolving consciousness and its physical expressions. It is thus critical that an understanding of spiritual matters begins to permeate our everyday lives as a counterbalance to our social materialism. As one thinker recently stated:

> We live in changing times whereby humanity is undergoing
> a transformation. Our consciousness, which has a vast
> potential for further development, must undergo a release
> from old, binding structures, and break out towards a rapid
> expansion ... We need to understand phenomena at deeper
> levels, and not just accept what we are told, or what is fed to
> us through well-structured social institutions and channels.
> We must learn to accept that our thinking is a great tangible
> spiritual force for change.[30]

In these years ahead it will be to our benefit if we try to develop a consciousness that is both open to spiritual impulses whilst simultaneously aware and attentive to the latest in scientific research. It is essential that we revitalize our collective sense of wellbeing and connectedness – our entanglement and empathy – as part of our shared human journey. Each person may be pushed or catalysed into balancing energies of both their inner and outer lives, and to strengthen their sense of connectedness, empathy and creative vision. It is possible that a new state of quantum consciousness will allow humanity access to an unimaginable *energetic field of information*. This would then open up new vistas of creative intelligence that could be the forerunners to the next stage along our ascending evolutionary path.

The *imaginal realm*, a term coined by Henry Corbin, suggests a state that is sensitized and open to alternate imaginative vision. We sometimes see this realm active in our children as they often tend to hover between fantasy and the physical world. Yet it is a discredit to our modern material cultures that this imaginal vision is conditioned out of our children as it is deemed contrary to 'normal' development. According to child therapist Bobbie Sandoz many indigenous cultures view the period from 6 to 12 years of age as the best time to teach children the powers of their psychic experiences, such as telepathically communicating with animals, nature and non-worldly entities. Sandoz explains that in modern cultures:

> … we have disdainfully labeled this a period of 'magical thinking' in which the child 'erroneously' believes that his thoughts have the power to actually influence the results of his world. Instead of honoring the power and value of this very real magic and its scientific basis, we have viewed it as an age-related phenomenon in need of being suppressed.[31]

Yet it appears that this pattern is now shifting as more and more reports from educators, therapists and social workers reveal the changing nature of our new generation of children. As one example, Dr Linda Silverman, a clinical and counselling psychologist who runs the Gifted Development Center in the US, has studied gifted children for over 45 years and notes that:

> I have been astonished by the children who have come into my life in recent years. It feels like they are a new breed … Their heredity and environment are not fundamentally different from all the children we've encountered in the past. Yet, there is a remarkable difference in these children from the children we've known in the past. The only explanation I can think of is evolution. I believe we are witnessing the evolution of the human species, and that this evolution is becoming apparent first among the gifted.[32]

The Gifted Development Center has assessed 800 exceptionally gifted children for over 25 years, with nearly all of them exhibiting 'whole brain' development and functioning; that is, left- and right-brain hemispheres operating as if an integrated whole. Psychologist Kenneth Ring uses the word 'Edglings' to describe such youngsters who he feels may be closer to a form of higher development in human potential than most of us. He likens these individuals to those who have undergone tribal sacred rituals that develop within a person a spiritual sensitivity and a sense of the sacredness of Earth.

Similarly, the social historians William Strauss and Neil Howe, who have originated theories about the recurrent cycles of generations in society, have noted a distinct characteristic of the new generations of young people. In their work *Millennials Rising: The Next Great Generation* they note how many children born between 1982 and 2001–03 are displaying a particular psychological temperament, one that manifests a civic-mindedness, optimism, fierce independence, a sense of purpose, and a centred form of personal energy.[33] Some of these young millennials are now expressing themselves with the slogan – '*I am important to the world. The world is important to me.*'

The 21st century may well be the time when the human species begins to bear witness to a new form of consciousness entering into the collective stream; an integrated field-type consciousness that no longer tolerates the old paradigm structure of ego-driven greed and materialist pursuits. Rather than being a full-frontal revolt, from the periphery of human consciousness will emerge a wave of reformist change: a new generation of young people driven to contribute to constructive social change, indifferent to the old hierarchical structures of control and power. Yet just who are these new children we may be talking about here?

In 1999 the book *The Indigo Children* was published and opened the lid on a new phenomenon that suggested humanity was witnessing the beginnings of a consciousness shift through the new generation of children being born, the new-paradigm forerunners. Yet why are these children being labelled as the 'Indigos'? After all, the name has a kind of New Age tint to it. Well, the story begins with a woman called Nancy Ann Tappe, who has a neurological condition known as synaesthesia, which means that her brain cross-wires two senses and the result, in her case, is that she is able to 'see' colours. This is different from the psychic ability to view auras; in Tappe's case it was simply that her brain picked up colours from people according to their set categories of behaviour. After monitoring this for a number of years, Tappe was able to intuit a person's character and way of being from the colour she 'saw' associated with them.

Then something happened – she began to see a 'new colour' coming into the world, and that this new colour was coming from the children.

It was an indigo-blue colour that was only appearing around children. For Tappe this represented a new kind of person that was being born on the planet, and suggested that the new generations were coming into the world with a slightly different range of feelings, behaviour, thinking; a different sense of presence.

Unfortunately, much misinformation has now sprung up concerning the subject of Indigo children. The most widespread misleading claim is that all Indigos are super-psychic children, some with glowing auras, who exhibit unique gifts of clairvoyance, healing, etc. Some claims even go so far as to say they are all incarnated space children being born now to help save the world. Such names as Star Children, Crystal Children and Rainbow Children are being cashed in and promoted, with centres popping up, and books being hastily written, to help parents and children come to terms with their new abilities. In the end, it's not about names, nor is it about trying to be different: the bottom line is that it seems that the younger generation of children are exhibiting a different form of consciousness, set of attitudes and perceptions about the world. For example, whilst many of the older generations grew up trusting and abiding by authority, without much questioning, the younger generation are finding themselves at odds with the system: it seems crazy to them and they want to question it. It is about value systems, and their values are making it difficult for them to fit into our obsolete programming and mindsets.

According to Tappe, 97 per cent of children under the age of 10 are Indigos, and 60 per cent of children older than 15 are as well.[34] Lee Carroll, who first wrote about this phenomenon in *The Indigo Children* (with Jan Tober), describes these new children as feeling entitled, and not ready to compromise to old systems and mind-sets. He notes that 10 years after publishing the first book it is finally being acknowledged that 'today's children represent an evolution of the human species'.[35] Indeed, recognition is spreading; there are now Indigo Children Centres throughout South America: Chile (Niños Indigo Chile); the Indigo Network (Red Indigo) with members in Argentina, Brazil, Columbia, Venezuela, Guatemala and Chile.

If Tappe is correct, then the great majority of people entering the world are being born with a new form of consciousness; yet it is neither super-psychic nor other-worldly; it appears to exhibit a different way of looking at the world. According to Jennifer Townsley, a college professor, some of these children require a new set of communication rules as they don't respond to the traditional threats of verbal or physical punishment. They also, say Townsley, have a stronger, more intuitive sense of community and of shared goals. These children expect respect and no longer adhere to established hierarchies; therefore communication can be difficult if an elder begins to talk down to them as they don't respond to this. Townsley further noted that many of these young children have little interest in validating the roles expected of them; they prefer to establish new and creative relationships rather than adhering to stereotypes.

Similarly, Julie Rosenshein, a psychotherapist and school consultant, notes that these young children are not so much *in*attentive as they are *selectively attentive*. In other words, when the school classroom forces them into activities that they consider meaningless or unimportant, they reject, pull away their attention or, at worst, revolt and lash out. The problem, says Rosenshein, is that many of these children who are at school are 'at the mercy of uninformed, old-paradigm parenting; schools that want kids to be under control; and paediatricians who are looking for quick behavioral fixes'.[36] The result is that many children are being incorrectly labelled with different disorders, with such names as 'oppositional defiant disorder' – just another linear old-paradigm category.

We just have to look at the list of today's child disorders to see that something *is* going on here: ADD (attention-deficit disorder); ADHD (attention-deficit-hyperactivity disorder), ODD (oppositional-defiant disorder); PDD (pervasive developmental disorder); AS (Asperger's syndrome); SID (sensory-integration dysfunction); ASD (autistic-spectrum disorder). In the US it has been estimated that 1 out of 10 children are categorized as mentally ill and more than 7 million have ADD; cases of ADHD are up 600 per cent since 1990 and autism is considered an epidemic.[37]

Children are now the fastest growing segment of the prescription drug market as they are over-supplied with Ritalin, Prozac, Risperdal, Concerta and other behavioural medicines. Julie Rosenshein, as a school consultant and witness to this situation, feels that these children are carrying around the 'rage of our planet', and as such they need support to process and deal with their rage, to direct it towards constructive ends. The tragic alternative, as Rosenshein reminds us, is an increase in extreme outbursts, such as that witnessed at the Columbine High School shootings, and others.

On the more positive side we are now seeing many of these early youngsters entering into business and career paths. The wave of new perceptive thinking is creeping into our social infrastructures and it will be from here, from within, that we will likely see constructive change. It will be here that the new energies of change, as opposed to the old energies of hierarchical power and control (*see* Chapters Four and Five), will gradually transform our cultural fabric over time. Bruce Doyle III, a business executive and consultant, is already noticing this change. He sees this new wave of young employees as wanting to work for people who respect them, and in a place where they can have self-expression. They seek flexibility in the workplace, and an atmosphere that fosters creativity: these are the employees of companies like Google and Facebook where employees wear jeans, work in brightly coloured environments, and have a shared network of camaraderie. Increased satisfaction in the workplace is now a must, or such work will be rejected. Again, Doyle notices that these young people are not concerned with stereotypes, or having to adhere to fixed roles, and they especially rebel against the orthodox judgments of others.

After noticing these characteristics in the new employees, Doyle decided to do his own survey, and to ask his own questions. What he found from the results was that these young people had a strong passion for self-expression, for helping others, for achieving life goals and for loving relationships. For example, when asked 'What are you committed to in your life?' the largest response category (57 per cent) included such replies as 'Changing the "systems" to help people in crisis'; 'Championing issues to quality of life as opposed to a more prevalent focus on quantity of life'; and 'Giving back to others and being a role model for children.' They also expressed strong personal values, such as being true to oneself, freedom and independence, trust, honesty, respect, empathy and loyalty. They appeared to attach less importance to material values and possessions, and more to achieving something of value in their lives.

Doyle noted, from his survey, that the overall top-five attributes of those questioned came in as:

1 Have strong empathy for others (84 per cent)
2 Have an obvious sense of self (73 per cent)
3 Often see better ways of doing things at home, school, or work (70 per cent)
4 Are a talented daydreamer and/or visionary (66 per cent)
5 Are very creative (66 per cent)

In concluding, Doyle writes that: 'The Indigos want to work in an environment that is fun, well organized, and efficient. They want responsibility, autonomy, and an atmosphere of flexibility.'[38] Doyle feels that this younger generation will drive forwards new visions with their creativity, and will supply the solutions required to 'move civilization to the next level of consciousness'. Already, there are signs that some of these young people are seeing more of the playing 'field' than the rest of us.

The Holographic Healing Field

Adam McLeod is no normal young man. As a young boy he exhibited unusual abilities to see into people's biofields; specifically, he began to realize that he could tap into the body's quantum information. Adam has now gone on to become a renowned international healer and speaker, as well as studying molecular biology and biochemistry in a bid to bring a scientific framework into his alternative healing practices.[39] What Adam says is that every physical object emits information in the form of quantum data. The body's field of quantum information is then accessed and assessed by the healer. Adam firmly believes that all particles are fundamentally connected to each other, and all information and knowledge is available in the quantum field.

For Adam, every physical object emits its own quantum hologram or image, regardless of where it is located, and he views the field of quantum information as a web of pathways connecting everything to everything else. It is this network of interconnections that Adam accesses when performing energy healing on someone. Of this he says that:

> Our consciousness and the universal consciousness is an interconnection of constant information exchange. Some

day, a truth as obvious as this won't have to be seen as self-revelation but instead will be readily accepted.[40]

Adam, as a young man, exhibits a great intuitive understanding of how a quantum holographic reality operates, regardless of his accolades as an alternative healer. It is worth noting here how Adam's own view on quantum reality sits squarely with what has already been said in previous chapters on biophotons and the quantum field.

Adam posits that the goal of every cell is to communicate in harmony with every other cell. This, he says, suggests that, when viewed on a larger scale, every living being is naturally inclined to want to be in communicative harmony with every other being. Thus, when people resonate together (in love, work, relationships, etc.) a synergistic effect naturally arises. This is because, Adam tells us, when we are conceived, biophoton emissions start coordinating the development of our cells. And as soon as light begins coordinating the formation of our cells, consciousness emerges. Our brains, however, act to access the quantum energy fields around us to organize, process and interpret this information so that it has local meaning for us. That is, direct nonlocal information is brought into a local, cognitive and meaningful reality for us. What appears as separate to us is only an illusion. Adam makes a profound statement in this regard when he says that:

> The barriers of individualism we have erected are nothing more than facades. A global shift in consciousness will erode these barriers as our evolution continues.[41]

Perhaps part of the empathy shift (*see* Chapter Seven) will involve an intuitive recognition of this fundamental human unity. After all, it appears that we all have the same capacity to access these nonlocal fields of information. Even on an individual bodily level it seems that our human biofields form a communicative web of emotions, thoughts, memory and data (as indicated in Rupert Sheldrake's hypothesis of morphic resonance). It is a question of whether we, as individuals, are able to decipher the information of the nonlocal fields into meaningful, conscious signals. If not, all this information will remain outside the remit of our senses. Adam suggests that we can each exercise our connection to the nonlocal quantum field just like exercising a muscle; he advises that we practise paying more attention to our intuition, or gut instinct. This may be an important point as our thoughts can affect the quantum fields around us, which may then have an effect on others nonlocally: our very thoughts are thus amplified beyond our normal conscious awareness and physical domains.

This is the very basis of Adam's healing – the nonlocal transference of intention. He claims that the light emitted from a healer's intentions enters another person, influencing a series of chemical reactions that benefit the person's health. Everything in this context is a complex array of vibrating frequencies, with certain frequencies having specific information. In this regard, consciousness does not reside solely in the brain, but is within every atom, cell and subatomic particle that constitutes the human body; this is exactly what some of the latest discoveries in the new sciences are finding out. Adam believes that the flow of energy/information, and our access to it, is constantly evolving and changing. With continued evolution, he notes, we will be able to access information from the field more easily. Most people have experienced, to some degree or other, the sense of intuition, and these intuitive abilities are likely to increase, the more we pay attention to them. To quote from the Persian poet Rumi's *Masnavi*: 'New organs of perception come into being as a result of necessity. Therefore, O man, increase your necessity, so that you may increase your perception.' Or, as Adam puts it:

> I believe that consciousness is becoming more complex
> all the time as the collective consciousness rapidly evolves
> to higher levels. People are becoming more aware of how
> consciousness functions and are making better use of it. They
> are deliberately manipulating their intuitive abilities to access
> information and therefore are developing stronger intuition,
> better mental telepathy and increased self-healing ability.
> Awareness increases the ease with which people can connect
> to the field.[42]

From Adam's writings, lectures and publically available materials, his core message is that healing must involve a person's own participation. Each individual's consciousness must combine with the intentions of everyone involved. In this regard, consciousness is a collective manifestation, and thus, in turn, influences everything else as we collectively form a web of connections between us and our environment. Perhaps this has answered our earlier question of whether human beings exist in a dynamic, living universe or in a lifeless, mechanical one. In the end though, this acknowledgement has to be a personal choice.

The world we are all living in now is undergoing vast and rapid change, and it may serve us well to reflect on this. Indeed, learning to know the world in a new way will be quite a task. Yet if we are part of an ongoing spiral of great ages (Yugas) then we will indeed keep arriving where we once started – and each arrival will be a new memory, and require us to learn anew. So if our present ascending Dwapara Yuga will bring humankind different forms of energy, technology, and 50 per cent of brain capacity, as Sri Yukteswar claims (*see* Chapter Six), then what reflections can we begin to make on this? That, I leave for the next chapter.

PART IV

Moving Forwards

CHAPTER TEN

Critical Thresholds:
An Emerging New Worldview

God wanted to hide his secrets in a secure place. 'Would
I put them on the moon?' he reflected. 'But then, one day
human beings could get there, and it could be that those who
arrive there would not be worthy of the secret knowledge.
Or perhaps I should hide them in the depths of the ocean,'
God entertained another possibility. But, again, for the same
reasons, he dismissed it. Then the solution occurred to Him
– 'I shall put my secrets in the inner sanctum of man's own
mind. Then only those who really deserve it will be able to get
to them.'

An anecdotal story by unknown persons in the Amazon

People are like stained-glass windows. They sparkle and shine
when the sun is out, but when the darkness sets in, their true
beauty is revealed only if there is a light from within.

Elisabeth Kübler-Ross

The empires of the future are the empires of the mind.

Winston Churchill

There is an oral folk tale, attributed to the fool Mulla Nasrudin, about an exchange with wise men on the subject of knowledge that goes something like this:

The philosophers, logicians and doctors of law were drawn up at Court to examine Mulla Nasrudin. This was a serious case, because he had admitted going from village to village saying: 'The so-called wise men are ignorant, irresolute, and confused.' He was charged with undermining the security of the State.

'You may speak first,' said the King.

'Have paper and pens brought,' said the Mulla. Paper and pens were brought.

'Give some to each of the first seven savants.' The pens were distributed.

'Have them separately write an answer to this question: "What is bread?"' This was done. The papers were handed to the King who read them out:

The first said: 'Bread is a food.'

The second: 'It is flour and water.'

The third: 'A gift of God.'

The fourth: 'Baked dough.'

The fifth: 'Changeable, according to how you mean "bread".'

The sixth: 'A nutritious substance.'

The seventh: 'Nobody really knows.'

'When they decide what bread is,' said Nasrudin, 'it will be possible for them to decide other things. For example, whether I am right or wrong. Can you entrust matters of assessment and judgment to people like this? Is it not strange that they cannot agree about something which they eat each day, yet are unanimous that I am a heretic?'[1]

An odd story to begin a chapter with perhaps; yet in our own ways we are all a mixture of wisdom and foolishness. And in the end who can really know the future? There are a great many clairvoyants, psychics, proclaimed mystics, gurus and future forecasters who make a living from predicting the future. With most people it ends up as a matter of perception and maybe an abstract grasp of the bigger picture too. Perhaps each of us has a piece of this bigger picture, yet not the whole scenario. For this reason the speculations and views I have expressed within these pages are meant, I hope, to at least stimulate thought. Further to this, I am attempting to present scenarios that pertain to my perception of events and these changing times we are so notably now passing through. As with everything, it is each person's responsibility to question the material they are presented with, and to question themselves. In the end, it is up to individuals what they make of the information they have, and the worldview they form from this.

One of the things I do take issue with is how many future forecasts are established upon the current consciousness or way of thinking. By this I mean that they extrapolate the future based upon what has gone before; there is a lack of ability to discern the uncertain, the unpredictable, and the unexpected. There are too many trend-based reports that fail to foresee unpredictable, chaotic and complex tipping-points. This lack of foresight continues to project that the world will go on developing within a relatively stable environment. Yet it is likely that the future will show different dynamics of development: not linear but the nonlinear dynamics of complex systems where energies are in a continual state of flux – or dynamic equilibrium. It is closer to the truth to say that humanity has managed to arrive at the 21st century through a growing series of critical thresholds, moving towards current global, social and environmental limits. And it is at such thresholds where new, often unexpected, arrangements are forced into being.

It is my understanding that our current transition will emerge through a mix of the following critical thresholds:

1   Violent political upheavals, such as in the Middle East due to deteriorating living standards, soaring food prices and corrupt regimes

2 Ad-hoc de-centralized and networked terrorist groups acting in guerrilla fashion

3 Rapidly changing weather patterns, affecting economies, food and populations

4 Growing organized anti-Western, anti-capitalism and anti-globalization movements

5 Shifting geopolitical players and relations such as those between China, India, Russia and Brazil

6 Collapse of the US position as the leading empire

7 Collapse of world financial markets and economies, etc.

These are just some of the scenarios that are already in play, and 2011, within its first month of January, saw many of these features highlighted through the uprisings in Tunisia, Algeria, Egypt, Yemen, Bahrain and Libya. Also in the early months of 2011 the world witnessed the torrential flooding of Queensland, Australia; the erratic heavy snowstorms over Europe and the North American continent; and the horrendous tsunami and radiation leak in Japan. The global economy continues to falter and sway dangerously close to a tipping-point of collapse. In terms of bankrupt sovereign states, and the incredible amount of debt held throughout the world, it is more a case now of the emperor's new clothes, and who will be first to point the finger towards our economic nakedness.

It is significant that in times of relative social stability, human consciousness plays a lesser role in the behaviour of society; yet when a society reaches the limits of its stability, and becomes chaotic and vulnerable, then that society becomes sensitive and responsive to even the smallest fluctuations in the consciousness of its citizens; in such changes as values, beliefs, perceptions and worldviews. Human consciousness becomes a significant stimulus and catalyst for change during these times of social instability. When order returns, people readapt to the changes, learn of the weaknesses, and generally show resilience in creating relations and institutions more in keeping with the new times, worldviews and challenges. It is these moments that shake us out of our lethargy and spur us into reflection and action. It should be said that no-one is perfect, and I wholeheartedly include myself here, yet we need to shift our thinking away from the familiar, the known comfort zones, and start to conceive, be inspired by, that which may lie just slightly beyond our standard frameworks.

Human history is also a form of collective amnesia; we only remember what has been agreed upon as being important to us, and in a manner that we are able to comprehend. This artificially constructed sense of our history often appears as a short line of linear progress rather than a far vaster historical pattern of sporadic leaps and cycles of growth and decline, like a grand year of seasons. A comparative view might be that supplied by Brian Aldiss's science-fiction series the *Helliconia* trilogy in which the planet Helliconia has a very long year (called The Great Year), which is equivalent to some 2,500 Earth years. Each book follows the rise and decline of civilization through each season (spring, summer, winter). By the end of summer, human civilization has developed to a level similar to that of advanced European Renaissance, only to inevitably regress once again when the centuries-long winter arrives. The trilogy also suggests that some elements of human society are able to preserve knowledge during the winter 'dark ages' that can be used in the coming season/cycle to once again develop a scientific-industrial civilization.

In a similar manner, it can be said that our global human civilization is in the early throes of its spring, casting off the old systems and infrastructures that have helped it achieve passage through the intervening 'winter' centuries. We may, after all, be responsible for nurturing the early seeds of a new cultural birth. The way ahead, for all of us, will surely be a challenging, yet deeply rewarding, journey and learning curve. However, we need to lose some of our evolutionary baggage during this transition of labour.

Psychologist Robert Ornstein and biologist Paul Ehrlich have noted that thanks to our evolutionary history we have a background in an 'us vs them' attitude to our world that we have brought with us into our present day. Also, that our antiquated ideas of family values divide the world into sets of us and them, divisions that are reflected in politics, in education, in national and international conflicts, and in the way we deal with the environmental crisis.[2] This division, once a natural human schism, no longer works for us; we first need to recognize that we are in need of changing some of our cultural conditionings. Yet human beings are largely social animals, not only in the sense of family and relations, but also in regard to our high degree of conditioning. Evolutionary biologists have long noted that the limitation on our head size at birth causes the modern human to be born 'premature', in the evolutionary sense. (This limitation is due to the fact that humans, as bipedals, have a narrow birth canal.) The head is not fully developed at birth, and for this reason human babies require more time of care than other animals before being able to look after themselves and be self-sufficient.

Much of our growth thus occurs after birth when we are in a social environment; hence humans are more susceptible to social conditioning and are largely 'wired' (neurologically patterned) in a social environment instead of being born 'ready'. It also takes many years after birth for a human being to fully develop their frontal lobes of the brain. This fact has not been lost as a metaphor for our global society, as Ornstein and Ehrlich note:

> Just as an adolescent has not fully developed the frontal lobes
> of its brain that supply social skill and restraint, our global
> society has not yet fully developed the institutions that would
> supply the same skill and restraint on an Earth-wide scale.[3]

This is referring to humans having existed for something like a fifth of the average life span of a mammalian species, and a fifth of a human life span is roughly the end of adolescence. As we are very much the social animal it is essential that in these upcoming years, as we restructure our social and psychological frameworks, we expand our connections and cooperation with our larger human family – after all, to varying degrees we are now in the same boat, and the current and ensuing problems facing us on this planet are common to us all. And this is exactly what has been occurring over the past several decades with the rapid rise of our technologies of communication and connection. Our human psyches have been undergoing preparation for a new era of social organization and communication.

A Psychology for the Third Millennium

The human psyche is able to adapt and evolve according to social and environmental impacts and influences. How we communicate as a 'social animal' wires our neuronal brains and forms our psyche. As was discussed in earlier chapters, the shift to information as an energy, and the exchange of information-energy, has helped to usher in not only new forms of social organization but has also influenced how we have 'wired' our brains. When our mind and attention are focused in specific ways we create neural firing patterns that link and integrate with previously unconnected areas of the brain. In this way synaptic linkages are strengthened, the brain becomes more interconnected, and the human mind becomes more adaptive.

According to psychologist Daniel Siegel the brain undergoes genetically programmed 'neural pruning sprees', which he says involves removing various neural connections to better organize brain circuitry. In other words, the neural connections that are no longer used become disconnected (deactivated), thus strengthening those regularly used synaptic connections, which helps the brain to operate more efficiently. As the phrase goes – *neurons that fire together, wire together*.

What is also significant is that the human brain is not solely an organ situated in the head. Physiologically the human mind is embodied throughout the whole body to regulate the flow of energy and information. Siegel tells us that neural networks throughout the interior of the body, around the heart and our various organs, are intimately interwoven and send sensory input/information to the brain. This input from the body forms a vital source of our intuition and, says Siegel, also influences our reasoning and the way we create meaning in our lives.[4] In this sense the body forms an extended mind, only that the brain is the receiver and interpreter of the signals. Again this corresponds to the 'field theory' of living systems discussed in Chapters Eight and Nine, where previously I suggested that conscious energies and electromagnetic forces constituted biofields and fields of conscious (holographic) information. In this context we see that physical organs, through their neural and sensory networks, form another type of extended brain, or distributed mind. In both cases living systems, rather than involving separate actions, are in fact a field-network of integrated processes. This type of knowledge, I suggest, will gradually come to represent how we view our dynamic, living universe – a relational system of integrated processes and energies.

Our modern sense of self-awareness, and our bodily extended mind, have clearly evolved to root us in our social world: a world of extended relations and social networks. Humanity, it can be said, has been hard-wired to extend its linkages, connections and communication networks. We are also hard-wired to adapt physically in response to experience, and new neural processes in our brains can come into being with intentional effort – with focused awareness and concentration. This capacity to create new neural connections, and thus new mental skill sets through experience, has been termed neuroplasticity. The human brain of today has to respond to the incredible amount of energy and information that is flowing through our environments and embedded in our cultural experiences. By being aware of our experiences and environmental impacts and influences we can gain a better understanding of how our brain and thinking become patterned. This awareness is what Siegel calls *mindsight*:

> In sum, experience creates the repeated neural firing that can lead to gene expression, protein production, and changes in both the genetic regulation of neurons and the structural connections in the brain. By harnessing the power of awareness to strategically stimulate the brain's firing, mindsight enables us to voluntarily change a firing pattern that was laid down involuntarily.[5]

Thus, how we focus our attention greatly shapes the structure of our brains; and the ability to grow new neural connections is available throughout our lives and not only in our young formative years. This knowledge encourages us to nurture our mindfulness, to establish greater self-awareness, and to pay attention to our intentions and thinking patterns. Neuroplasticity also encourages us to be more reflective over our connections with others, and to develop our social skills that underlie empathy and compassion. These new 'wired connections' are exactly what are becoming activated through the rise of new media and communication tools.

Information is our current dominant form of energy, and as mentioned earlier in the book, each new energy revolution stimulates also a revolution in human communications; in turn catalysing new patterns and organization within the human psyche. Examples of this process include the introduction of cuneiform tablets at Sumer that ushered in early city organization; and Gutenberg's printing press that helped to democratize Europe and encourage distributed information-sharing. The Gutenberg printing press was a dramatic revolution in that it made information more available within the public domain, and affected the physical and physiological condition of those exposed to printed information. Not only did the general masses take up reading on a large scale but also the very act of reading (which for Latinized Western cultures was left-to-right) stimulated parts of the human brain hitherto underused.[6] The sudden increase in a reading public put emphasis upon the need for greater social organization as the written word became responsible for promoting increased individualism and instances of opposition to ruling structures (as is very much the case today).

And so today our distributed digital networks of communication are re-wiring and re-patterning human consciousness through their diverse and pervasive interconnections. Such international connections breach cultural and national borders and force us to self-reflect on our identity, values and ethics. With more and more people accessing connections outside of the heavily corporate-controlled mainstream media, gaining information from a social media that is more distributed, independent and alternative, more people are being exposed to a wide range of viewpoints, beliefs and narratives. This exposure to new patterns of information helps us to break out from rigid, narrow and myopic scenarios.

It is my hypothesis, as I have previously expressed, that humankind is on the threshold of a great shift in its collective psyche; however, this may be preceded by a series of traumatic events – a global near-death experience as suggested in Chapter Three. This potential transition has been 'visioned' by Christopher Bache, an educator in transpersonal psychology, who whilst in an altered state of consciousness underwent an amazing series of visions. In these visions he witnessed a global system collapse, followed by the gradual crystallization of a new planetary culture. Bache speaks of a social awakening that is coming, a time when we will shift from 'the atomised cells of our historical past' towards a more integrative and inclusive communion. Everything we are currently undergoing, in our personal lives and on a global level, he says, is paving the way for this future. In his series of visions Bache saw that:

> ... out of the seething desires of history, out of the violent conflicts and of the scheming of individuals and nations, there was now driving forward a new awareness in human consciousness. Its birth in us no less difficult or violent than the birth of a new continent through volcanic upheaval. It drives upward from the floor of our being, requiring a transposition of everything that has gone before to make room for its new organisational patterns.[7]

Bache also had the understanding that mind/consciousness is primary, and that humanity is nearing an era whereby physical experience will be more influenced through the 'power of "coherent consciousness"' (Bache's terms). This, however, would not manifest at the level of 'egoic-consciousness' but would require a deeper integral style of consciousness.

The visions of Christopher Bache are just one example of many indications that we may be moving towards a restructuring of our psychological and social structures, on both local and global scales. Our own human nature – our inner psyche – may be undergoing a restructuring (or rather rewiring) as we are pushed and/or encouraged to evaluate how we consider ourselves not only within our local environments, the physical world at large, but also in a grander, cosmological sense. Does the human evolutionary journey have meaning? What are our responsibilities for now and the generations to come? A re-patterning of the self can lead to new priorities in our lives, to be more in balance with our needs rather than swamped by our wants. Perhaps we will be compelled to orientate ourselves towards needs rather than wants in order to have a more focused path upon which to drive forwards.

This re-patterning and restructuring of social relations incorporates new styles and modes of interpersonal connections and communications. It heralds a new set of shared values, understanding, empathy and respect. As a global family we have already suffered enough from egocentric systems and a world driven by power, greed and control. These institutions are now archaic and destructive to our continued survival. They are the dregs of an old mode of existence, one that is unsuitable for a world to come. The ideal set of relations would be that which honours the Golden Rule: social exchanges based on mutual trust and respect. We may be a long way from this, yet the seeds have been planted, and are growing in firm soil around the world – in projects, communities, social networks and organizations.

The world systems for a new era are not likely to emerge from an elite base, like the Medici-influenced Renaissance that sprang up in Florence in the Late Middle Ages, but rather from a groundswell of people-centred change. The new 'renaissance' will come from the periphery or from the bottom up, a distributed and networked emergence of conscious individuals and groupings. Like ink dots on blotting paper, these conscious and creative centres will spread their influence through decentralized channels and processes until a time will come when the ink dots begin to fill the blotting paper. The social changes of the future are likely to come from revolutionary movements from the people; a shift catalysed within the hearts, spirit and minds of the people.

Movements for social and spiritual change are already growing, adding more pressure to the older institutions, which will be forced to adapt or die off. Paul Hawken's *Blessed Unrest* details some of these activist/ actionist movements with over one million of such groups worldwide. More and more people are already insisting on increased social responsibility from business, as people become more choosy according to their values. The old mind/old world energy systems of scarcity and control are ripe for change. The new revolutions in psyche and action will be more in tune with the new energies, and no longer tolerant of the old systems.

We are transitioning from the older linear mind of the industrial-globalization 'modernity project' of the last two centuries into a life-sustaining, ecological-cosmological new world mind. We are fostering values that will be inherited by the world to come and thus have an obligation to rewire ourselves to a more integral, empathic world. Part of the role of our global communications has been to adjust our minds into functioning across nonlinear relations; to become accustomed to dealing with multiple connections rather than single ones; and to become immersed in varied and diverse relations and not just local families and communities. We are now beginning to embody myriad viewpoints, beliefs and identities. As a species we are beginning to fuse; although we are still fragmented and rife with cracks and schisms.

The initiation from our species infancy into adolescence will require a moral and ethical growth. We are called to respond differently to the world around us – not in fear or with anxiety, with trepidation or apprehension; but with robustness, energy, flexibility, creativity and positive intentions. The world in which we live is an ecology of which we are a part – we must learn to respect this, to feel it, and to develop our lives around it. The world we are moving into requires of us that we both inspire and be inspired. What we are witnessing, now for the first time as a planetary species, is a transition between world ages, from one mode of psychic reality to the next. Our scope for shared collective consciousness and intention will continue to have a greater capacity to affect our environment and our potential futures. Just as the use of electricity has altered our industrial skylines, so we can learn to use the energy of our collective psyche to transform our world into the community skylines we wish to see for the future. In the words of psychologist Daniel Siegel:

> As patterns of energy and information flow are passed among people within a culture and across generations, it is the mind that is shaping brain growth within our evolving human societies. The good news about this perspective from science is that we can use an intentional attitude in our modern lives to actually change the course of cultural evolution in a positive direction. Cultivating mindsight in ourselves and in one another, we can nurture this inner knowing in our children and make it a way of being in the world. We can choose to advance the nature of the mind for the benefit of each of us now and for future generations who will walk this earth, breathe this air, and live this life we call being human.[8]

Like never before, our connective and communicative environments are becoming embedded with our bio-psycho-social influences. We are establishing what Siegel terms 'interpersonal neurobiology'; how our social relationships influence and affect our nervous system. We are unable to separate the neurological functioning of the human being from the environment. Our various social and cultural impacts, influences and experiences are rewiring our neural circuitry. It is thus imperative that we have positive and constructive external stimuli with which to foster and support conscious development. The scale of adjustment to live differently may be enormous, or will be to those without adequate preparation.

It is no understatement to say that the human species has entered a period of profound, fundamental and unprecedented change. As such, we need to acquire new skills in order to co-exist with a world seeking to develop more integral and profound relations with the larger fabric of life: planetary, solar and cosmic. Every evolutionary/revolutionary change requires a change in consciousness; this has always been the case. We are slowly beginning to recognize this fact and to notice a change in our psychology and consciousness. Philosopher and humanist Ervin Laszlo has outlined what he calls the 'Ten Benchmarks of an Evolved Consciousness', which he lists as:

1 Live in ways that enable all other people to live as well, satisfying your needs without detracting from the chances of other people to satisfy theirs.

2 Live in ways that respect the lives of others and that respect the right to the economic and cultural development of all people, wherever they live and whatever their ethnic origin, sex, citizenship, station in life, and belief system.

3 Live in ways that safeguard the intrinsic right to living and to an environment supportive of life for all the things that live and grow on Earth.

4 Pursue happiness, freedom and personal fulfilment in harmony with the integrity of nature and with consideration for the similar pursuits of others in society.

5 Require that your government relate to other nations and peoples peacefully and in a spirit of cooperation, recognizing the legitimate aspirations for a better life and a healthy environment of all the people in the human family.

6 Require business enterprises to accept responsibility for all their stakeholders as well as for the sustainability of their environment, demanding that they produce goods and offer services that satisfy legitimate demand without impairing nature and reducing the opportunities of smaller and less privileged entrants to compete in the same marketplace.

7 Require public media to provide a constant stream of reliable information on basic trends and crucial processes to enable you and other citizens and consumers to reach informed decisions on issues that affect your and their life and well-being.

8 Make room in your life to help those less privileged than you to live a life of dignity, free from the struggles and humiliations of abject poverty.

9 Encourage young people and open-minded people of all ages to evolve the spirit that could empower them to make ethical decisions of their own on issues that decide their future and the future of their children.

10 Work with like-minded people to preserve or restore the essential balances of the environment, with attention to your neighborhood, your country or region, and the whole of the biosphere.[9]

These benchmarks of an evolved consciousness, as Laszlo outlines, suggest a transcendent mind that forms relations and ties both locally and globally, both physically and non-physically. These, again, support the precepts of a quantum-field consciousness that embraces the local field of the person as well as having nonlocal influence. The traits may form what is increasingly being viewed as an ecological identity; perhaps even the stirrings of the cosmic self? The person acts and behaves both as an individual and as a part of the greater connected whole. These multiple relations form a more varied, rich and complex life; what psychology professor Mihaly Csikszentmihalyi terms as essential for an evolving self. Csikszentmihalyi believes that a truly fluid evolving self needs to seek out and be involved in a range of activities and relations that stretch the self; to find new challenges and the commitment to develop new skills and learning.

Another trait of an evolving transcendent self, notes Csikszentmihalyi, is the 'mastery of wisdom and spirituality'; meaning the ability to see beyond the appearance of things, and to see through déceptions: to 'grasp the essential relationship between the forces that impinge on consciousness'.[10] Also important in Csikszentmihalyi's framework for harmonious evolution is our ability to 'invest psychic energy in the future'. By this he means that a person should not only have trust in what is to come, but also to actively engage with 'unforeseen opportunities' to build towards a positive and constructive future.

What both Laszlo and Csikszentmihalyi are effectively saying is that a transcendent, evolving consciousness develops through those who engage in human activity that expresses both greater individuation and a greater sense of oneness and unity. An evolving consciousness also reflects the understanding that conscious energy is primary, and the need to be aware and open to ideas and impacts of evolutionary and spiritual thinking. The view that consciousness is a primary force/energy in our reality is the key to helping people expand their consciousness and identify with ever more nonlocal ties and responsibilities: from one's family and community to the world, all life on Earth, and eventually to all life in our known universe. It is our materialistic thinking that has become dysfunctional and which now forms the backbone of a type of social pathology, which has little idea or social index of how to measure our quality of life.

These days, a country's GDP only serves to indicate its economic inefficiency and says nothing about the wellbeing of its citizens. Negative social attributes have become rewards for our global economic system and for the modern way of life. Our social relations have for too long been representative more of an exchange of economic values and goods rather than our empathic wellbeing. It seems as if we have been living within a 'topsy-turvy' upside-down reality.

In an interesting study that links brain science to investment behaviour, researchers concluded that people with an impaired ability to experience emotions could actually make better financial decisions than other non-impaired people. The research is part of a new academic interdisciplinary field called 'neuroeconomics' that explores the role biology plays in economic decision-making by combining insights from cognitive neuroscience, psychology and economics. This new study, published in the journal *Psychological Science*, shows that people with brain damage that impaired their ability to experience emotions outperformed other people in an investment game. The study suggests that a lack of emotional responsiveness gives people an advantage in economic circumstances as emotionally impaired people are more willing to take high risks because they lacked fear. Players with 'normal' brain wiring, however, are more cautious in their dealings and interactions. A co-author of the study has even suggested that people who are high-risk takers or good investors may possess a form of 'functional psychopathy'.[11]

There we have it then – neuroeconomics has confirmed that our upside-down world is partly run by people who are social psychopaths. No wonder the old systems are failing us, and our so-called 'modern societies' are suffering from the effects of embedded socio-cultural disorder, disequilibrium and disharmony. It makes us wonder how our systems of politics and economics would be different if we all accepted and understood that consciousness is primary and that our thoughts are at the root of everything that manifests in our lives. In other words, how would human life be if we shifted from being 'functional psychopaths' to being transcendental evolutionary agents?

New Thinking for a New World

We are in need of new global leadership in the sense of respected citizens or spokespeople to step up to be our evolutionary drivers. This new catalytic impetus will not necessarily come from the top-down governments but is more likely to be from awakened sectors of the masses. Like the fall of the Berlin Wall, much change will come without guns yet with human force; the power of human will for change and transformation. Governments and many current authorities are not able to fully understand, or apply the changes needed. Many controlling political bodies and corporate institutions are too static or have too much invested in the status quo to implement flexible and sometimes radical change.

This is why social networks, non-governmental organizations (NGOs) and civil bodies are more likely to push the new agenda forwards. Alongside the heavyweight political meetings like the G8 and G20 we have the NGO-centred Global Forums and a vast array of other civil-society organized meetings. It is estimated that there are around 40,000 internationally operating NGOs, with some countries having a far higher number operating domestically, such as India with over 3 million NGOs internally. These are some of the forces operating on the ground, physically; yet transition is also about managing a shift psychically, in how we think.

Albert Einstein famously remarked that 'Everything has changed except our way of thinking.' Our thought systems are still stuck within old patterns; the problem with patterns is that once stuck in their groove it is hard to break out, like water that has carved its channel and flows nowhere else. We need to shift our thinking away from many past 'grooves' and towards new value creation. Edward de Bono, who teaches people how to think, says that we can analyse the past but we need to design the future. That, he says, is the difference between suffering the future and enjoying it.

Sadly, many of our educational programmes veer to suffering the future as they promote the storage and regurgitation of information rather then the absorption, creative evaluation and reinterpretation of information and knowledge. As an educator myself for many years I have witnessed first-hand the bureaucracy that strangles academic vitality. I have seen the appalling drop in standards in the British university system where now departments are afraid to fail students because they fear dropping down the league table of successful graduates. I have personally known cases of students who have blatantly plagiarized essays, time and time again after repeated warnings, yet were never 'allowed' to fail because the department needs each student to pass. On the other hand, I have had students coming to me asking what to write for their essays; they ask what type of arguments and opinions am I looking for? And when I reply that it is for them to be creative and argue according to their own ideas and opinions, they complain that they will fail if they don't write according to what is expected of them, as in other classes. In this manner students fear being creative and relying on their own judgements as they believe the 'system' will only pass them for showing agreement with accepted ideas. Sadly, in many cases this may be true, although certainly it wasn't the case in my classes!

Our schools and educational systems lack educators who are able to teach people how to align with a higher purpose, hold a positive intention, and develop their will so they can accomplish constructive goals effectively. Much teaching is still linear and individualized and neglects the role of contributing to a larger need. Our Western systems of schooling were originally established to be modern forms of the workhouses, preparing youngsters to be just literate enough to enter the workforce. Today this has come full circle to the point where many employers no longer look for graduates or see them as preferable employees because they say they lack the necessary life skills. Many employers now prefer to take on people without a formal university education so that they have more opportunity to learn from a living environment. Our way of thinking, and our way of teaching thinking, needs to shift away from the learning of standard situations and the standard ways of dealing with them. We require creative minds that can think out-of-the-box, away from established patterns.

Considering neuroplasticity and our brain's ability to rewire itself according to new experiences and impacts, if we continually entrain ourselves with established and standardized patterns and thought processes then this is how we will measure the future. After all, the human brain can only see what it is prepared to see; as a result, we will react to the new in terms of the old. As de Bono says:

> If everyone is going in the same direction, then anyone who
> is going in a different direction is 'wrong'. The other direction
> might be better – but it is still wrong.[12]

It may sound grand to say we are in need of new millennial thinking patterns and processes, yet this is indeed the case. We now require thinking habits that are different from our traditional ones; such older habits were useful in bringing us to our present stage but have now outlived their usefulness. There is an Eastern proverb that roughly translates as, 'You may ride your donkey up to your front door, but would you ride it into your house?' In other words, when we have arrived at a particular destination we are often required to make a transition in order to continue the journey. In this sense we may need to shift to more appropriate thinking patterns. Cleverness has been likened to a sharp-focus camera whereas wisdom is more of a wide-angle lens. What this suggests is that many clever people are not wise, and yet many people who are not especially clever in the conventional sense *are* wise.

Perhaps wisdom is more about learning to deal with myriad life experiences, complex arrangements, and being flexible to changing circumstances when they present themselves. And, as the wide-angle lens suggests, being able to see, understand and act upon the bigger picture. Poor thinking is often caused by inaccurate perception, and our mainstream institutions (educational/media) do a good job of promoting lazy thinking and ideas. It doesn't matter how loudly one shouts a bad idea, it's still going to remain a bad idea however far it travels through our global communications. Part of our inability to perceive the bigger picture lies in how Western civilization, especially, has largely ignored the development of the right-hemisphere working of the brain, opting instead to focus more on a left-brain rational functioning that operates as mechanical, linear, competitive and narrow. The abstract right-brain, with its magical world of creative visionary thinking, has been mostly sidelined throughout our recent history. Whilst logical thinking certainly is essential, it requires balancing with a more creative, visual and abstract style of perception. To put it simply, the left-brain likes to work with logic and facts whilst the right brain works more with perception, design and possibilities. It has been noted that for centuries certain inner teaching traditions have provided stories, tales, jokes and riddles etc., as a way to stimulate right-hemisphere activity. In these traditions it has been long known that providing unbalanced brain stimulation will result in incorrect perceptions. As one ancient anecdote (attributed to Miraza Ahsan of Tabriz) says: 'Show a man too many camel's bones, or show them to him too often, and he will not be able to recognize a camel when he comes across a live one.'

Edward de Bono rightly asks why thinking isn't taught in our schools: 'Is it because thinking is not considered important? Is it because many people believe that thinking cannot be taught? Is this because we believe we are already teaching thinking?'[13] I don't know, I have no answer to this.

In truth, no-one actually 'teaches' us how to think. We may have classes in philosophy (patterns of thinking); in linguistics (the study of language); in epistemology (the theory of knowledge); yet no-one actually shows us *how* to think. Perhaps one solution to this is to provide a balanced and far-ranging curriculum and as broad a spectrum of knowledge in our schooling as possible. For example, the following is a list – which in no way claims to be exhaustive – of some potential ideas to be included in an educational curriculum.[14]

- **Early School**: at an early stage our young children are taught
  – by algebra and alphabet – to use predominantly the left portion of their brain rather than abstract patterns. Before linear language, spend more time with games and puzzles; shapes, sounds, colours. Also, why not begin with being taught creation myths from different cultures: learn folk songs; stories/tales; dance/drama; poetry and rhymes. As children develop they could be introduced into notions of the self: self-actualization and a sense of identity, and be supported and encouraged to work in groups, for work and games. Aim to develop collaborative and co-solving activities.

- **Society & Culture**: introduce young learners to the notion of systems: how things of the world are related, natural ecosystems, and natural cycles. Also, discuss ancient anthropological human history – of early cave dwellers and their sacred art/cave paintings and abstract sense of the 'beyond'. Examine what constitutes 'culture'?; how hunter-gatherers formed the first agrarian societies; the emergence of early civilizations; priestly caste and power hierarchies, and the shift into patriarchal societies. Look at the wonders of the world and architectural monuments of past civilizations: Egypt, South America, Asia, South Asia, Arabia, etc., including the Chinese, Persian, Arabic, Ottoman, Indo-European, Mongolian, Aztec, Mayan etc., empires and cultures. Teach how Arabic learning, knowledge and science came into the West. Examine Western feudal and aristocratic societies, early city states, and the rise and fall of complex societies. Examine the shift from the Dark Ages/

Medieval times to the Renaissance; the rise of the modern
nation-states; the discovery of the New World and the history
of colonialism and colonial nation states. Study revolutions –
French, American, English, Bolshevik, Orange, etc. – as a means
of examining the rise of individuals within society and the notion
of social liberty; the presence and function of warfare within the
rise of nations and empires. Look at modernism, the Industrial
Revolution, and the transition to modernity and the 20th century:
technology and the rise of mega-cities. The age of radical seeking
– ideas of spiritual movements, especially late 19th century to
21st century; the age of acceleration – emergence of a new world,
1960s onwards. The rise of a global civilization: aspects of the
ethics of a planetary culture – sustainability and integral systems;
individual and collective responsibility. Post-modernity and
multi-culturalism.

- **World Philosophies & Teachings**: world religions – Christian,
  Jewish, Islamic, Buddhist, Tao, Confucius, etc.; classic
  philosophies of, for example, Plato, Aristotle, Pythagoras,
  Zoroaster, Swedenberg, Wittgenstein, etc.; and the question of
  what are morality and ethics? Discuss wholeness and empathy and
  value systems. Self, ego and the social construction of identity.

- **Environment**: geological cycles and a history of global natural
  catastrophes; history of great migrations; ice ages;
  extinctions, etc. Biodiversity and ecosystems; fossil fuels and
  resource depletion; sustainability and alternative energy; climate
  change and its global effects, etc. Discuss Lovelock's Gaia Theory;
  emergent communities; holism, ecology and systems theory.

- **Communication**: the Gutenberg Press – the social effects of
  printed books. A history of communication technologies:
  telegraph, telephone, radar, radio, TV, Internet. Ideas on the
  democratization of information. Global travel – the rise of
  transport. The rise of networks and decentralized and
  distributed communications. Modern digital social networks;
  digital identities; non-governmental organizations.

- **Finance**: the origins of money and transactions; how money is created and utilized; the origins of the banking industry and types of banking. Teach the basics in financial practices.

- **Science**: how scientific revolutions and discoveries changed the world. As well as the existing basics in biology, chemistry and physics, etc., add some information on: complex systems, quantum mechanics, holography, string theory, neuroscience, nanotechnology, quantum biology, astronomy and facts of the universe, stars and galaxy formation, genetics and latest DNA research.

- **Computing**: basic training in the major programming languages; discussions on bio-machines/artificial intelligence (smart/natural computing); bioinformatics; biomimicry; and DNA computing.

- **Metaphysics**: consciousness studies and latest psi research; different models of human consciousness. Global consciousness, conscious evolution and the noosphere. Discuss the near-death experience and its effects on people. Is there an afterlife? Shamanism and other indigenous teachings.

- **Music**: the genres and their celebrated artists and musical movements.

- **Art**: the periods, movements and their celebrated painters.

These are only some ideas, and are not meant to cover the whole spectrum of possible learning. Learning should be a two-way process where the teachers, as conscious communicators, should also be open to learning new things from their students. Students in the future are likely to be less willing to swallow rote learning, handed out parrot-fashion, and more inclined to respond to a mutual flow of ideas, experimentalism and flexible teachings. In this manner the teacher-communicator must be open to accepting that they might not know everything after all! Learning should be open to questioning, interpretation and dialogue – not the usual one-way 'this is the truth – take it or leave it' antiquated style.

What is learned in the classrooms of the future should have a practical application outside in life. It is important that learning shifts away from its historical roots in the workhouse, orientating and training youngsters for the factory, and begins to represent a body of understanding with knowledge that helps to integrate all learners into a meaningful and changing global world. This issue of education needs to be an ongoing debate, with ideas endlessly flowing in order to stimulate open and flexible minds. New channels need to be opened up for the flow of emerging youthful rivers, away from their old-patterned and dry river-beds.

In response to this need there are already new institutions of learning emerging throughout the world that utilize new technologies of communication and are aimed at a distributed, diverse range of students. One example is the Giordano Bruno GlobalShift University, a global online university whose Chancellor, Ervin Laszlo, has stated that the aim is to offer an educational programme that integrates fields of knowledge rather than promoting disciplinary divisions. The PhD programme pioneers disciplinary hybridization with its Consciousness Studies programmes linked to both natural sciences and humanities. This new online university plans to promote a vision of the world as a planetary community, examining issues of consciousness and sustainable transformation. It is certain that more centres of learning like this will become established to deal with a need for 'wholeness' learning; knowledge that is trans-disciplinary rather than fragmented by divisions and hierarchical specialism. This is just one example of how shifts within a civilization can assist in promoting change and transformation.

One way or another, change will happen; those civilizations in the past that either could not or did not adapt, finally fell by the wayside. There are many varied reasons why societies and civilizations succumb to collapse.[15] Yet what is significant now about this current transition era is that we, for the first time in our known history, are close to forming a planetary civilization. In other words, we are in the midst of the emergence, the birth pangs, of a planetary era. At the same time, many of our current infrastructures and global systems are in meltdown (*see* Chapters Four and Five), whilst our planetary communications systems are fostering the manifestation of a collective empathic psyche amongst the citizens of the world. Our energy resource situation is in dire need of a revolution, a tipping point into a new era of energy use, whilst we are in the midst of a communications revolution as protestors worldwide make use of the Internet and mobile phones to organize and orchestrate their rallies, such as the 'Occupy' movements that began in September 2011. The energy of resources and communications is shifting along with energies of human consciousness – these are truly revolutionary times. At the same time, it may be fortuitous that planet Earth is going through its own ascending arc of energetic renewal, as depicted in the Hindu Yugas. We are today witnesses to the new revolutions for our small planet.

Global Revolution as a Global Rebirth

In view of what has already been said concerning the nature of cyclic change and the need for balance and sustainability within our global ecosystems, then humanity's frantic technological pursuit of unlimited economic growth, exploitation of non-renewable resources, and exponential increase of industrial pollution appears to be dangerous insanity. Looking around us we can see that materialism and technologies of control have become the dominant paradigm. The Internet can be either a self-organizing means of true democracy and freedom of information, or the largest top-down spy network. Technology needs to be utilized with the correct spirit and intention for it to work *for* us and *with* us, rather than against us.

Yet at the present time we are also drowning in national and consumer debt; there has been a corruption of science and religion through hierarchical institutions; and our belief systems are forced into false dialectics, such as 'good' vs 'bad'; 'friend' vs enemy'; and 'Darwinism' vs 'Creationism'. If we take a cursory glance at our global politics we find evidence that there are many psychopathic activities at work. As a species we still manifest an immature consciousness. It has been said that the main obstacle to our human development is our lack of knowledge about consciousness itself, and the idea that many of our actions are based on thoughtful decisions is just a grand delusion.

As I outlined in Chapter Four, planet Earth is a finite resource and yet our energy-intensive lifestyles (especially in the industrializing nations) show an unhealthy addiction to oil. Our modern global energy system is now so integrated that components, equipment, etc. are outsourced and involved in an elaborate oil-dependent chain of transport and delivery. Furthermore, oil prices play a key role in the global economy, through inflation with its knock-on effects. We are also beset by food and water supply concerns, with many agricultural growing regions now affected by climatic change, topsoil erosion, desertification, etc., not to mention the political mechanisms at work to control the global food supply chains. These developing concerns have not gone unnoticed. Already in 2011 we saw the 'Arab Spring' revolutions, the many protests in European countries (such as *los indignados* in Spain) and the 'Occupy' protests that began in the US and have spread worldwide.

What this perhaps shows is that we are collectively an immature consciousness that is waking up to the injustices and absurdities of the situation. The study of psychohistory, a discipline that applies the findings of psychology and psychoanalysis to the study of history and political science, reveals that many wars have begun because of the psychological history of key political leaders, their system of values and process of decision-making. Psychohistorians have analysed how the nature of revolutions may in fact be related to the influence of child-rearing practices of that particular historical period. Lloyd deMause, a scholar who has researched psychohistory for the past four decades, has outlined a psychohistorical theory of history, applying it to politics, culture and warfare, showing the connections between childhood and the evolution of the psyche and society. Our present human psyche, being at an infant or child level, has created a global civilization that in terms of aggression, warfare, greed and control, is likewise infantile. For example, the atomic bomb dropped over the Japanese city of Hiroshima during WWII carried the painted nickname 'The Little Boy', and the agreed-upon message sent to Washington as a signal of successful detonation was 'The baby was born'.

Carol Cohn, who wrote the paper 'Sex and Death in the Rational World of Defense Intellectuals',[16] spent a year immersed in the almost entirely male world of defence intellectuals. She collected some extremely interesting facts confirming the perinatal dimension in nuclear warfare. In her research she confirms the significance of the motif of 'male birth' and 'male creation' as important forces underlying the psychology of nuclear warfare. For example, Cohn notes how in 1942, Ernest Lawrence sent a telegram to a Chicago group of physicists developing the nuclear bomb that read: 'Congratulations to the new parents. Can hardly wait to see the new arrival.' At Los Alamos, the atom bomb was referred to as 'Oppenheimer's baby'. This, amongst many other historical examples, shows how even as grown 'mature' individuals, including some of the greatest scientific minds, we still manifest infantile behaviour, like boys playing with their baby toys.

According to the new insights of psychohistory, along with consciousness research, it is revealed to us that we all carry in our deep unconscious, powerful energies and emotions, many of which are associated with the trauma of birth that we have not adequately processed and assimilated. These unprocessed emotions often play out on the global stage, confirming that much of our social distress originates from an immature psyche. We have exteriorized in the modern world many of the essential themes of the death–rebirth process that a person involved in deep personal transformation has to face and come to terms with internally. Transpersonal psychologist Stanislav Grof notes that:

> It seems that we are all involved in a process that parallels the psychological death and rebirth that so many people have experienced individually in non-ordinary states of consciousness. If we continue to act out the destructive tendencies from our deep unconscious, we will undoubtedly destroy ourselves and all life on our planet. However, if we succeed in internalizing this process on a large enough scale, it might result in evolutionary progress that can take us as far beyond our present condition as we now are from the primates.'[17]

It is for this reason that it is imperative that the upcoming years, the 'birth' journey through the collective near-death experience, be an initiation into a new period of psychological growth and evolution of human consciousness.

Out of the epiphany of awakening, as experienced in such moments as a transpersonal experience, comes the inner desire, the spontaneous emergence, to develop our deep sense of humanitarian and ecological concerns. With a growth in human consciousness often comes the need to get involved in service for some common purpose. This appears to be based on an intuitive awareness that each of us is ultimately entwined and connected within the entire web of existence. Yet before the emergent awareness of our collective humanity becomes global, there will be seen many outbursts of revolution. This is why I am suggesting that before humanity emerges from this darker patch (our metaphorical underworld journey), the vestiges of the 'old mind' will attempt to increase their grip of power over our social lives. In other words, to combat a rising tide of collective human consciousness towards betterment and a more harmonious world order, many nations, regimes and power structures will increase their restrictions upon human freedoms of speech, expression and liberty. However, as Terence McKenna once put it, very succinctly: 'The history of the silly monkey is over, one way or another.'[18] For the revolutionary change to come, we need to throw off our 'silly monkey' minds and self-cultivate a heightened, more aware expression of conscious living.

Consciousness may well be the energy of the future that fuels our global society into adolescence and renewed growth. It will be the collective strength of our combined intentions and mindful actions that will pull us up by our bootstraps from the metaphoric – and literal – old-energy regimes of black goo and the dangerous blackened coal pits. The revolutions currently occurring on our small yet beautiful planet will pave the way for a psychophysical transformation of life on Earth. I believe that the human race is in line for some great changes, as a more creative, empathic, collectively integrated field of consciousness emerges into being; or rather, *into awareness*. Again, Stanislav Grof notes that:

> We seem to be involved in a dramatic race for time that has no precedent in the entire history of humanity. What is at stake is nothing less than the future of life on this planet. If we continue the old strategies, which in their consequences are clearly extremely destructive and self-destructive, it is unlikely that the human species will survive. However, if a sufficient number of people could undergo the process of deep inner transformation, we might reach a level of consciousness evolution where we would deserve the name we have so proudly given to our species: *Homo sapiens sapiens.*[19]

Humanity is in the midst of a dramatic race towards a goal for evolutionary development within this crucial window of time where a great many changes are hanging in the balance. This moment in our world history offers not only potential for great social change, but also necessary adaptation through great natural upheaval and disruptions. Cultural and psychological conditions for improvement will emerge alongside physical pressures for change; such as messy resource wars, natural disasters and catastrophes, dictatorial suppression, economic hardships and civil unrest.

At the same time, however, the global revolution occurring at this time is also a revolution in our sciences, our understanding of consciousness, and our way of thinking. The upcoming years and decades will provide much opportunity for discovering and learning more about the 'finer' energies available in our physical and psychic realms. For example, it is possible that our science will gain an understanding of how to utilize the dark energy of the universe or similar means of harnessing energy from the untapped universal energies within our physical cosmos. There may also be advances in understanding how to control quantum energy fields, electromagnetic fields and vacuum energy fields, as well as increasing use of magnetism. We have also to consider advances in nanotechnology and microtechnology. Our sustainable futures are likely to increasingly shift towards a new generation of clean and safe energy, away from the dirty, heavily financially motivated fossil fuels and towards a more egalitarian form of energy supply, distribution and use. As more clean energy processes are developed there will be a geopolitical power shift amongst our nations. This is also likely to occur alongside much needed systemic change in our global systems of economy, food and planetary resources.

As I have attempted to explain within the pages of this book, we are now entering a period of opportunity for change and betterment like never before in our recent history. Such unique historical moments may never be present again at exactly the right time when they are so badly needed; well, perhaps not in our lifetimes. What we may now be witnessing in these tumultuous times is the rise of intuition, empathy, greater connectivity to the world and to people, and a sense of 'knowing' about what each given situation demands. At the same time, both our sciences and our human intuition are beginning to awaken to the understanding that consciousness is primary within what we perceive to be a materially ordered universe. Within these new paradigms we are gaining insight into a field-perception of living systems; that is, biological life and consciousness both coexist within nonlocal fields of energy. Our latest scientific discoveries and technological innovations are helping to prepare humanity for the realization that meaningful relations can operate at a distance, stimulating empathic relations in global contexts through nonlocal fields of information transfer and exchange. It would appear that humanity may indeed be more prepared than we realize within the psychophysical transformation now occurring on planet Earth.

This shift in understanding moves us towards the acknowledgement that humanity plays a small yet meaningful part within a much grander and epic dynamic, living cosmos. This may be part of an evolutionary catalyst within humanity to steer us towards a revitalized, compelling and harmonious human future within the natural order of cyclic change.

CHAPTER ELEVEN

The Way Ahead:

Reflections on the Coming Years

The dreams of magic may one day be the waking realities
of science.

Sir James Frazer

No pessimist ever discovered the secrets of the stars
or sailed to an uncharted land or opened a new heaven
to the human spirit.

Helen Keller

We are living through an extraordinary passage of change, whereby what we do for the next two decades, from now to 2030, will create the template for the future. And what happens between now and 2050 will be a crucial period for establishing these patterns of change and getting them in place to serve for the long run. Right now, as a collective family, we are juggling the various elements of our planetary future. I am firmly in the camp that says the future is assured – we are going to survive as a species on this planet. That means also that our dear planet – our Mother Earth – is also 100 per cent guaranteed her future. The only uncertainties that remain are the type, frequency and consequences of the obstacles that must be overcome.

The quantity and quality of the change ahead will depend very much upon the degree to which human consciousness is able to change. Humans have always had a 'consciousness-relation' with the planet, since the resonance of the planet is very much aligned with the quality of consciousness on the planet, and both energy frequencies are integrated. To this end we have to wonder to what degree human consciousness can influence the direction of events and processes here on Earth, and whether it can have a meaningful role in adapting (and adapting to) the coming physical changes. In this way we can take on a responsibility to form a way forwards that is beneficial to all, and in harmony with all systems, instead of humanity racing egoistically, and often blindly, ahead upon its selfish destructive path. It is imperative that we now need to be a part of the change – to work, understand it, and to move with it. Consciousness is a state that can be developed daily, as well as over generations. We should thus start thinking and observing in *groups of generations* and not simply *year to year*. Many of us now realize that human culture and consciousness co-evolve and although it is difficult to step outside the perceptual paradigms of our respective cultures, and to develop awareness of our social conditioning, it is nonetheless time for a more objective consciousness and human society to evolve together.

As previously pointed out, some of these stirrings have recently been witnessed in Arab revolutions (known as the 'Arab Spring') – the dissatisfaction of three generations against outmoded authoritarian regimes. These 'new revolutions' emerged as a rising wave of shared, communal consciousness that was opposed to the old energy consciousness and was more conceptual than linear. Such 'new revolutions' that have occurred in the early decades of the 21st century will not automatically replace one kind of dictator/regime with another. The authoritarian regimes are falling, and will continue to fall piece by piece, because the new energies spreading across the planet and through human consciousness can no longer support their way. The 'old mind', as I have previously referred to it, is no longer in resonance with the changing energetic social arrangements. In addition to the Arab lands, some of this shift has already occurred in South America where the once-hotbed for dictatorial regimes has now formed a region of developing nations that are putting in place moderate, effective leadership that is making a mark upon the global stage. This region is expected to be an important and strategic player in the coming decades. I anticipate that there will be a significant shift from now until 2030, with the next two decades marking the route that many nations will take, and the changes that will emerge as leading indicators. This chapter will take a brief look at some of these 'change indicators' that may serve to be major factors in the 21st century, and to offer some reflections on these coming years.

A key factor during the next couple of decades is that three generations of people will be sharing an activated awareness of the emerging perceptual shift. The teenagers and young people who were around during the Harmonic Convergence of 1987, who heard of it and maybe even followed its happening, were some of the first wave to tune into the shift of the new energies. Their parents, who were the war generation, have largely been unable to recalibrate for the energetic change. The 'Harmonic Convergence' generation, who were perhaps 15–30 at the time, will now be in the 40–55 age bracket. Many of these will have already begun families and thus seeded a new generation, who may be somewhere in the 15–30 age bracket (if we take 25 as the average age for beginning a family). At present this 2nd generation is the most 'consciously aware' of the perceptual and energetic change now occurring since they were already born into a planet with a different energetic signature. Thus, they arrived already 'hard-wired' for the change. It is this generation that I referred to in Chapter Nine as the 'new children' (sometimes referred to as the 'Indigos'). Over the next couple of decades this aware generation will seed the third generation who will become even greater agents of change as they will all arrive with a completely different range of consciousness, entirely suited to the new energies of the 21st century.

Therefore, by 2030, a time I see as an important crux in humanity's evolving transition, the three generations of the new energy will look something like this:

1st Generation: 58–73
2nd Generation: 33–48
3rd Generation: 8–23

Three generations of 'change agents' will have the presence and soul-force required to bring in and implement the necessary change for the future of planet Earth and of humanity's next phase. Such 'change agents' will foster a shift in how societies perceive the current situation and its implications for the future. That is, a change will organically occur in how we *see* the world.

Our perception of reality depends upon our 'habits of perception', which we develop throughout our lives. These perceptual habits – or markers – are often constructed and/or validated throughout the socio-cultural institutions of a given era. To move on, to break with these perceptual habits and push for an emerging new paradigm of thought, requires from us that we are open to questioning our frameworks of belief and knowledge. By not questioning the existing structures we are forfeiting our right to consciously evolve our patterns of understanding. And it needs to be recognized that a consciousness shift is now underway as the world has come to a point where it cannot continue without a shift in perceptual reality. The world that humanity inhabits is, as never before in our recorded history, globally and integrally connected; as such it is at a 'phase change' between a fragmented planetary culture and a unified planetary culture (from a Type 0 to a Type 1 civilization). One of the phases of this transition to a planetary culture is the step-by-step process of unification.

A Shift Towards Unity

Humanity's historical past worked with and utilized an older, 'heavier' energy. It was an energy that defined separateness, ego and identity. This energy of division allowed humanity to form, create and to evolve to the stage where we now find ourselves. Yet it was also an energy that cut humanity off from the integral wholeness of all systems, cosmic and natural. The new energy that is now manifesting, and spreading across the planet, is a 'lighter' energy that unifies, not divides. It is likely that we will see more and more examples of a unifying energy manifesting in our social, cultural and financial arrangements. Some elements of this unifying force have already surfaced in the convergence of nations and currencies, such as the European Union and the euro. The United States was also a model along these lines, to show that a unity of states could exist together. The European Union model, in particular, shows that nations which are dependent on one another economically don't make war on each other. Although currently there are financial problems arising within the EU (Greece, Ireland, Portugal, Italy, for example), these issues belong to the older dysfunctional global economic system. As such, before the euro can fully develop into a strong global currency for the long term, a worldwide financial reorganization is required. However, as in all worthy endeavours, the seeds have to be planted at an earlier stage. The next step may be for South America to issue its own shared currency, with perhaps Africa following by the middle of the century. An outrageous idea?

It is feasible, and also very likely, that South America will consider its next move along the model of the European Union. That is, dissolved borders for fluid travel through all territories; and a single currency. If this happens, the world will witness a new great power emerging onto the global playing field: a region of immense natural resources, a population of millions wanting to share in the zeitgeist of change and new world values, and a fresh energy coming in to balance the now stale energy of the older empire-building nations. The countries of South America are already beginning to form various well-intentioned collaborations, and are showing a great deal of social stability in comparison with past (and often brutal) regimes. Such great change can take place within one or two generations. This will be further accelerated when we reach the moment where the world has three generations of 'change agents' active in the world – around 2030 – at which point there will be dramatic and radical adjustment within a single generation.

If we take a look back, only 70 years ago we were at a time when great nations were at war with one another; and now these same nations are trusted trading partners. Within 60–70 years our most formidable enemies have become our closest trading allies, making many of the items we buy and rely on daily. This is just one example of how we have collectively been moving from a divisive to a unifying energy. Humanity has been going to war over division (God, beliefs, ideology, territory, power) for as long as we have had historical data. It is a record repeating itself – the needle stuck in the groove. Yet this phase of human history is set to end; the parameters are being shifted. And the younger generations instinctively know this – they 'get it' – and are already working to see the shift manifest on this planet within our lifetimes. Even the young generation in the Middle East whose conditioning is teaching them to hate; many of them are instead opting for connection, collaboration and positive change through meaningful dialogue and actions. They no longer listen to their governments, to the speeches of anger and violence – they opt for solutions through the new, lighter energies. There is already a worldshift happening.

Each entity attempting to strengthen its power within the old energies of the status quo will have to compete, and brace itself, against the rising tide of free thinkers and innovators who will usher in rapid and often unexpected change. Those institutions (including nations) that don't re-evaluate themselves within this new light will find themselves unable to maintain stability within a world, and its peoples, forging ahead with a renewed spirit. Human consciousness is set to usher in great change, and the potential lies ahead for each one of us. The future will no longer be dictated to us through our past; it will be created anew along a totally different paradigm, forming unity through purpose and shared empathy. The old energy may at first seem to be leaving slowly, yet within the next few decades we will witness this inevitable transition and the birth of a new planetary phase – the mythical hero's journey home.

The upcoming decades will more likely be based around *potentials* rather than linear trends, forecasts and certainties. Nothing is certain; yet we can project upon particular paths based upon the most promising, or emerging, potentials that are either beginning to manifest, or lie within our capacities. One de-limiting aspect of our current situation is the lack of vocabulary we have to describe these 'potentials', since our human vocabulary is mostly geared towards describing what *is*, rather than that which *can be* beyond our current frames of reference. Much of human language has been developed around the concept of duality since we have had to live within this reality of duality for so long. The increasing shift towards unity, towards a new paradigm of connectedness – a quantum state – is lacking in accurate terms of reference. As mentioned in Chapter Seven, the rise of empathy – of shared compassion – is one of the features that mark the transition from duality to unity (from 'old mind' to 'new mind'). This period of change will force many people to confront the need to develop some new terms of reference. This can be illustrated by the following allegory of the many-coloured room:

> There is a large room known only as the many-coloured room; and in this room all the colours of the rainbow present themselves one at a time, changing colour every few thousand years. The many-coloured room has always existed and will continue to exist as long as there is a need for it. For thousands of years the room is yellow; then it turns to blue; then to red; then the purples; then the greens: slowly, the room goes through all the colours of the rainbow.

> Within this large many-coloured room reside a group of smart, intelligent beings, all of whom were born during a time when the colour in the room was red. Their parents were also born during the red cycle, and even their grandparents. In fact, as far back as their recorded history goes the room has always been red. It is the only room colour they've ever known. You could say then that they have a *red consciousness* and they expect red. Everywhere they go, they work with red. They are, quite simply, the red people.

> Over time, the many-coloured room starts to do what it always has done and slowly begins to move into its next colour – the colour purple. What happens to those beings who have always known red? The first thing they experience is fear. The red beings say, '*Here comes something odd and*

unusual, and it has never happened before! It's dark and somehow scary. We must have done it. We must be responsible. There is no other explanation! Therefore, we must find ways to stop the purple. It's supposed to be red. Purple is bad.'

But even among the red beings there are those few who say, *'We welcome the purple. We don't know why it is here, but we recognize that it is appropriate. Although we've always been red and we don't understand the purple, we're not afraid of it. Even some of our ancient wise elders spoke of a time when a shift in the red colour would come. Let us work with the purple!'*[1]

This allegory of the many-coloured room expresses how cycles of change may occur naturally, yet still be beyond the scope of our known recorded history. We may in fact relate such cycles within the many-coloured room to the Yuga cycles discussed in Chapter Six. Human consciousness, we might say, is changing colours. Whilst the future cannot be known precisely, we can perhaps at least have an inclination that the potentials are there within, for example, the colour purple. It is these potentials that can be worked with to better understand the way ahead.

Past historians have attempted to make a map of known trends, which has resulted in some insightful indications. In this regard I make reference to British historian Arnold Toynbee who, from his extensive meta-historical study on the rise and fall of civilizations, came up with his 'Law of Progressive Simplification'. By this, Toynbee indicated that civilizational growth was not so much measured by material resources but rather by its ability to transfer increasing amounts of energy and attention towards non-material growth, such as culture, education, artistic pursuits, wellbeing, etc. Toynbee also coined the term 'etherialization' to describe the historical process whereby a society learns to accomplish the same, or more, using less time and energy.

The noted visionary architect Buckminster Fuller expressed a similar notion when he wrote of 'ephemeralization' which noted how there is a technological trend that moves ever closer towards the ethereal/ephemeral; such as the shift from heavy cables and towers/masts to fibre optics, then to space satellites and wi-fi transmission. This transforms a civilization from heavier materiality towards lighter, more subtle, forms of connectivity and functionality. The material side of life becomes increasingly associated, or converges, with subtle energies and channels of transmission. Furthermore, new and emerging forms of collaboration and reciprocity arise that utilize these new forms.

This line of thinking reinforces what has been said in previous chapters of this book about how revolutions in communications and energy (forms of technology) go together with shifting forms of human consciousness. There is thus a relationship, I argue, between dramatic and revolutionary advances in science and technology and increasing capacities of human consciousness. With this in mind, however, it should also be noted that the parallel state of human consciousness has not always been at a level whereby it could have made best use of the advances in science and technology. One wonders, then, how this will play out in the coming decades.

Reflections on the Coming Years

Each time that a new form of technology gives humanity a changed perspective upon the universe, its worldview is irreversibly altered, or rather it expands. Humanity's worldview was catalysed when Galileo used optical telescopes to map the stars and planets. Much later, when radio telescopes came into operation, our minds were introduced to a much vaster, more active universe, with black holes and supernovas. Now that we are in the 21st century with a new generation of the latest telescopes that can detect gravitational waves, humanity's perspective may be further expanded into vistas of multiverses and multidimensions. Our socio-cultural evolution as a sentient species relies heavily upon the notion of perspective; our sense of what 'reality' is relies upon how we formulate our perspectives and perceptions. In general there has been a diffusion pattern of how mass technologies have evolved through society; this is a pattern that moves from scarcity and privilege to mass distribution and eventually to being available everywhere. We can see this pattern working through the technological medium of paper. Initially paper was used in the form of sacred scrolls that were guarded under heavy secrecy by priests; this later changed as the public printing press was introduced and people became literate; subsequently there was a great leap to almost any book being now available in our supermarkets; and finally, paper being thrown away mindlessly as waste. Likewise with computers we can see how the first computers belonged to high-ranking organizations, guarded in rooms and shared with only a handful of selected scientists/engineers. Later this developed into the first large, stand-alone desktop computers that began to adorn our homes. Recently the Internet has linked, or rather networked, our computers into a distributed virtual environment. Now we have our computer networks in our pockets, on our phones, and with us everywhere we go. Soon this technology will be ubiquitous and embedded into our environments and everyday objects.

This evolution of technology from the scarce to the ubiquitous also reflects how energy moves from a concentrated form to a more dispersed, finer, and distributed medium. This shift in energy consumption is a significant marker in socio-cultural evolution as, in general, the rise and fall of human civilizations can be measured in terms of their energy production and consumption. For most of recorded human history, our societies were limited to 1/5th horsepower; or rather, the power of our bare hands. Early humans lived nomadic lives, as hunters and gatherers, living daily within hostile environments. Then, around 10,000 years ago, a great transition occurred when the end of the Ice Age arrived. This opened the way for the rise of agriculture, and for the domestication of horse and oxen, which increased human energy production to one horsepower. As larger areas of land were cultivated and harvested, they generated surplus food/energy stores which supported an expanding population. Soon after, relatively speaking, the domestication of animals led to the establishment of the first stable human settlements. Then, as recently as 300 years ago, the Industrial Revolution shifted energy production and use once again away from human hands and animal energy into the power of machinery and the birth of modern technology. This lifted energy production and usage to new levels.

At our current stage in this process, humanity has stepped into the era of the finer, more subtle energies of information and the quantum field. The Earth now has a digital membrane as well as a quantum connection to living beings. The next level will arise when humanity has better understood these finer, quantum energies, and how to use them correctly and in line with more balanced energy requirements.

It is telling that physicists rank civilizations by the amount of energy they consume. According to Russian astrophysicist Nikolai Kardashev civilizations throughout the cosmos are likely to be socially and culturally different from us, yet they would all have to consume energy, and therefore obey the universal laws of physics. With this in mind Kardashev proposed three theoretical types of civilization (known as the Kardashev scale):

- Type I: planetary – consuming the sunlight that falls on their planet (about 10^{17} watts)

- Type II: stellar – consuming all the energy that their sun emits (10^{27} watts)

- Type III: galactic – consuming the energy of billions of stars (about 10^{37} watts)

At present humanity is a Type 0 civilization as we get our energy mostly from dead plants (fossil fuels). Theoretical physicist Michio Kaku estimates that we will attain a Type I civilization in roughly 100 years, based on the average rate of our economic growth. The early signs of this transition, according to Kaku, are:

- **The Internet**: a planetary communication system. Also allowing for a distributed network of news and movements.
- **Global language**: several languages are manifesting as global – such as English, Chinese, Spanish – this is encouraged by our global communication systems.
- **Global economy**: financial trade agreements; economic blocs; economics beyond nation states.
- **A planetary culture**: cultural trends are dispersed globally – films, music, food, fashion, sports, etc.
- **Environmental issues**: threats and consequences are now global, with knock-on effects being felt worldwide, whether from disasters or campaigns.
- **Travel**: mobility and tourism and now allowing for planetary contact, exposure and experiences.
- **Boundaries**: a weakening of the nation state, and a blurring of boundaries; also, larger international political blocs (eg. the EU).[2]

Both our energy production and usage signify that we are a Type 0 civilization, and in order to progress to a Type 1 civilization it is likely, according to the Kardashev scale, that we need to organize ourselves as a planetary civilization. The signs are already there, as Kaku indicates, with our human systems, technologies, communications and consciousness all moving in a unitary planetary direction. What we are in need of is a new wave of innovators, bringing in 'disruptive innovations' that will drive/catalyse a new form of human mental-spiritual-perceptual energy for an evolutionary impulse towards a human planetary society. Kaku notes that 'the transition between our current Type 0 civilization and a future Type I civilization is perhaps the greatest transition in history'.[3]

It is important, however, to point out here that the concept of a planetary society is one that may come about from:

1 A development in the type of energy source utilized and the form of its consumption. This is estimated to require the shift from finite to infinite energy sources, which are natural and can be fairly distributed to maintain a global civilization.

2 Ubiquitous global communications that allow fair and egalitarian access for all peoples to engage in free and open communication and connection worldwide.

3 The emergence of an increased empathic, compassionate collective consciousness that exhibits greater intuitive reasoning and ethical responsibility.

These points are critical when discussing notions of a potential planetary society, as without these in place (as well as other factors) we may witness the formation of a one-world government that is undemocratic, authoritarian, and more along the lines of what is talked about in conspiracy circles as the 'New World Order' (NWO). This is definitely not what is being discussed in these pages. The concept of unity that may be an increasing feature of the 21st century will come about in stages as part of increasing human awareness, consciousness, and the desire for human social evolution and betterment.

However, the immediate transition may seem far from anything representing unity. In the short term, until we have sorted out our global energy sources, it may seem that we are heading towards increased localism in terms of community-based groupings and resources. In the long term, over the next century, if we are able to shift from consuming fossil fuels (finite) towards solar, wind, sea, geothermic sources (infinite), then we have a better chance of developing into a planetary society. In other words, the energy issue is key. Right now we are living amidst the most extraordinary of times – a pivotal epoch in our ongoing human journey.

We cannot, however, continue along a path of increasing returns as we inhabit a finite planet. As a Type 0 civilization we are beset with the problems confronting the beginnings of a planetary society: politics, trade, finance, culture, food, warfare – and more – are all being revolutionized by the emergence of our planetary civilization. These problematic events will spiral into further chaos unless we can raise ourselves, as a planetary species, to a new level of understanding and utilization of energy, technology and consciousness.

Recently the Fukushima nuclear disaster in Japan that occurred after the tsunami that hit on 11 March 2011 is likely to put a halt on developing nuclear power. It is recognized as being the largest nuclear accident to have occurred since the 1986 Chernobyl disaster, and is considered to be a more complex disaster due to the multiple numbers of reactors and spent fuel pools involved. As they say, nuclear reactors are the world's most expensive and dangerous steam engines. The international outcry from this monumental disaster is likely to put nuclear energy off the table for many, in terms of a viable future energy source. Instead, more research and emphasis in the upcoming decades will likely be placed upon solar power; wind- and water-generated energy; geothermal energy; magnetic energy; and possibly fusion power.

In recent years there has been a boost of investments in desert real estate, for building state-of-the-art solar farms. This includes the Chinese who are pouring millions into such alternative energy sources. For example, the Chinese government has invested in a huge 2-billion-watts solar park to be built in Inner Mongolia as part of their wind, solar, biomass and hydroelectric energy growth. On a similar tack the Japanese Trade Ministry announced a plan to investigate the feasibility of Space Solar Power (SSP); that is, to place huge solar-radiating satellites in high earth orbit 22,000 miles in space. Likewise, a consortium of

Japanese companies was in talks to join a $10 billion programme aimed at launching a solar power station into space to generate billions of watts of power that could be beamed back to Earth for human needs. The urgency of this is now more evident after the Fukushima nuclear disaster.

There are also many projects underway to develop wind power. Generating energy from wind power grew globally from 17 billion watts in 2000 to 121 billion watts in 2008 as new wind turbine technology is now making it a more viable and profitable option.[4] Many countries in both Europe and Asia are investing heavily in wind power as an alternative energy source (arriving full circle from the old wooden windmills of early Europe). One example of this is the Atlantic Wind Connection (AWC) that is planning to create a vast array of wind farms off the mid-Atlantic coast with hundreds of miles of these wind farms being connected and networked under the sea. Similarly, tidal and wave-generated power are being seen as viable alternatives, especially as some of the largest and most populated cities on Earth sit near the ocean, making this power source ideal. An extra incentive is that such a natural power source presents no danger to humans living close by.

Another natural energy source that is, quite literally, right beneath our feet, is geothermal energy. And if a disaster, such as an earthquake or explosion, occurs at a geothermal plant then the worst part will be the rebuilding of it and little else. Our natural world has given us a huge abundance of energy sources that ebb and flow, steam and blow, within the context of our everyday environments. Why not make use of them?

It is also my feeling that magnetic power will come more to the fore within the upcoming decades of the 21st century. The truth about most energy today is that a large percentage of it goes into overcoming friction, causing a great part of the power to be wasted rather than utilized. Magnetism, as a power source, would permanently reduce both energy use as well as energy waste and pollution. Examples of the use of this today are magnetic levitating trains (maglev) that hover above a set of rails containing magnets. Countries leading the way in this technology are Japan, Germany and China. Already maglev trains have set world records, such as the MLX01 maglev train in Japan that set a record speed of 361 mph in 2003. Magnetism as a future power source is likely to gain a huge boost once our scientists have developed room temperature superconductors; that is, superconductors that do not require any refrigeration so they can create permanent magnetic fields of enormous power, eliminating virtually all forms of friction. Magnetism could also be used for desalinating sea water and providing much needed water resources.

There is a large body of research, at various levels of scholarship and credibility, which suggests that forms of 'free energy' devices have been invented yet are suppressed by governments, corporations and elite bodies, in order to maintain a stranglehold over current energy sources. Such free-energy devices are thought to exploit perpetual motion, electromagnetic energy, and extracting/utilizing zero-point, or vacuum, energy. It has also been stated many times that legendary inventor Nikola Tesla invented free-energy devices that were suppressed, and thus never made commercially available. There is a large question mark over whether, at some point in our future, we will make discoveries into such free-energy as humanity learns more about the presence and properties of quantum energies. If such were to be the case, this would indeed herald an unprecedented energy revolution that would transform civilization as we know it. However, for the time being, this remains a question mark.

Another, somewhat controversial, form of future energy could come from fusion power. There are currently many grand expensive fusion projects underway (most of them under direct government/military control). The European Fusion Development Agreement (EFDA), an agreement between European fusion research institutions and the European Commission, aims to demonstrate that nuclear fusion is a viable long-term, safe, and environmentally benign future energy option. The EFDA currently funds the Joint European Torus (JET) which is Europe's largest fusion device. Fusion is a current reality, but currently it requires more energy input than it produces. Although unlikely to be commercially viable for many decades to come, many scientists apparently feel it is within our grasp. As physicist Michio Kaku states:

> The critical period will be the next few decades. By mid-century, we should be in the hydrogen age, where a combination of fusion, solar power, and renewables should give us an economy that is much less dependent on fossil fuel consumption … The danger period is now, before a hydrogen economy is in place.[5]

These investigations into physical energy sources, however, neglect to foresee the advances in our human understanding of quantum energy. As previously discussed, the next stage in our understanding of finer energy could be the scientific verification of the quantum energy field that pervades our known universe. Further, that this underlying, ubiquitous energy field not only acts as a crucial element for evolution but is also a conscious energy force that could be utilized to play a part in our physical lives, energy needs and wellbeing. I have also speculated that this quantum field is in constant communication with human DNA. Moreover, the interaction between human quantum fields affects the planet's energetic state, which reflects back and influences the coding of human DNA. Within this perspective it can be seen that humanity has an energetic relationship with the planet, and this is processed through the DNA. This relationship between man and the environment is, in principle, a form of information processing. Indeed, renowned astronomer Carl Sagan suggested that civilizations should not only be ranked by energy consumption but also by information processing. As civilizations evolve they are increasing their energy consumption as well as their information processing capacities. This brings us back to consider the future of technological computing, and whether there will be marked advancements in line with the trajectory of finer energy sources and consumption.

Already we are in an era of profound scientific upheaval, with the pace of discovery accelerating exponentially. We should be careful not to underestimate the pace of science and technology, as when Charles H Duell, the commissioner of the US Office of Patents, said in 1899 that 'Everything that can be invented has been invented.' Perhaps more (in) famous is Thomas Watson's remark when, as chairman of IBM, he said in 1943 that 'I think there is a world market for maybe five computers.' We can appreciate this exponential change ourselves by realizing that those singing birthday cards we sometimes receive (that sing 'Happy Birthday' to us in an annoying tone) contain a chip that has more computer power than all the Allied Forces of 1945. And what do we do with it after a few obligatory listens? We just throw it away! It is said that our average mobile smart phone today has more computer power than all of NASA back in 1969 when it placed two astronauts on the Moon. Our technologies have been getting more powerful and at the same time they have become ever tinier. Can this relationship continue indefinitely? The answer, it seems, is no.

There may be a ceiling on the growth of physical computing power, so far continuing to operate according to Moore's Law, which states that computing power doubles more or less every 2 years (or 18 months according to some accounts). This is due to a limit on how tiny the integrated circuits can become before they are too miniscule to be operable. Yet there are at present thousands of industries, as well as our global technology infrastructure, which are predicated on this continued growth. Ever so slowly the computing industry is waking up to these realities. This would be a significant reality as:

> ... the collapse of Moore's law is a matter of international importance, with trillions of dollars at stake. But precisely how it will end, and what will replace it, depends on the law of physics. The answers to these physics questions will eventually rock the economic structure of capitalism.[6]

It may be that such old-paradigm growth will be replaced by new findings in physics. What may replace integrated-circuit technology is quantum computing, such as is strongly advocated by inventor and futurist Ray Kurzweil. This may be a forerunner to a more extensive, immersive mind–matter interface between the power of human thought and the control of matter. It is within the remit of our current technological paradigm to extend the reach of the human mind so that it would have the potential to interact directly upon our material environments. For example, if the human mind were to have greater contact with external magnetic fields, we would have greater control over matter. If superconductors were, one day, to be embedded within objects, then they could create magnetic fields that could be controlled by human thought.

Yet the future may be more about the expansion of human consciousness than it is about the rise of 'intelligent machines'. One of the most sophisticated super-computers in the world – the 'Dawn' computer based at the Lawrence Livermore National Laboratory in California – was able in 2006 to simulate 40 per cent of a mouse's brain; and in 2009 broke all records when it allegedly simulated 1 per cent of the human cerebral cortex. To do so the Dawn computer consumes 1 million watts of power and generates so much heat it requires 6,675 tons of air-conditioning equipment in order to provide 2.7 million cubic feet of chilled air every minute – and only to model 1 per cent of the human brain! Using this as reference we can calculate that the energy needed, according to current trends, to model the human brain would thus be 1 billion watts. Not only is this equal to the energy produced from a nuclear power plant, but the super-computer itself would occupy the equivalent of many city blocks in size. By comparison the human brain uses just 20 watts, and no power source other than our daily food, water and the air we breathe.

This illustrates one of the fundamental issues for our future decades: we lack the vocabulary and vision to comprehend beyond our current models. Thinking linearly we can see that a super-computer would need a nuclear power station to model the human brain. Yet this is old-paradigm thinking smacked onto the top of future forecasting. Not only will the future be about discovering and utilizing newer, finer forms of energy, I contend, but it will be a case of expanding upon the capacities inherent within the human mind and consciousness rather than attempting to simulate it through unconscious machinery.

One vision of the future provides us with a ubiquitous, embedded technological-based environment where humans interface with the 'Net' through contact lenses or glasses; interactive touch-screen walls and furniture; flexible electronic paper; and the buildings we walk through. The other vision is one where human consciousness evolves its capacities to connect with the quantum energies that enfold and inform our physical environment, forming an expanded awareness and interaction with energetic forces. How technology evolves is, in the end, anyone's guess. The bottom line for technology is energy, for if we do not secure sustainable energy sources for our world then there will be no planetary civilization, and the plug on our computers will be pulled, literally.

It all goes back to the same equation: can energy, communication and consciousness evolve in balance with each other? Out of balance, we remain on insecure footing. The other question is: will we progress beyond a point where we have the vocabulary or the vision to comprehend just where we are? This situation, or event, has been dubbed the *singularity*. In truth, we must ask ourselves whether as a species we are consciously mature enough to begin playing around with the atoms of creation. Nanotechnology – the manipulation of individual atoms – is just such a science. Whilst the promise of molecular engineering heralds a new era of super-strong, super-light materials with incredible conducting, electrical and magnetic properties, it also opens the way for meddling at a level that humankind is spiritually, mentally and emotionally unprepared for.

The materialist's view on the future is that by 2050 our world will be awash with the gains of nanotechnology, albeit hidden from view as we walk down the street and notice nothing unusual. Perhaps those of us still alive will never know to what degree nanotechnology has changed our world. Yet will we have managed to mark a change, a positive shift, in our inner world? As the later chapters in this book have discussed, our physical world is a sea of quantum forces that we do not perceive. Solidity is an illusion, created by the forces of repulsion that exist at a quantum level. The reality is that we do not in actual fact 'touch' anything; rather we only make an energetic contact between our own and another's quantum forces. Will the 21st century be the epoch when humanity finally (or once again) comes into alignment with a living universe and comes to understand our energetic connections?

Our Human Future?

Humanity will find itself faced with decisions, turning points, and crucial 'critical' moments in the upcoming decades of the 21st century that will test our maturity as a species. We may find ourselves responding nobly to such events as we take a step closer to regaining our position within a living, conscious universe. As visionary thinker Duane Elgin writes: 'a key test of our maturity as a species as we move into this next major phase in humanity's evolution is how well we manage to integrate the many polarities that currently divide us.'[7] Elgin continues on this theme by outlining six tasks that he considers vital for our human evolutionary journey, these being:

1   Co-creating our story of awakening
2   Cultivating reflection and reconciliation

3 Living simply and sustainably
4 Creating new kinds of community
5 Becoming media-conscious citizens of the earth
6 Bringing our true gifts into the world[8]

In common with Elgin, I feel that the focus for our collective human future lies in psychological stability, happiness, wellbeing and a sense of human belonging.

A note of caution is that we are perhaps overly concerned at present with the struggle of independence vs dependence – a rush for independence and autonomy that is driving our communities and societies closer to a hive of isolated individuals. Also, the increased reliance and dependence on material gains may lead people further into a form of self-indulgence; even a type of introspection through materiality. This draws people into a narrow perceptual field that may encourage them to withdraw into material distractions in times of uncertainty. Like an addict that escapes into the realm of drugs, more and more people in the developed world may find themselves retreating or indulging in the realm of 'form' for temporary satisfactions. This is why it is crucial that our technological innovation empowers us and adds to our humanity rather than taking away from it; it will, I feel, be a central issue of the 21st century. After all, technological growth will not provide satisfaction nor give us meaning if we have increased anxiety, stress and personal suffering.

A question to ask ourselves is whether technology can help us to learn how to live more fully, with less – perhaps a type of tech-enabled voluntary simplicity? In Chapter Two of this book I described how modernity had created a 'technological state of mind' that was overly rational, hierarchical, and focused on managing control. This 'heavy' technological presence is neither sustainable nor the model for the future. It is imperative that if we are to move into a sustainable global future, alongside technology, then we will need a completely different relationship to our technological environment. It will need to be a fluid, empowering relationship; not a disempowering, controlling one.

What is clear, at least to me, is that the years ahead need to involve a search for the self – an expression of our humanity. And yet this *search for the self* need not be purely an inner one – it may also involve reconnecting with lost skills, such as producing our own food, etc.; taking more care over our nutritional needs and diet; and striving to live a more harmonious and balanced, natural lifestyle. There are myriad ways each person could undergo their search for increased personal happiness and fulfilment.

A sense of personal balance, satisfaction and fulfilment may be a necessary endeavour for each individual as the 21st century is likely to see an increased deterioration in the influence and power of institutional religion. With the role and presence of religion in decline, this could lead some people to speculate on the loss of a spiritual authority – to lose sight of the need for inner development. This may itself be part of the transitional phase (the underworld journey). At the same time, however, there is a strong possibility that the coming years will witness a renewed connection between science and spirituality – the merging of the 'two cultures'.[9] What is necessary for the future is to foster an alliance between science and the great traditions of spiritual wisdom. Humanity is not only a collective of rational beings; inherent to us also is the element of gnosis, of the inner connection to a deep source of nourishment and, for many, guidance. If we can bring these two aspects together we can form a broader, more integral understanding of the world around us.

With a combination of science and spirituality we can move beyond a purely sense-driven perception of our environment into a more expansive perception of how we are connected to a world, a universe, at a deeper, more fundamental level. Through spirituality we are able to perceive connections that are otherwise unavailable through solely rational, scientific means. Similarly, through science we are able to learn how physical and energetic connections arise and are maintained. With the very latest findings in quantum physics we are seeing a closer convergence between what has been taught for generations in the wisdom traditions and what is arising under the most advanced scientific observations. We are discovering that every part of what is in existence is intrinsically connected within the fabric of the whole. If we can bring this knowledge together, and realize that science can verify this, we can begin to close the artificial gap that has existed for too long – the gap that categorizes people as either a follower of science or as a 'spiritual dreamer'.

This dangerous gap is indeed being dissolved, as we move into the 21st century, by the new sciences that recognize the insights of spirituality have a real basis within the physical universe. Likewise, our modern understanding of spirituality is mature enough to recognize that we have tremendous faculties of reason and rational enquiry, and together both these aspects of human nature are able to form a more completed human being, more capable of taking charge of the responsibilities required to participate in our inner and outer evolution.

The gulf between science and spirituality is not only an historical, socio-political division; it is also a perceptual one. All we know of the world comes to us through experience, and human experience (the subjective perspective) has more facets than we presently acknowledge or give due credit to. To grasp a little more of these facets would go a long way towards a more holistic understanding. It is a time in our history where we are forced to reflect upon our value systems and modes of thought. Every one of us lives as part of an interconnected, whole-system world; yet many of us continue to act as if we were separate entities, out to please only ourselves, and ready to subordinate everything and everybody in the material quest for an instant accumulation of wealth and power. As a species, this means a loss of coherence, which translates as a loss of viability. However, it is my feeling that the 21st century will be the meeting point where the wisdom of ancient traditions can find a synthesis with modern science. If this is the case then humanity may come to recognize that whilst technology is a tool, and science a powerful authority, without an inner wisdom and maturity also guiding humanity there will remain an imbalance and many limitations.

The challenge is to benefit from a scientific, technological advancement and material comfort, whilst securing our wellbeing, happiness and inner growth. This will be the great challenge in the 21st century. We must ask of science and technology that it aids us in catalysing our compassion and inner security, as opposed to fuelling humanity's greed and selfishness. The need to develop internal resources is just as important as the need to develop those external resources that are best suited to long-term human progress. The discovery, understanding, and ultimate utilization of finer energies for our physical survival and the growth of civilization are only a part of the equation. Just as important – perhaps more so – is the parallel discovery, understanding, and utilization of the finer energies within each of us; that is, the faculties of consciousness, perception and gnosis (inner wisdom). If we live our lives purely externally, without an inner dimension, we will be lacking in the full and complete development of qualities needed to bring a harmonious and sustainable long-term future into being.

The ultimate revolution needed for this small planet of ours is a spiritual revolution – or rather a re-evolution of consciousness; a revolution in our inner gnosis, understanding, and our inherent conscious selves. If this occurs parallel to revolutions in our understanding and application of energy and technology, as well as within the context of our grander celestial revolutions, then all together they belong to a design that sets the stage for the new revolutions that are to occur on our small planet.

Afterword

Throughout this book I have repeatedly stressed how many of our current struggles are between a world that is transitioning between an 'old mind', with its status quo and territorial struggles, and that of a 'new mind' rising that looks more towards an integral, sustainable and egalitarian planetary era. Despite the surface tensions I feel it is safe to say that a global consciousness that reflects a universal sense of responsibility and compassion is more available to us today than it was earlier in the 20th century. This shows the shift in our maturity as a collective species in only a few decades – an incredibly short span of time. Just as the communications revolution has spurred this global consciousness, we are now closer to a consciousness revolution that will impact our collective spiritual hearts – this will be the true mark of the maturity of our species. No true sense of physical unity (from nation blocs to planetary society) can come into being if we are unable to cultivate and nurture the 'being' of unity within our very own internal states. Our internal state is a measure of our own strength, forbearance and fortitude. We need to cultivate this focus, this ability for calmness within change and adversity, in order to manage our maturity into the next phase of our evolutionary development.

Human dreams can exercise great power, yet they must have focused intention if they are to manifest and exert influence in the physical world. We should be mindful of how each day brings new impacts, emotions and learning opportunities. We live in a vast, dynamic, living school – nothing is static. We are not machines, robotic automatons that respond to applied stimuli. We are complex emotional and spiritual beings that have myriad encounters, events and experiences from which to learn, grow and evolve. We should strive to always remember this, and to avoid those things that negatively affect us. We are here now to be empowered; not suppressed, oppressed, nor repressed.

It is my sense that many of the younger generation instinctively know this – they 'get it' – and are already working to see the shift manifest on this planet within our lifetimes. There is already a worldshift happening.

The world we are moving into requires of us that we both inspire and be inspired. Change will come through the living spirit of people. When a sincere intention is placed into the world, it can, and does, move matter into its alignment. In these times of great transition it is our human obligation to hold onto and focus our integrity, our balance, our compassion and our positive strength for moving beyond these temporary disturbances and aligning ourselves with a future that we wish to be a part of. Together, we can build upon our collective spirit of love. Let us be calm, balanced, and hold the truth.

And let us also not forget, there are many wonders still to come …

The Lighthouse

> There was once a man who began building a lighthouse in the middle of the desert. Everyone started to make fun of him and called him crazy.
>
> 'Why a lighthouse in the desert?' everybody wondered.
>
> Yet the man would not listen and kept on quietly doing his work. One day he finally finished building his lighthouse. At night, without moon or stars in the sky, the magnificent lighthouse started spinning its light in the darkness of the air, as if the Milky Way had become a carousel.
>
> And it happened that as soon as the lighthouse began to give its light there suddenly appeared in the desert a sea lit by a river of light, with beautiful ocean-going ships, sail boats, submarines, whales, dancing dolphins, merchants of Venice, the pirate Barbarossa, mermaids, sirens, and many more …
>
> Everyone was amazed, except the builder of the lighthouse: for he knew that if someone turns on a light in the darkness, from the brightness of that light will spring up many wonders.

Notes

Introduction
1. Thompson, W I, *Transforming History: A New Curriculum for a Planetary Culture*, 2009, Lindisfarne Books, p14
2. Cited in Harman, W, *Global Mind Change: The Promise of the 21st Century*, 1998, Berrett-Koehler, p129

Chapter One
1. Tarnas, R, *Cosmos and Psyche: Intimations of a New World View*, 2007, Plume, p4
2. Tarnas, R, *Cosmos and Psyche: Intimations of a New World View*, 2007, Plume, p4
3. Tarnas, R, 'Is the Modern Psyche Undergoing a Rite of Passage?', 2001, http://www.cosmosandpsyche.com/Essays.php
4. Tarnas, R, 'Is the Modern Psyche Undergoing a Rite of Passage?', 2001, http://www.cosmosandpsyche.com/Essays.php
5. Cited in Thompson, W I, *Passages About Earth: An Exploration of the New Planetary Culture*, 1974, Harper & Row, p155
6. Thompson, W I, *Passages About Earth: An Exploration of the New Planetary Culture*, 1974, Harper & Row, pp119–20
7. Tarnas, R, 'Is the Modern Psyche Undergoing a Rite of Passage?', 2001, http://www.cosmosandpsyche.com/Essays.php

Chapter Two
1. Mitchell, W J, *E-Topia: Urban Life, Jim – But Not As We Know It*, 1999, MIT Press, p132
2. Kern, S, *The Culture of Time and Space: 1880–1918*, 2000, Harvard University Press
3. Kern, S, *The Culture of Time and Space: 1880–1918*, 2000, Harvard University Press
4. Cited in Kern, S, *The Culture of Time and Space: 1880–1918*, 2000, Harvard University Press, p15
5. *See* Tainter, J A, *The Collapse of Complex Societies*, 1988, Cambridge University Press
6. This subject has been dealt with in greater detail in my book *The Struggle for Your Mind*
7. Jean-François Lyotard's 'incredulity towards meta-narratives'
8. *See* the work of Jean Baudrillard
9. Laszlo, E, *Evolution: The General Theory*, 1996, Hampton Press
10. Negroponte, N, *Being Digital*, 1995, Alfred A Knopf

[11] Russell, B, *The Impact of Science on Society*, 1985/1952, Routledge
[12] Black, E, *IBM and the Holocaust: The Strategic Alliance Between Nazi Germany and America's Most Powerful Corporation*, 2001, Crown Publishing Group
[13] Marcuse, H, *One-Dimensional Man: Studies in the Ideology of Advanced Industrial Society*, 2007/1964, Routledge
[14] McLuhan, M, *Understanding Media*, 2002/1964, Routledge
[15] Baudrillard, J, *Simulacra and Simulation*, 1994, The University of Michigan Press
[16] Shah, I, *Reflections*, 1969, Octagon Press
[17] Heinberg, R, *Peak Everything: Waking Up to the Century of Decline in Earth's Resources*, 2007, Clairview Books
[18] Tarnas, R, *Cosmos and Psyche: Intimations of a New World View*, 2007, Plume, p40

Chapter Three

[1] Rifkin, J, *The Empathic Civilization: The Race to Global Consciousness in a World in Crisis*, 2010, Polity Press
[2] An extract from the writings of G I Gurdjieff taken from http://www.gurdjieff.org/needleman2.htm
[3] Heinberg, R, *Memories & Visions of Paradise: Exploring the Universal Myth of a Lost Golden Age*, 1990, The Aquarian Press
[4] Grosso, M, *The Final Choice: Playing the Survival Game*, 1985, Stillpoint Publishing, p5
[5] Tarnas, R, 'Is the Modern Psyche Undergoing a Rite of Passage?', 2001, http://www.cosmosandpsyche.com/Essays.php, p19
[6] *Dark Night of the Soul* is the title of a poem and treatise written by 16th-century Spanish Roman Catholic mystic Saint John of the Cross
[7] Elgin, D, *Awakening Earth: Exploring the Evolution of Human Culture and Consciousness*, 1993, William Morrow & Company, p24
[8] Elgin, D, *Awakening Earth: Exploring the Evolution of Human Culture and Consciousness*, 1993, William Morrow & Company, p121
[9] Elgin, D, *Awakening Earth: Exploring the Evolution of Human Culture and Consciousness*, 1993, William Morrow & Company, p150
[10] Snow, C B, *Mass Dreams of the Future*, 1989, McGraw-Hill
[11] Snow, C B, *Mass Dreams of the Future*, 1989, McGraw-Hill, p50
[12] Ring, K, *The Omega Project: Near-Death Experiences, UFO Encounters, and Mind at Large*, 1992, William Morrow, p190
[13] Cited in Ring, K, *The Omega Project: Near-Death Experiences, UFO Encounters, and Mind at Large*, 1992, William Morrow, p170
[14] Heinberg, R, *Memories & Visions of Paradise: Exploring the Universal Myth of a Lost Golden Age*, 1990, The Aquarian Press, p117
[15] Heinberg, R, *Memories & Visions of Paradise: Exploring the Universal Myth of a Lost Golden Age*, 1990, The Aquarian Press, p119

16 An alternative view of the Yuga cycle and time scale was taught by the 19th/20th-century Indian yogi Swami Sri Yukteswar Giri. By his interpretations humankind is currently within the Dwapara Yuga.

17 Heinberg, R, *Memories & Visions of Paradise: Exploring the Universal Myth of a Lost Golden Age,* 1990, The Aquarian Press, p116

18 Lovelock, J, 'The fight to get aboard Lifeboat UK', *The Times,* 8 February 2009

19 Rees, M J, *Our Final Century,* 2003, Heinemann, pp23–4

20 Rees, M J, *Our Final Century,* 2003, Heinemann, p74

21 de Rosnay, J, *The Symbiotic Man: A New Understanding of the Organization of Life and a Vision of the Future,* 2000, McGraw Hill

22 Rees, M J, *Our Final Century,* 2003, Heinemann, p61

23 Rees, M J, *Our Final Century,* 2003, Heinemann, p186

24 Laszlo, E, *Quantum Shift in the Global Brain,* 2008, Inner Traditions, introduction

25 Ring, K, *The Omega Project: Near-Death Experiences, UFO Encounters, and Mind at Large,* 1992, William Morrow

26 Grosso, M, *The Final Choice: Playing the Survival Game,* 1985, Stillpoint Publishing

Chapter Four

1 Tainter, J A, *The Collapse of Complex Societies,* 1988, Cambridge University Press

2 Diamond, J M, *Collapse: how societies choose to fail or survive,* 2005, Allen Lane

3 Tainter, J A, *The Collapse of Complex Societies,* 1988, Cambridge University Press

4 Rifkin, J, *The Empathic Civilization: The Race to Global Consciousness in a World in Crisis,* 2010, Polity Press

5 Greer, J M, *The Long Descent: A User's Guide to the End of the Industrial Age,* 2008, New Society Publishers, p19

6 Hirsch, R; Bezdek, R; Wendling, R, 'Peaking Of World Oil Production: Impacts, Mitigation, & Risk Management', SAIC (Science Applications International Corporation), 2005

7 Hirsch, R; Bezdek, R; Wendling, R, 'Peaking Of World Oil Production: Impacts, Mitigation, & Risk Management', SAIC, 2005

8 Hirsch, R; Bezdek, R; Wendling, R, 'Peaking Of World Oil Production: Impacts, Mitigation, & Risk Management', SAIC, 2005

9 Greer, J M, *The Long Descent: A User's Guide to the End of the Industrial Age,* 2008, New Society Publishers; Kunstler, J H, *The Long Emergency: Surviving the Converging Catastrophes of the 21st Century,* 2006, Atlantic Books

10 Ruppert, M C, *Confronting Collapse: The Crisis of Energy & Money in a Post Peak Oil World,* 2010, Chelsea Green Publishing Company

[11] *See* the work of John Michael Greer, *The Long Descent: A User's Guide to the End of the Industrial Age*, 2008, New Society Publishers

[12] Engdahl, F W, *Seeds of Destruction: The Hidden Agenda of Genetic Manipulation*, 2007, Global Research, p50

[13] Engdahl, F W, *Seeds of Destruction: The Hidden Agenda of Genetic Manipulation*, 2007, Global Research, cited p63

[14] Rockerfeller and Ford Foundation funding of the Harvard University study titled 'Harvard Economic Research Project on the Structure of the American Economy' (led by Wassily Leontief) helped to identify US corporate interests and expansions.

[15] Engdahl, F W, *Seeds of Destruction: The Hidden Agenda of Genetic Manipulation*, 2007, Global Research, p138

[16] Engdahl, F W, *Seeds of Destruction: The Hidden Agenda of Genetic Manipulation*, 2007, Global Research, cited p146

[17] Dixon, P, *Futurewise: Six Faces of Global Change*, 2007, Profile Books, p71

[18] *See* http://edition.cnn.com/2010/BUSINESS/09/22/un.food.security. poverty/index.html

[19] Rifkin, J, *The Empathic Civilization: The Race to Global Consciousness in a World in Crisis*, 2010, Polity Press, pp36–7

[20] McLuhan, M, *The Gutenberg Galaxy: the making of typographic man*, 1962, Routledge & Kegan Paul

Chapter Five

[1] Ellul, J, *The Technological Society*, 1964, Vintage Books

[2] Marcuse, H, *One-Dimensional Man: Studies in the Ideology of Advanced Industrial Society* 2007/1964, Routledge, p10

[3] *See* Burrows, W E, *Deep Black: Space Espionage and National Security*, 1986 Random House; Laidler, K, *Surveillance Unlimited: How We've Become the Most Watched People on Earth*, 2008, Icon Books

[4] Laidler, K, *Surveillance Unlimited: How We've Become the Most Watched People on Earth*, 2008, Icon Books, cited p127

[5] Laidler, K, *Surveillance Unlimited: How We've Become the Most Watched People on Earth*, 2008, Icon Books

[6] Laidler, K, *Surveillance Unlimited: How We've Become the Most Watched People on Earth*, 2008, Icon Books, cited p98

[7] http://www.guardian.co.uk/uk/2002/oct/13/humanrights.mobilephones

Chapter Six

[1] Shah, I, *Thinkers of the East*, 1971, Jonathan Cape, p123

[2] Heinberg, R, *Memories & Visions of Paradise: Exploring the Universal Myth of a Lost Golden Age*, 1990, The Aquarian Press, xxviii

[3] Cited in Heinberg, R, *Memories & Visions of Paradise: Exploring the Universal Myth of a Lost Golden Age*, 1990, The Aquarian Press, p49

[4] Cited in Heinberg, R, *Memories & Visions of Paradise: Exploring the Universal Myth of a Lost Golden Age*, 1990, The Aquarian Press, pp68–9

[5] Eisler, R, *The Chalice and The Blade: Our History, Our Future*, 1987, Harper & Row

[6] Cited in Heinberg, R, *Memories & Visions of Paradise: Exploring the Universal Myth of a Lost Golden Age*. 1990, The Aquarian Press, p210

[7] Eliade, M, *The Sacred and the Profane*, 1961, Harper & Row

[8] Heinberg, R, *Memories & Visions of Paradise: Exploring the Universal Myth of a Lost Golden Age*. 1990, The Aquarian Press, pp240–1

[9] de Santillana, G & Von Dechend, H, *Hamlet's Mill: An Essay on Myth and the Frame of Time*, 1970, Macmillan

[10] Pratt, L, 'Astrological World Cycles', *East West Magazine*, 1932

[11] For a concise and comprehensive summary of the binary star theory read Walter Cruttenden's *Lost Star of Myth and Time*

[12] Men, H, *The 8 Calendars of the Maya: The Pleiadian Cycle and the Key to Destiny*, 2010, Bear & Company, pp66–7

[13] Yukteswar, S, *The Holy Science*, 2010, Self-Realization Fellowship

[14] Pratt, L, 'Astrological World Cycles', *East West Magazine*, 1932

[15] Yukteswar, S, *The Holy Science*, 2010, Self-Realization Fellowship, p14

[16] Pratt, L, 'Astrological World Cycles', *East West Magazine*, 1932

[17] Shah, T (ed), *The Middle East Bedside Book*, 1991, The Octagon Press

[18] *See* the work of Rupert Sheldrake, especially his book *A New Science of Life*

[19] Miller, R A and Miller, I, 'The Schumann Resonances and Human Psychobiology', *Nexus Magazine* 10 (3), April–May 2003

[20] Miller, R A and Miller, I, 'The Schumann Resonances and Human Psychobiology', *Nexus Magazine* 10 (3), April–May 2003

[21] Cruttenden, W, *Lost Star of Myth and Time*, 2006, St Lynn's Press, cited p183

[22] Yukteswar, S, *The Holy Science*, 2010, Self-Realization Fellowship, p8

[23] For a concise and comprehensive summary of the binary star theory and its influence upon the life of humanity read Walter Cruttenden's *Lost Star of Myth and Time*.

[24] Cruttenden, W, *Lost Star of Myth and Time*, 2006, St Lynn's Press, p192

Chapter Seven

[1] Scott, E, *The People of the Secret*, 1985, Octagon Press, p248

[2] For a more in-depth study of the great transformative changes in human history that have occurred in relation to changing cycles I would refer the reader to Richard Tarnas's *Cosmos and Psyche*.

[3] For an in-depth study of the rise of occult movements at this time I refer the reader to James Webb's *The Occult Establishment*.

[4] *See* my other book *The Struggle for Your Mind* for more on the adverse uses/effects of technology.

5   Lévy, P, *Cyberculture*, 2001, University of Minnesota Press, pp174–5
6   Teilhard de Chardin, P, *Building the Earth*, 1969, Avon Books
7   Rheingold, H, *Smart Mobs: The Next Social Revolution*, 2003, Perseus Publishing
8   Rifkin, J, *The Empathic Civilization: The Race to Global Consciousness in a World in Crisis*, 2010, Polity Press
9   Gardner, H, *Five Minds for the Future*, 2009, Harvard Business School Press
10   Cited in Strassman, R, Wojtowicz, S, Eduardo Luna, L, Frecska, E, *Inner Paths to Outer Space: Journeys to Alien Worlds through Psychedelics and Other Spiritual Technologies*, 2008, Park Street Press, p112
11   Rifkin, J, *The Empathic Civilization: The Race to Global Consciousness in a World in Crisis*, 2010, Polity Press, p604
12   Lyrics from the song 'Ballad of a Thin Man', taken from the album *Highway 61 Revisited*

Chapter Eight

1   The Milky Way, our home galaxy, is estimated to contain a hundred billion or so stars. It is part of a local group of 19 galaxies (each with 100 billion stars), which in turn is part of a larger local super-cluster of thousands of galaxies. Astronomers currently estimate that there are perhaps 100 billion galaxies in the observable universe.
2   Cited in Pfeiffer, T & Mack, J E (eds) *Mind Before Matter: Visions of a New Science of Consciousness*, 2007, O Books, p96
3   Elgin, D, *Promise Ahead: A Vision of Hope and Action for Humanity's Future*, 2000, William Morrow, p67
4   Rees, Alun, *Mail on Sunday*, London, August 8, 2004
5   Hancock, G, *Supernatural: Meetings with the Ancient Teachers of Mankind*, 2006, Arrow, p591
6   Hancock, G, *Supernatural: Meetings with the Ancient Teachers of Mankind*, 2006, Arrow, p600
7   Lewis-Williams, D, *The Mind in the Cave: Consciousness and the Origins of Art*, 2004, Thames & Hudson
8   Cited in Hancock, G, *Supernatural: Meetings with the Ancient Teachers of Mankind*, 2006, Arrow, p602
9   Hancock, G, *Supernatural: Meetings with the Ancient Teachers of Mankind*, 2006, Arrow, p202
10   Cited in Hancock, G, *Supernatural: Meetings with the Ancient Teachers of Mankind*, 2006, Arrow, p356
11   Cited in Hancock, G, *Supernatural: Meetings with the Ancient Teachers of Mankind*, 2006, Arrow, p756
12   Strassman, R, Wojtowicz, S, Eduardo Luna, L, Frecska, E, *Inner Paths to Outer Space: Journeys to Alien Worlds through Psychedelics and Other Spiritual Technologies*, 2008, Park Street Press, p80

13 Scott, E, *The People of the Secret*, 1985, Octagon Press, p237

14 Pfeiffer, T & Mack, J E (eds), *Mind Before Matter: Visions of a New Science of Consciousness*, 2007, O Books, p229

15 James, W, *The Varieties of Religious Experience*, 1983/1902, Penguin, p388

16 Huxley, A, *The Doors of Perception*, 1994/1954, Flamingo, p11

17 Cited in Loye, D, *An Arrow Through Chaos: How we see into the future*, 2000, Park Street Press, p171

18 Mcfadden, J, *Quantum Evolution: Life in the Multiverse*, 2000, Flamingo, p295

19 Becker, R O & Seldon, G, *The Body Electric*, 1998, William Morrow

20 *See* my book *The Struggle for Your Mind* for more discussion on this subject.

21 Mcfadden, J, *Quantum Evolution: Life in the Multiverse*, 2000, Flamingo, p314

22 Bischof, M, 'Introduction to Integrative Biophysics' in Popp, F-A & Beloussov, L V (ds) *Integrative Biophysics*, 2003, Kluwer Academic Publishers

23 *See* Hammeroff, S R, 'Quantum coherence in microtubules: A neural basis for emergent consciousness?', *Journal of Consciousness Studies* 1:91118, 1994; Marcer, P J, Schempp, W, 'Model of the Neuron Working by Quantum Holography', *Informatica* 21:519534, 1997; and Penrose, R, *The Emperor's New Mind*, 1999, Oxford University Press

24 *See* Capra, F, *The Web of Life: A New Synthesis of Mind and Matter*, 1996, HarperCollins; Capra, F, *The Hidden Connections*, 2002, HarperCollins; Chaisson, E, *The Life Era: Cosmic Selection and Conscious Evolution*, 1987, Atlantic Monthly Press

25 Capra, F, *The Turning Point: Science, Society and the Rising Culture*, 1985, Fontana

26 Sheldrake, R, *A New Science of Life: The Hypothesis of Morphic Resonance*, 1981, JP Tarcher

27 http://www.sheldrake.org/Articles&Papers/papers/morphic/morphic_intro.html

28 Sheldrake, R, *Seven Experiments That Could Change The World*, 1994, Fourth Estate; Sheldrake, R, *The Sense of Being Stared At: and other aspects of The Extended Mind*, 2003, Hutchinson

29 Kuhn, T, *The Structure of Scientific Revolutions*, 1996/1962, The University of Chicago Press

30 Sheldrake, R, *The Sense of Being Stared At: and other aspects of The Extended Mind*, 2003, Hutchinson

31 Radin, D, *The Conscious Universe: The Scientific Truth of Psychic Phenomena*, 2009, HarperOne

32 Sheldrake, R, *The Sense of Being Stared At: and other aspects of The Extended Mind*, 2003, Hutchinson, p283

[33] Ostrander, S & Schroeder, L, *Psychic Discoveries: The Iron Curtain Lifted*, 1997, Souvenir Press
[34] Vasiliev, L, *Mysterious Phenomena of the Human Psyche*, 1965, University Books
[35] Dr Shafica Karagulla, cited in Ostrander, S & Schroeder, L, *Psychic Discoveries: The Iron Curtain Lifted*, 1997, Souvenir Press, p306

Chapter Nine
[1]   Popp, F-A, Li, K H, Mei, W P, Galle, M & Neurohr, R, 'Physical Aspects of Biophotons', *Experientia*, 1988, 44, 576–85
[2]   Ho, M-W & Popp, F A, 'Gaia and the Evolution of Coherence', *3rd Camelford Conference on The Implications of The Gaia Thesis: Symbiosis, Cooperativity and Coherence*, 1989, The Wadebridge Ecological Centre, Camelford, Cornwall
[3]   Bischof, M, 'Synchronization and Coherence as an Organizing Principle in the Organism, Social Interaction, and Consciousness', 2008, *NeuroQuantology*, 6, 440–51
[4]   Bischof, M, 'Synchronization and Coherence as an Organizing Principle in the Organism, Social Interaction, and Consciousness', 2008, *NeuroQuantology*, 6, 440–51
[5]   Ho, M-W, *The Rainbow and the Worm: The Physics of Organisms*, 1998, World Scientific, p116
[6]   Becker, R O, *The Body Electric*, 1998, William Morrow
[7]   Siegel, D, *Mindsight: Transform your Brain with the New Science of Kindness*, 2010, Oneworld Publications, p43
[8]   Siegel, D, *Mindsight: Transform your Brain with the New Science of Kindness*, 2010, Oneworld Publications, p52
[9]   Krishna, G, *Kundalini: The Evolutionary Energy in Man*, 1997, Shambhala, p226
[10] Laszlo, E, *Science and the Akashic Field: An Integral Theory of Everything*, 2004, Inner Traditions
[11] Narby, J, *Cosmic Serpent: DNA and the Origins of Knowledge*, 1999, Phoenix
[12] Narby, J, *Intelligence in Nature*, 2006, Jeremy P Tarcher
[13] Cited in Ornstein, R & Ehrlich, P, *Humanity on a Tightrope*, 2010, Rowman & Littlefield Publishers, p14
[14] Bischof, M, 'Man as a Cosmic Resonator: Re-Imagining Human Existence in the Field Picture', *11th Annual International Research Consciousness Reframed Conference for Art and Technology 'Making Reality Really Real'*, 2010, Trondheim, Norway
[15] Cited in Pfeiffer, T & Mack, J (eds), *Mind Before Matter: Visions of a New Science of Consciousness*, 2007, O Books, pp78–9
[16] Ede Frecska is chief of psychiatry at the National Institute of Psychiatry and Neurology in Budapest; he is specifically interested in the

neurobiological mechanism of initiation ceremonies and healing rituals and similar states of altered consciousness.

[17] Strassman, R, Wojtowicz, S, Eduardo Luna, L, Frecska, E, *Inner Paths to Outer Space: Journeys to Alien Worlds through Psychedelics and Other Spiritual Technologies*, 2008, Park Street Press

[18] Strassman, R, Wojtowicz, S, Eduardo Luna, L, Frecska, E, *Inner Paths to Outer Space: Journeys to Alien Worlds through Psychedelics and Other Spiritual Technologies*, 2008, Park Street Press

[19] Hancock, G, *Supernatural: Meetings with the Ancient Teachers of Mankind*, 2006, Arrow

[20] Strassman, R, *DMT: The Spirit Molecule: A Doctor's Revolutionary Research into the Biology of Near-Death and Mystical Experiences*, 2001, Inner Traditions

[21] Narby, J, *Cosmic Serpent: DNA and the Origins of Knowledge*, 1999, Phoenix

[22] Strassman, R, *DMT: The Spirit Molecule: A Doctor's Revolutionary Research into the Biology of Near-Death and Mystical Experiences*, 2001, Inner Traditions

[23] Hancock, G, *Supernatural: Meetings with the Ancient Teachers of Mankind*, 2006, Arrow, p222

[24] Ring, K, *The Omega Project: Near-Death Experiences, UFO Encounters, and Mind at Large*, 1992, William Morrow, p168

[25] Ring, K, *The Omega Project: Near-Death Experiences, UFO Encounters, and Mind at Large*, 1992, William Morrow

[26] Cited in Strassman, R, Wojtowicz, S, Eduardo Luna, L, Frecska, E, *Inner Paths to Outer Space: Journeys to Alien Worlds through Psychedelics and Other Spiritual Technologies*, 2008, Park Street Press, p191

[27] Strassman, R, Wojtowicz, S, Eduardo Luna, L, Frecska, E, *Inner Paths to Outer Space: Journeys to Alien Worlds through Psychedelics and Other Spiritual Technologies*, 2008, Park Street Press, p196

[28] Bucke, R, *Cosmic Consciousness: A Study in the Evolution of the Human Mind*, 1972/1901, The Olympia Press

[29] Krishna, G, *Higher Consciousness and Kundalini*, 1993, F.I.N.D. Research Trust, p166

[30] Gulbekian, S E, *In the Belly of the Beast: Holding Your Own in Mass Culture*, 2004, Hampton Roads, p251

[31] Atwater, P M H, *Beyond the Indigo Children: The New Children and the Coming of the Fifth World*, 2005, Bear & Company, p80

[32] Cited in Atwater, P M H, *Beyond the Indigo Children: The New Children and the Coming of the Fifth World*, 2005, Bear & Company, p134

[33] Strauss, W & Howe, N, *Millennials Rising: The Next Great Generation*, 2000, Vintage

[34] Carroll, L & Tober, J, *The Indigo Children 10 years later*, 2009, Hay House

35   Carroll, L & Tober, J, *The Indigo Children 10 years later,* 2009, Hay
     House, ix
36   Cited in Carroll, L & Tober, J, *The Indigo Children 10 years later,* 2009,
     Hay House, p86
37   Atwater, P M H, *Beyond the Indigo Children: The New Children and the
     Coming of the Fifth World,* 2005, Bear & Company
38   *See* http://www.indigoexecutive.com/page/page/3616153.htm
39   *See* his website at http://www.dreamhealer.com
40   Adam, *Complete Dream Healer,* 2009, Piatkus, p174
41   Adam, *Complete Dream Healer,* 2009, Piatkus, p307
42   Adam, *Complete Dream Healer,* 2009, Piatkus, p403

Chapter Ten

1   Shah, I, *The Exploits of the Incomparable Mulla Nasrudin,* 1985,
     Octagon Press, p27
2   Ornstein, R & Ehrlich, P, *Humanity on a Tightrope,* 2010, Rowman &
     Littlefield Publishers
3   Ornstein, R & Ehrlich, P, *Humanity on a Tightrope,* 2010, Rowman &
     Littlefield Publishers, p30
4   Siegel, D, *Mindsight: Transform your Brain with the New Science of
     Kindness,* 2010, Oneworld Publications
5   Siegel, D, *Mindsight: Transform your Brain with the New Science of
     Kindness,* 2010, Oneworld Publications, p42
6   McLuhan, M, *The Gutenberg Galaxy: the making of typographic man,*
     1962, Routledge & Kegan Paul
7   Bache, C M, *Dark Night, Early Dawn,* 2000, Suny
8   Siegel, D, *Mindsight: Transform your Brain with the New Science of
     Kindness,* 2010, Oneworld Publications, p261
9   Laszlo, E, *The Chaos Point: The World at the Crossroads,* 2006, Hampton
     Roads, pp80–1
10   Csikszentmihalyi, M, *The Evolving Self: A Psychology for the Third
     Millennium,* 1993, HarperCollins, p248
11   Spencer, J, 'Lessons from the Brain-Damaged Investor', *The Wall Street
     Journal,* July 21, 2005
12   De Bono, E, *New Thinking for the New Millennium,* 2000, Penguin, p45
13   De Bono, E, *New Thinking for the New Millennium,* 2000, Penguin, p279
14   Some of these ideas were inspired from reading Thompson, W I,
     Transforming History: A New Curriculum for a Planetary Culture, 2009,
     Lindisfarne Books
15   *See* Diamond, J M, *Collapse: how societies choose to fail or survive,*
     2005, Allen Lane; Tainter, J A, *The Collapse of Complex Societies,* 1988,
     Cambridge University Press
16   Cohn, C, 'Sex and Death in the Rational World of the Defense
     Intellectuals', *Journal of Women in Culture and Society,* (12), 1987,
     pp687–718

17   Grof, S, *The Holotropic Mind: The Three Levels of Human Consciousness and How They Shape Our Lives*, 1993, HarperCollins, p220

18   McKenna, T, *Food of the Gods – The Search for the Original Tree of Knowledge*, 1992, Bantam, New York

19   Grof, S, 'Roots of Human Violence – Psychospiritual Perspective on the Current Global Crisis'. Presented at a conference at the Eranos Foundation in Ascona on Lago Maggiore in the Swiss Alps in June 2008

Chapter Eleven

1   Adapted from a parable presented by Kryon during one of his numerous talks. A collection of these talks is available online at http://www.kryon.com/k_25.html

2   Kaku, M, *Physics of the Future: How science will shape human destiny and our daily lives by the year 2100*, 2011, Doubleday

3   Kaku, M, *Physics of the Future: How science will shape human destiny and our daily lives by the year 2100*, 2011, Doubleday, p347

4   Kaku, M, *Physics of the Future: How science will shape human destiny and our daily lives by the year 2100*, 2011, Doubleday

5   Kaku, M, *Physics of the Future: How science will shape human destiny and our daily lives by the year 2100*, 2011, Doubleday, p234

6   Kaku, M, *Physics of the Future: How science will shape human destiny and our daily lives by the year 2100*, 2011, Doubleday, p38

7   Elgin, D, *The Living Universe*, 2009, Berrett-Koehler Publishers, p143

8   Elgin, D, *The Living Universe*, 2009, Berrett-Koehler Publishers, p159

9   A reference to C P Snow's lecture 'The Two Cultures' (1959) which spoke of the gulf between science and the humanities.

Index